TEACHING
Numeracy

TEACHING
Numeracy

9 CRITICAL
HABITS TO
Ignite
MATHEMATICAL
THINKING

MARGIE PEARSE // K.M. WALTON

Foreword by ARTHUR HYDE

CORWIN
A SAGE Company

CORWIN
A SAGE Company

FOR INFORMATION:

Corwin
A SAGE Company
2455 Teller Road
Thousand Oaks, California 91320
(800) 233-9936
Fax: (800) 417-2466
www.corwin.com

SAGE Ltd.
1 Oliver's Yard
55 City Road
London EC1Y 1SP
United Kingdom

SAGE India Pvt. Ltd.
B 1/I 1 Mohan Cooperative Industrial Area
Mathura Road, New Delhi 110 044
India

SAGE Asia-Pacific Pte. Ltd.
33 Pekin Street #02-01
Far East Square
Singapore 048763

Acquisitions Editor: Carol Chambers Collins
Associate Editor: Megan Bedell
Editorial Assistant: Sarah Bartlett
Permissions Editor: Adele Hutchinson
Production Editor: Jane Haenel
Typesetter: C&M Digitals (P) Ltd.
Proofreader: Susan Schon
Indexer: Terri Corry
Cover Designer: Scott Van Atta

Printed in the United States of America

Library of Congress Cataloging-in-Publication Data

Pearse, Margie.

Teaching numeracy: 9 critical habits to ignite mathematical thinking/Margie Pearse and K. M. Walton; foreword by Arthur Hyde.

p. cm.
Includes bibliographical references and index.

ISBN 978-1-4129-9223-7 (pbk.)

1. Numeracy—Study and teaching.
2. Mathematical ability. I. Walton, K. M. (Kathleen M.) II. Title.

QA141.P275 2011 510.71—dc22 2010053208

This book is printed on acid-free paper.

11 12 13 14 15 10 9 8 7 6 5 4 3 2 1

Contents

Foreword   vii
Arthur Hyde

Preface   xi

Acknowledgments   xiii

About the Authors   xvi

Introduction: Numeracy: What Is It, and Why Is It Important?   1

PART I. THE 9 CRITICAL HABITS TO IGNITE
NUMERATE THINKING   7

Habit 1. Monitor and Repair Understanding   9

Habit 2. Develop Schema and Activate Background Knowledge   18

Habit 3. Identify Similarities and Differences,
Recognize Patterns, Organize and Categorize
Ideas, Investigate Analogies and Metaphors   29

Habit 4. Represent Mathematics Nonlinguistically   36

Habit 5. Predict, Infer, Recognize Trends, Use Patterns,
and Generate and Test Hypotheses   53

Habit 6. Question for Understanding   68

Habit 7. Summarize, Determine Importance,
Synthesize: Using Note Taking and Journaling   79

Habit 8. Develop Vocabulary   102

Habit 9. Collaborate to Learn   117

**PART II. THE 5 ESSENTIAL COMPONENTS OF
A NUMERACY-BASED MATHEMATICS LESSON**   125

Component 1. Purpose and Focus   127

Component 2. Ignition   130

Component 3. Bridge to the Learning   137

Component 4. Gradual Release in Mathematics   149

Component 5. Debrief: Tying It All Together   168

Conclusion: *Our* **Debrief**   177

Appendix A. Sample Numeracy-Based Lesson Plans   179
    Sample Lesson 1: Introduction to Division (Grades 2–3)   180
    Sample Lesson 2: Elapsed Time (Grades 5–6)   188
    Sample Lesson 3: Surface Area of a
        Right Rectangular Prism (Grades 7–8)   195

Appendix B. Anticipation Guide: The 2010 Census   203

Appendix C. Clock Reproducible for Clock Partners 204

References and Further Reading   205

Index   216

Foreword

What kind of a day was today? A day like any other day, filled with those events that alter and illuminate our times. And you are there.

—Walter Cronkite

Today some educators and politicians in the United States are salivating at the prospect of national K–12 curricula in mathematics. Is this the culmination of the so-called Math Wars? The Common Core School Standards in Mathematics (CCSS), written by a handful of people and hastily reviewed and adopted by states, will now require an intense rearguard action by those of us who care about what the curriculum really is and how it actually gets implemented in the millions of classrooms around our nation. The CCSS is long on content and comparatively silent on process.

Does anyone remember why the National Council of Teachers of Mathematics (NCTM) developed their initial standards for curriculum in 1989, revised them in 2000 with extensive treatment of both content and process, and then developed preK–8 grade-level-specific Focal Points for the critically important concepts in 2006?

Think back to the Third International Mathematics and Science Study, especially the videotaped component that by 2003 had analyzed thousands of hours of 100 eighth-grade teachers in each of seven high-performing countries as compared to 100 U.S. teachers. The researchers discovered several things:

- Each country had its own particular "culture of teaching mathematics."
- Teachers in each of the other seven countries had a typical way of helping students grapple with conceptually rich math problems through some form of active questioning and dialogue. There were characteristic patterns of engaging students' thinking and making connections among the concepts of the problem.

- However, none of the 100 U.S. math teachers exhibited any such behavior. Instead, they told the students what procedures to use to get the right answer, turning the rich, conceptual task into a plug and chug, computational exercise. In fact, a third of the time, they merely gave them the answer!!!

Is it any wonder that so many of our U.S. students believe that math is a hodge-podge of rules to memorize, procedures that one simply *does without thinking?* I am not chastising our math teachers; they are teaching the way they were taught.

The culture of math teaching in the United States includes the following patterns of behavior:

- Showing students what procedure to use to get the right answer rather than helping them understand underlying concepts.
- Suggesting that students look for the key words (e.g., "altogether" to cue them to add the numbers, or "difference" to mean that they should subtract). The teachers do not realize that the message kids get is, "don't bother reading the problem or thinking about what is going on."
- Using mnemonic tricks to help memorize procedures, for example, "Please Excuse My Dear Aunt Sally" where PEMDAS signifies the order of operations (parentheses, exponents, multiply, divide, add, subtract). Students thus focus on the order rather than the *meaning* of the operations.

Perhaps the epitome of our U.S. culture of teaching math was shared with me by a sixth grader. When confronted with the exercise of dividing a fraction by a fraction, he stated, "Ours is not to reason why, we just invert and multiply!" Alfred Lloyd Tennyson, roll over in your grave! With our God-given capability of abstract thought and reasoning, are we not better served by asking *why*?

In Algebra class, how many denominators must be mindlessly "rationalized"?

How many polynomials must be factored without reference to a context?

Or "Here is an equation, young fellow. Make a table of values for it. Then graph it. Okay, you are finished." "What? You want to know what this is an equation OF?" "Why, it could be many different things, sputter, sputter. Don't ask such ridiculous questions."

Where do we start?

I talk to a lot of parents and teachers each year. I tell them that there are three ideas one must entertain:

1. Arithmetic is not synonymous with mathematics. It is part of math, one of its many branches. *Mathematics is the science of patterns.* There are many wonderful patterns in mathematics that even young children can appreciate.

2. The goal of teaching mathematics is to understand concepts, not to memorize procedures. To teach mathematics for conceptual understanding, teachers must *use principles from cognitive psychology* to help students learn how to think. By their very nature, concepts organize information and help students discern patterns. Concepts in mathematics are abstract relationships that are understood by wrestling with lots of examples. When someone else (teacher, parent, or older sibling) merely tells a child what to do or shows him or her how to do it, the child is denied the experience of *thinking through* what is going on here. The child may remember the procedure but not know when to use it appropriately.

3. Most humans, most of the time, think with language. Reading, writing, speaking, and listening are integral to doing thoughtful mathematics. The teacher must have a *dynamic dialogue* with the students, discussing, debating, and thinking about how they are conceiving of the mathematical tasks they are doing. They must be able to read mathematics texts and story problems with full comprehension. They need time to think and write about their conceptions and strategies.

Like the 1001 Arabian Nights of Scheherazade, Margie Pearse and K. M. Walton have written a book that gives teachers 1001 suggestions of where to start. They have organized these suggestions around nine *critical thinking habits,* which will be familiar to educators who have studied literacy and developed a love for language and literature of all genres. These nine critical thinking habits are cognitive processes—habits of mind, thought, and imagination. They encompass reading comprehension strategies, and the authors show how these can help students comprehend mathematics. They include the five fundamental processes of doing mathematics advocated by NCTM (problem solving, reasoning and proving, making connections, communicating one's conceptions, and creating representations). The authors illustrate how to use metaphors and analogies (metaphorical and analogical thinking) to reach even the recalcitrant math student . . . like my daughter.

My daughter, Alicia, was doing fine in mathematics through eighth grade but was becoming increasingly indifferent to it each year. The performing arts were her passion. She excelled in language and literature, but acting, singing, dancing, writing, and directing (which she did in high school and college) were her raison d'être. In college she was required to take one math course. The most basic one allowed was Finite Mathematics. Before she panicked, she found out that she could take Finite Math at the local community college when she was home in the summer (and I could help her). Before she registered, I went to the college bookstore to see what texts were being used by the five different instructors. She signed up for the fellow who was using a text that provided relatively good contexts, offering a modicum of motivation.

The course contained a fair amount of probability. During the first week, we got out a deck of cards to explore poker hands (Critical Thinking Habit 2: Develop Schema and Activate Background Knowledge). A dim recollection stirred. We looked at the first problem: What is the probability of a heart flush? I turned to look at Alicia sitting next to me. She was totally spaced out. "Earth to Alicia. Come in, please."

"Heart flush. Heart flush," she muttered. "What a great title for a poem!" Whereupon, she wrote a haiku by that title.

I dragged her back to the poker game, complete with manipulatives. "Okay, there are 52 cards, and 13 of them are hearts. So the probability of the first card being a heart is 13 out of 52 or ¼. The probability that a second card would also be a heart would be 12 out of 51." And so on. We walked and talked through the problem. "So figure out the probability of all five cards in the hand being hearts. What would it be?"

Her response was immediate, guileless, matter of fact: "Oh, I don't know. One in a million."

She thinks in metaphors. So do most humans. Try to go an entire day without using a metaphor.

Margie Pearse and K. M. Walton have spent a decade devouring the research on best practice in teaching mathematics and testing out this work in classrooms. Much of this research base was ignored by the presidential panel in 2008 that was charged with reporting on teaching and learning in math. The panel examined only studies that met the standards of experimental or quasi-experimental research (e.g., the random assignment of students to treatment and control groups). Excellent qualitative research studies, which also include appropriate statistics, describing and analyzing *what* students learn as well as *how* they learn, were readily available. They would have provided the panel with a powerful foundation. Instead, with one swipe of a hand, any research that might have been inspired by Piaget (e.g., clinical observation) was dismissed. Similarly ignored was the landmark synthesis of research on how students learn mathematics sponsored by the National Research Council (2005).

Fortunately, Margie Pearse and K. M. Walton have extensively referenced the practices that they explored, and they supply solid documentation for their suggestions. They have chosen *numeracy* as their flagship concept, and it's a grand one. Their intent is to draw attention to the fundamental building blocks of mathematical meaningfulness that children must develop to construct higher-level mathematics. In *Early Numeracy*, Wright, Martland, and Stafford (2003) carefully establish the validity of their Learning Framework in Number (LFIN) model, the basis of their Math Recovery program of assessment, intervention, and teaching. They show that the development of initial numeracy by young children ages 4 to 9 years old is absolutely critical to later mathematical success. The practices, activities, and problems Margie Pearse and K. M. Walton elaborate on can provide a mathematically rich environment in which numeracy can flourish.

—*Arthur Hyde*

Preface

A merican students are losing ground in the global mathematical environment. There, we said it. Now that we've put it on the table, we assume you're not surprised. If you bought this book, you probably feel it in your mathematical bones, so to speak. That knowledge gnaws at teachers, administrators, board members, and politicians; it is a truth that is slowly eating away at the American student's chances of taking the mathematical lead in deep thinking.

We are a world leader, with government-funded public education, highly trained teachers, a vast majority of involved parents, and millions of students who genuinely want to learn. How can we be so far behind the rest of the world mathematically?

The answer is quite simple: because our students have a weak number sense. Many students know how to *do* the math but do not know how to *think through* the math. There is an enormous difference.

As educators, we kept asking ourselves one question: How can we empower American students to think? That question, and many more, drove us toward research, and through our research we discovered a movement that is basically uncharted territory in American classrooms but is the driving force in many of the same countries that consistently outscore us. That movement is called *numeracy*.

This book is the result of over 10 years of research in the field of numeracy. Using this research as a springboard, we've tried everything offered in this book in the math classroom. What we discovered was staggering: When offered the opportunity, students were empowered to think critically and became truly numerate. In this book, we lay a clear and well-researched path that we hope will empower teachers to fill their mathematics instruction with numeracy and deep thinking. Research mixed with practical ideas is, in our opinion, a magical brew for teachers.

The focus on literacy over the last decade has positively affected American education, of that there is no doubt. But our question is, why did America wait so long to commence our literacy initiative when New Zealand and Australia had been reaping the benefits for years? We fear America is repeating the same mistake in mathematics. We cannot allow that to happen; we must look to countries consistently outscoring us on international tests and investigate what they're doing. The time is now for us to use the knowledge gained through the literacy focus and the use of literacy strategies and merge them with deep thinking and sense-making in mathematics—no matter what math concept is being taught.

What makes a student numerate? Numeracy encompasses deep thinking, meaning-making, and sense-building. Students, when numerate, do not simply do math; they are taught how to think through the math. As a nation, we have our students do math, then do the same math over and over until it is memorized. More often than not, students are not encouraged to think through the math and make sense of it. Many students don't know when they have a wildly wrong answer.

Nationally, our students need to be taught that, when mathematicians process, they have an inner conversation with the math; they listen to the voice in their heads as they process, allowing them to construct a true understanding of the math—numerate understanding. Only when they have an inner conversation (questioning, visualizing, and making connections) will they notice when their answer is illogical or where they went wrong in their calculations.

We invite you to roll up your sleeves and help us revolutionize American mathematics instruction—one classroom at a time.

Acknowledgments

We extend our deepest gratitude to the following people who helped strengthen this book. First, thank you to our amazing editor, Carol Chambers Collins, who believed in us from day one. Thank you to the genius, otherwise known as Arthur Hyde, for giving two unknowns a chance. Thank you to the volunteer reviewers who spent their precious time giving us incredible feedback—we hope you see the fruits of your labor in the book! Thank you, Megan Bedell, for your help and continued enthusiasm; both meant a great deal to us. Sarah Bartlett, permissions guru extraordinaire, thank you for your patience and guidance along the way. Jane Haenel, thank you for pulling it all together; you are a wonder. Christina MacRae, thank you for creating many of the graphics throughout the book. Thank you to Kathie de la Vergne for your brilliant ideas and your endless hours of reading and rereading. To Dr. Rina Vassallo, thank you for always pushing us as professionals and thinkers. Thank you to Chamise Taylor and Dr. Denise Ray for supporting us. To the teachers at Scott Middle School, thank you for opening your classrooms and your minds to us. Finally, thank you to everyone else who helped, guided, and encouraged during this journey.

I am forever grateful for my husband, Chris, and my children Christopher, Drew, and Gloria. Thank you for pushing me to be a better me. Your faith in me kept me writing. I would also like to thank my four siblings, Linda, Joanne, Nancy, and Joe, and my lifelong friend, Mo. They see me for me and love me anyway. I think the world of you! Thanks, Mom and Dad, for living a life of integrity and love. You taught me how to persevere. To my sweet little angel, Ayden, you give meaning to the saying, "my cup runneth over." You fill my heart with smiles. I am especially thankful for my dear friend and coauthor, Kate Walton. I have never worked so hard and giggled so much at the same time. You are a gifted writer and a wonderful friend. U R the best!

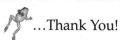…Thank You!

—*Margie Pearse*

I would like to thank my husband, Todd, and my sons, Christian and Jack, for their unwavering belief in me and this book—and for affording me the countless hours I spent lost in numeracy land. Thank you to my mother, Mary Anne, for being my biggest cheerleader, building my confidence, and making me truly believe in . . . me. To my three younger sisters, Meghan, Nikole, and Christina, thank you for the best support known to sisterhood—love. And last, but certainly not least, thank you to Margie Pearse for including me in her brilliant ideas and for being the best writing partner and friend anyone could ask for (especially for a language arts teacher cowriting a book on mathematics)!

—*K. M. Walton*

PUBLISHER'S ACKNOWLEDGMENTS

Corwin gratefully acknowledges the contributions of the following peer reviewers:

Susan Birnie
Curriculum Specialist for Mathematics
Alexandria City Public Schools
Alexandria, VA

Judy Filkins
K–8 Math and Science Curriculum Coordinator
Lebanon School District, SAU 88
Lebanon, NH

Barbara Fox
Mathematics Coach
City of Cambridge
West Medford, MA

Debbie Gordon
Third Grade Teacher
Madison Simis Elementary School
Phoenix, AZ

JoAnn Hiatt
Mathematics Instructor
Olathe East High School
Olathe, KS

Noël Klimenko
Middle School Mathematics Specialist
Instructional Services
Fairfax County Public Schools
Fairfax, VA

Joy Weiss
First Grade ELD and Technology Mentor/Trainer
Balsz Elementary School
Phoenix, AZ

About the Authors

 **Margie Pearse** has spent the last quarter century as an educator and researcher. She has a master's degree in multicultural education and over 23 years of math teaching experience. Margie is presently working as an instructional coach in Coatesville, Pennsylvania. Her educational philosophy can be summed up as, "Why NOT reinvent the wheel. Yesterday's lessons will not suffice for students who need to succeed in tomorrow's world." Her current research focuses in the untapped area of numeracy. Her passion for research and best practice drove her to coauthor this book.

 **K. M. Walton** has taught at both the elementary and middle school levels for 12 years. Although K. M.'s primary passion and expertise is with language arts, she feels numeracy transcends and is, at its very core, deep, logical thinking, which she has always encouraged in her classroom. She believes that a well-crafted lesson and a healthy obsession with creativity are the keys to inspiring students to think deeply. She currently coaches teachers and conducts original professional development days on best practices. Her passion for cutting-edge instructional practices drove her to coauthor this book.

Introduction

Numeracy: What Is It, and Why Is It Important?

We need to help our students delve deep to find the concepts that underlie all mathematics and thereby better understand their significance in the world.

—Lynn Arthur Steen (1990)

Our students have a weak number sense. How many times have you asked measurement questions only to discover that the students have no sense of what the measurement means? How many times have you had your students work through word problems just to watch them skip a crucial step and come up with a wrong answer? We'll go out on a limb here and answer for you—countless times (if you'll forgive the expression).

The word *numeracy* was introduced in Britain more than two decades ago, and the UK Department for Education and Skills defines numeracy as follows:

- Numeracy is a proficiency developed mainly in mathematics but also in other subjects. It is more than an ability to do basic arithmetic.
- Numeracy develops confidence and competence with numbers and measurement; it requires understanding of the number system, a number sense.
- Numeracy demands understanding the way in which data are gathered by analyzing and evaluating, as presented in graphs, diagrams, charts, and tables.
- Teachers of numeracy develop critical thinking and foster behaviors that enable students to make sense of numerical information in their world.

- Numeracy is about applying mathematical concepts in sophisticated settings.
- Numeracy is about making sense of numbers and understanding the effect numbers have in the world around us.

According to the Program for International Student Assessment (PISA, 2007), two key characteristics of a numerate individual are

1. the ability to use mathematics in everyday life and

2. the ability to understand and appreciate information presented in mathematical terms.

PISA further states that numeracy looks less at what mathematics a student knows and more at what the student can do with the mathematical knowledge he or she has acquired.

We think numeracy can be described as a fundamental literacy that is crucial to people's engagement with the world in which they live. We can thus say that it is not a discipline but, rather, a language crucial to most disciplines. The ability to adapt mathematical ideas to new contexts in everyday life is the signature of numeracy.

Numeracy has become an "in-vogue" term in many European and Australian educational circles, and many governments have been explicitly pressing for a numeracy agenda. In English-speaking nations outside the United States, the word *numeracy* is widely used in commentary about mathematics education. In both Australia and New Zealand, numeracy has generally been paired with literacy in research, policy and program development strategic action, school development, and accountability measures (see *Literacy and Numeracy Across the Curriculum* available at http://www.thenetwork.sa.edu.au/files/links/Numeracy_formatted.pdf).

The past decade in American education has been spent focusing on literacy: literacy across the curriculum, critical literacy, digital and media literacy, and so on. We are certainly not diminishing this focus; it was clearly essential for our country. Many American students have benefited from the literacy focus, and to that we say, "Fantastic!" We are also not suggesting there should be a "literacy versus numeracy" mentality in our nation's schools.

But hear us: American mathematics needs to take its turn as the primary focus of educational reform. It is time.

In Scotland, Australia, England, and New Zealand, where students consistently outscore American students, literacy and numeracy across the curriculum share the top priority when creating new initiatives in the educational field (PISA, 2007). Alan H. Schoenfeld observed that, in the past, what students learned in mathematics classes rarely connected with their literacy learning. Now, however, these skills are largely thought of and taught as overlapping. In an age dominated by numbers, individuals who lack the ability to think and reason numerically can neither make wise decisions nor participate fully in civic life (Schoenfeld, 1994).

The National Council of Education and the Disciplines (NCED) hopes to make numeracy a priority for schools and colleges across the United States. Its 2003 report (Madison & Steen, 2003) states the following:

- Numeracy skills are socially distributed. That is, people who are regarded as insufficiently numerate are predominantly working class, are disproportionately female, and are more likely to be members of certain ethnic and racial minority groups.
- Perceptions about the numeracy demands of particular tasks and, consequently, of what sorts of people succeed with them will have a powerful effect on who gets chosen and who chooses themselves for certain life opportunities at home, at work, and in public life.
- From business decisions and personal finances to government policy and environmental monitoring, the need for school graduates to understand and be capable of using numeracy has never been greater.
- Daily headlines use numeracy measures to report on public opinion, financial markets, school test scores, risks of disease, consumer prices, and refugees from ethnic wars.
- Anyone who wishes can obtain data about clinical trials of new drugs, educational expenditures in local schools, projections of government budgets, and indicators of climate change.

Of course, numeracy is of value not only for earning a living but also for leading an informed life (Madison & Steen, 2003). Numerate citizens will be better equipped to understand the many forces that shape their lives, including

- how different voting procedures (e.g., runoff, approval, plurality, preferential) can influence the result of an election;
- the difference between rates and changes in rates (e.g., a decline in prices as compared to a decline in the rate of the growth in prices); and
- how small samples can accurately predict public opinion, how sampling errors can limit reliability, and how sampling bias can influence results (Steen, 2001).

These applications are quite different from those of traditional mathematics. They require greater understanding of chance and data, or percentages and risks. These quantitative aspects of citizenship are less those of algebra and geometry than of logical thinking, number sense, and data interpretation. Our unprecedented access to numerical information in the digital age will inevitably place more power in the hands of individuals and serve as a stimulus to democratic discourse and civic decision making. Without appropriate understanding, however, access to vast amounts of quantitative information can as easily mystify as enlighten (Steen, 2001).

Poor numeracy can reduce employment opportunities and career progress. In *Does Numeracy Matter? Evidence From the National Child Development Study on the Impact of Poor Numeracy on Adult Life* (Bynner & Parsons, 1997), numeracy is recognized as a key skill in the employment opportunities of pupils at all levels of attainment. Evidence shows that poor numeracy skills are a greater impediment to life chances than poor literacy skills and that by raising standards of numeracy we will be improving the career prospects of our pupils (Groves, 2001).

There are two paramount criteria for the effective teaching of numeracy:

1. Development of conceptual understanding

2. Engagement in a critical analysis and evaluation of how numbers affect our everyday lives

Many students in the United States have given up on ever knowing *why* things work in mathematics. When they get an answer correct by simply following a procedure, regardless of conceptual understanding, they are satisfied. One problem is that, for most of us, this lack of conceptual understanding is cumulative, and eventually, it all catches up with us (Hyde, 2006, p. 92).

Psychologists are now seeing that people who have conceptual understanding and organized knowledge are able to "conditionalize" what they know. Conditionalized knowledge does not come from memorizing things you don't understand. It comes from generalizing from a variety of similar contexts, representing one's conception, creating mental models, communicating with others, and consciously reflecting on what you are doing (Hyde, 2006, p. 93). Building conceptual connections is at the heart of numeracy. Meaning is not passively received; it is actively constructed. Numeracy is "braiding" together mathematics, language, and thinking (p. 1).

Numeracy is thus an appreciation of common numerical sense with a depth of reasoning and critical thinking around how numbers change our world. There is little doubt that literacy and numeracy are connected. In other words, being numerate requires the person to be literate to understand numbers in context. However, being literate by itself doesn't help the reader interpret the mathematics.

Being numerate means being able to use mathematics in life by being a confident mathematician. As students come to understand and expect to make sense of mathematics, and as they build a repertoire of strategies, they can begin to develop confidence in their ability to do mathematics (Allsopp, Kyger, & Lovin, 2007).

Even individuals who have studied calculus often remain largely ignorant of common abuses of data and all too often find themselves unable to comprehend the nuances of quantitative inferences (Steen, 2001). What does this look like in everyday life? When you're numerate, you understand how to navigate through the world with a practical sense of how and why numbers affect you. For instance, a numerate individual can interpret data with a critical eye: Who wrote the graph, and why are they presenting it that way? How does that affect the decisions I have to make? Every graph is a sales pitch from someone, and we, as responsible members of society, need to understand that fact. That understanding includes using metaphors and analogies effectively to make better sense of the data (Wormeli, 2009).

Numeracy is an individual's capacity to identify and understand the role mathematics plays in the world, to make well-founded judgments, and to engage in mathematics to meet the needs of that individual's current and future life as a constructive, concerned, and reflective citizen (PISA, 1999). Numeracy is about applying elementary tools in sophisticated settings. It includes the capacity to identify similarities and differences through categorizing and organizing information (Marzano, 2007).

There are sufficient parallels and connections between literacy and numeracy for us to look to literacy work over the past 20 years for advice on future development work in numeracy. In literacy best practice, the teachers' knowledge and understanding of literacy development and their content knowledge in other learning areas come together into a symbiotic relationship. The same is true of good practice in numeracy. We need to find ways of unlocking the best practices that teachers know and use to develop student critical literacy and apply them to numeracy development. We also need to learn from recent research in student understanding of key mathematical concepts and apply this knowledge at the same time we are developing our approach to numeracy.

Lynn Arthur Steen states the following in *Mathematics and Democracy: A Case for Quantitative Literacy* (2001):

- Considering the deluge of numbers and their importance in so many aspects of life, one would think that schools would focus as much on numeracy as on literacy, on equipping students to deal intelligently with quantitative as well as verbal information. But the evidence shows that they do not.
- Numerate citizens need to know more than formulas and equations.
- Numerate citizens need to understand the meaning of numbers, to see the benefits of thinking quantitatively about commonplace issues, and to approach complex problems with confidence in the value of careful reasoning.
- Numeracy empowers people by giving them tools to think for themselves, to ask intelligent questions of experts, and to confront authority confidently.
- The consequence in the United States is a generation of students who feel alienated from mathematics and who therefore leave the educational system innumerate.

STANDARDS CAN HELP

The Common Core States Standards Initiative is an innovative, state-led effort to improve mathematics education in the United States. These standards are currently being adopted by many states across the nation. The common core standards focus on core conceptual understandings. They allow students to become progressively more proficient in understanding and using mathematics. We think that sounds a lot like numeracy.

The standards of mathematics practice follow:

- Making sense of problems and persevering in solving them
- Reasoning abstractly and quantitatively
- Making viable arguments and critiquing the reasoning of others
- Looking for and making use of structures
- Modeling with math

This book concentrates on *why* and *how* to bring these practice standards to life.

We fully embrace the power of numeracy. We acknowledge that numeracy can end the disturbing alienation from numbers by making mathematics real for students. When students are taught to be numerate thinkers, it's nearly impossible for them to feel unconnected to the math because it becomes such a natural way of thinking. When you're truly numerate, you're thinking conceptually. It is a change in the educational mindset. A mathematical revolution.

America was founded on upheaval and rebellion. We say, with as much zest and passion as possible, let's get going!

Are you with us?

THIS BOOK CAN HELP

This book will explore each critical thinking habit and its relation to numeracy and share hundreds of practical ways to incorporate the habit into your instruction tomorrow. *Practical* ways to bring it into your classroom . . . tomorrow. (We thought that deserved repeating.)

We're all about practical. Each of the chapters in Part I share important research findings, key ideas, and teaching strategies that can be implemented immediately in any K–8 classroom. Part II contains our recipe for making your classroom truly numerate. We take you through our lesson planning step by step. In Part I, you will find many practical tools to ignite mathematical thinking. In Part II, we show exactly how and when these tools are best used in a numeracy-based lesson. Finally, in Appendix A, we share three numeracy-rich lesson plans, complete with clear directions and student handouts.

PART I

THE 9 CRITICAL HABITS TO IGNITE *NUMERATE* THINKING

All mathematicians at any grade level use the following nine critical habits when highly engaged and thinking deeply—in other words, when exhibiting true numeracy:

1. Monitor and Repair Understanding

2. Develop Schema and Activate Background Knowledge

3. Identify Similarities and Differences, Recognize Patterns, Organize and Categorize Ideas, Investigate Analogies and Metaphors

4. Represent Mathematics Nonlinguistically

5. Predict, Infer, Recognize Trends, Use Patterns, and Generate and Test Hypotheses

6. Question for Understanding

7. Summarize, Determine Importance, Synthesize: Using Note Taking and Journaling

8. Develop Vocabulary

9. Collaborate to Learn

These nine critical habits are a distillation of 10 years of research and classroom experimentation by Margie Pearse. My journey began with a sense of disequilibrium. I noticed my students had a general lack of number sense and reasoning and an inability to use mathematics in everyday decisions. I didn't know how to intervene.

I turned to the in-depth knowledge of Pearson and Gallagher (1983) on what proficient *readers* do. I wanted to know if this thinking could apply to proficient mathematicians. And if it could, how? I continued to read works by Ellin Keene and Susan Zimmerman (2007), Cris Tovani (2004), Stephanie Harvey and Anne Goudvis (2007), Adrienne Gear (2008), Arthur Hyde (2006, 2009), Marilyn Burns (2007), Robert Marzano, Debra Pickering, and Jane Pollock (2001), Janet Allen (1999, 2000, 2004), Lynn Arthur Steen (1988, 1990, 2001), and Rick Wormeli (2009). The nine critical habits were created from internalizing this wealth of research, combining it with my willingness to experiment in my math classroom, and having many discussions with my coauthor, K. M. Walton. These nine habits are tried and true and are what we believe it takes to become a deeply numerate thinker. Each of the chapters in Part I is devoted to one of the nine habits.

Habit 1

Monitor and Repair Understanding

Five out of four people have trouble with fractions.

—Steven Wright

When readers read, they have an inner conversation with the text. They listen to the voice in their heads speaking to them as they read, which allows them to construct meaning. Only when they are having an inner conversation will they notice when they stray from it (Harvey & Goudvis, 2007).

Now, don't throw this book across the room, snarling, "I thought this was a book about mathematics!"

Let us rephrase: When mathematicians process, they have an inner conversation with the math. They listen to the voice in their heads speaking to them as they process, which allows them to construct an understanding of the math. Only when they are having an inner conversation will they notice when their answer is illogical or recognize where they went wrong in their calculations.

We're sure mathematics teachers everywhere would agree that, to be a true mathematician, students must possess this ability to reason through the math. If you've been in the classroom for more than a week, you know that logic escapes many young people. We need to bring it back. Many American students have no number sense, which means they need to be taught how to realize when they're way off in their thinking or calculations. Who will show them? The teacher.

Every reader has read a particular passage, closed the book or the article, and then wondered what he or she just read. This happens to everyone occasionally, but it happens to our students in math much more frequently. You think they get it, but when it is time to apply the learning, you get "I'm lost" looks. Most discouraging is when students don't know how far off they are or at what point they went wrong—like when a student writes 53 as the answer when the correct answer should be over 4 million, and he simply moves on without a thought to the unreasonableness of his answer.

That experience demonstrates why we're writing this book. As teachers, we were witnessing a dissonance: How was it that students in a district with such a strong literacy push couldn't transfer their proven ability to monitor their understanding in reading to mathematics? Why didn't students grasp when they were way off track mathematically? We were inspired to find the answers. We wanted to empower teachers who would, in turn, empower their students to reason and think critically in mathematics—to become numerate as well as literate.

We all struggle with comprehension at times. The truth is, meaning doesn't arrive fully dressed on a platter. We all need fix-up strategies (Harvey & Goudvis, 2007). The best fix-up strategy is to cultivate awareness; when engagement starts to waver, like a car veering from its lane, we immediately recognize it and take steps to get back on course. That is the beginning of the numeracy challenge—to provide the tools for students to realize that they are not getting it and why. As Hyde (2006) says, the main goal of mathematics should be to deeply understand the concepts, not just memorize facts and procedures.

When we monitor our comprehension in literacy, we pay attention to whether or not we are understanding what we are reading. The same must happen in a mathematics classroom. Richard Allington, in *What Really Matters for Struggling Readers* (2006), says that we need to teach students to read beyond their math textbooks and start thinking like mathematicians. Students must have inner conversations with the text and listen to that voice in their heads speaking as they read; it allows them to construct meaning. If the inner conversation is missing, students typically have no idea when understanding has broken down.

BEGIN WITH ESTIMATING

In mathematics, that inner voice should begin with a reasonable answer, a "Guesstimate," an "I think it should be around . . ." thought. Estimating helps lead students in the right direction. Taking the time to teach estimating is invaluable and will empower your students to become critical thinkers for life.

Let's say your students are calculating the mean. First, have them "check out" the data and try to make sense of it. What do they think the mean should be? Why do they think that? These are questions easily included in daily instruction that have a big payoff for students. It is a way to activate prior knowledge. Next, have students record their predictions and reasons behind their thinking before they start to calculate. Give students an opportunity to talk about their estimates, thus allowing them to take responsibility for their own learning.

Estimating also provides a meaningful starting point for you: Who understands the concept of mean? Who needs support? Next, try data with an outlier. Do students understand how an outlier affects the mean? Use their estimates as feedback as you continue the lesson. The more teachers stimulate students to be aware of and to monitor their own thinking, the better mathematical problem solvers they will become (Hyde, 2006, p. 15).

THEN TRY REPAIRING

When we *repair our understanding*, we figure out what to do when we are confused. To describe how this works in mathematics, imagine sitting in the dentist's chair. (Just go with this, you'll see . . . .)

> The dentist pulls up her chair to work on your teeth; she then rolls her tray of assorted dental instruments over. You think, *Is she really going to use all of those tools today? I just came here for a cleaning!* Throughout your cleaning, she repeatedly grabs the "just right" tool when she needs it. How does she always know which tool to grab? It's simple; she's completely familiar with all the tools and knows which tool will do the job in the best way.

Well, "fix-up" tools in mathematics are similar. Students won't need all their tools all the time, but they will need some of them some of the time. Just like the dentist knows which tool to grab to get the job done, a deep-thinking mathematician knows what intellectual tool to choose at the right time to help make meaning or to repair understanding. It's so logical, yet it isn't happening in many American classrooms.

Fix-up tools proficient mathematicians use if they do not understand:

- Make a logical "guesstimate." Predict what you think the answer would be and understand why you think that would be a close enough guess. You can do this by rounding, estimating, visualizing, and making personal connections to the problem. (Guesstimation is numerate thinking in action. When students ask themselves if their guesstimate is logical or reasonable, they are processing as numerate thinkers.)

- Slow down! There is sometimes too much information for a mathematician to take in quickly.
- Go back and reread or look again. Sometimes that's enough.
- Read or look ahead to clarify meaning, pausing and revisiting your original predictions.
- Identify what it is you don't understand—is it an expression, equation, concept?
- Do a quick summary to get back on track. Ask yourself, "Does what I'm doing make sense so far?"
- Seek help from an outside source.
- Engage in "positive self-talk" through the assessment or problem. Build stamina and keep interested through constant monitoring and repairing to stay focused. (Model this method by using a think-aloud. This practice will definitely pay off during standardized testing!)
- Connect the reading or problem to background knowledge.
- Try to get a picture in your mind.
- Raise new questions throughout the problem solving. The best questions to continue to ask are, "Does what I am doing now make sense?" and "Does what I'm doing go along with what I originally thought?" Why or why not?
- Make inferences. To do so may mean that you must identify patterns and relationships.
- When you come up with an answer, revisit your original guess. Are you close? Why or why not? Check your answer using the following questions: Is my answer reasonable? Why or why not? Does it make sense in the problem? Why or why not? If not, where did I go wrong? What happened to get me off track? How do I get back on track?
- Try solving the problem a different way and check what you come up with. This process may clarify any questions you still have.

HOW CAN I DO THIS IN MY MATH CLASS . . . TOMORROW?

If a student(s) is stuck, do not tell her what is wrong, as hard as that may be. Arthur Hyde says that interventions are best done with questions that help a student or group rethink and repair on their own. When students rethink and repair themselves, they own the learning. It is actually the essence of deep understanding.

Help build good estimating sense with these measurement ideas:

Measurement Ideas: Early Elementary

What's as Big as Me?

Take the height of each child using string. Cut the string and have the students use it to discover what else is as big as them in the classroom.

Have students categorize things that are smaller, the same, and larger than themselves.

Oh, That'll Take About a Minute

Start a stop watch and ask students to clap when they think a minute is up. Talk about how close they were. Now do jumping jacks and ask students to stop when they think a minute is up. Continue with different ways to help students make sense of a minute.

Oh, That'll Take About an Hour

Have students talk with family members to figure out activities that take about an hour to do. They should draw illustrations of two examples and bring them to class to share. Have groups talk about their findings and then identify different times during the day that an hour has passed. Discuss all the things that happened during that hour.

Measurement Ideas: Upper Elementary/Middle School

Measurement Scavenger Hunt

Students love a good measurement scavenger hunt. For your Ignition (see Component 2 for more on Ignition), place some "mystery measures" on the board and have them guess what in the room is that length, perimeter, area, volume, and so on. For example, you can ask, What in this room is 50 cm long? The next day ask, What is 20 cm long and weighs 10 grams? Then, how about, What is 20 cm long, weighs 10 grams, and is 5 cm in height? Make sure that what you are asking them to find are different objects. Students will then be challenged to consider the relationship among length, weight, and height. You will learn very quickly who has a good sense of measurement and who does not.

Mystery Staff Member

Another really fun idea is to have a "mystery staff member." Put the mystery person's measurements (height, arm span, shoulder span, whatever) out in the hall and make it a school challenge. Don't forget to switch up the unit of measure. Challenge the students to "think outside the inches box." It is a blast. Don't forget to include the custodial or cafeteria staff or principal. It's endless! This activity will really help build number sense, which really helps in monitoring and repairing math understanding.

"Size 'em Up": Measuring Angles

Students often get confused about how to use a protractor properly. Alleviate this problem by having the students first "size-up" the angle before using the protractor. Use an "under 90°, over 90°" estimate. Then model using the protractor. Your estimate will lead you to the right measurement without any confusion. This method is very meaningful compared to some of the "catch phrases" used to teach measuring angles (e.g., "come right in or be left out"). Catch phrases are quick fixes without the reasoning. An estimate will automatically bring in reasoning and meaning.

Estimation Moment

Select a single object such as a box, a watermelon, or a jar (or you can select a person like the principal). Each day, choose a different attribute or dimension to estimate: length, weight, volume, surface area, and so on (Van de Walle & Lovin, 2006, p. 235).

Create Math Sense Moments

- A million drops of water equal how many liters? Discuss this idea in small groups. Draw and/or explain the process of discovery.
- Name a fraction that is close to 1 but not more than 1. Explain how you know this fraction is close to 1. Now write another fraction that is closer to 1 than the first one you picked. Explain how you know this fraction is even closer to one. Try one more. Do you see a pattern? Explain your findings in writing. Turn and talk to a partner and share your explanation. Would you like to revise your answers? If so, what did you change? Why?
- Make a case for why each of a series of numbers does not belong (e.g., 24, 12, 2, 11). Do this as an Ignition when the students come in. At the end of the class, as a Debrief, put up the series again and challenge the students to include the following concepts in their explanations: prime, composite, divisible, multiple, factor, whatever you are teaching at the time.
- Chips-Ahoy cookies claim to have 1,000 chips per box of cookies. How could your determine whether this claim is true without counting the chips in every cookie (Schuster & Canavan Anderson, 2005)? Identify the pattern so that you can discover the number of chocolate chips in "X" boxes.

Encourage Students to Monitor and Repair Their Understanding by Providing a Working Answer Key

Working Answer Keys help alleviate the meaningless nightmare of checking homework during valuable class time. Now hear this: We are certainly not saying that you should remove homework from the mathematics classroom. However, homework must induce deep thinking and not devour half your math class the following day and not allow you to provide meaningful feedback to your students. Tall order, right? Not really. Here's how Working Answer Keys were born.

Margie Pearse: My son's brilliant precalculus teacher provided the answer to a problem I was struggling with as a teacher. My son would come home with five problems to complete each night. Attached to his assignment was an answer key. Now, the answer key did not simply have the answers, it included the process as well. I hate to admit it, but my first thought was, "Wow, that was dumb to give to the kids. He's just going to copy the problems and be done with it." However, that is not what happened at all. I did realize that, without the proper setup by the teacher, it probably would not have worked, but this teacher had obviously taken the time to empower his students to value their own learning. My son wanted to discover the process and to succeed. I watched him try a problem and then check his work against each step on the answer key. I heard him wonder aloud why he was wrong. Then he'd discover where his mistake was and what he needed to do to be correct. It was amazing. He said he wished he had another classmate there to discuss the process. Watching my son sparked an idea about how to solve *my* homework nightmare! That night, I worked out the problems I had assigned my students for the next day. I learned something valuable by doing the assignment myself: Assigning 10 thoughtful problems was more meaningful than assigning 20 or 30 repetitive problems. The next day, I placed what I dubbed Working Answer Keys in a labeled bin and started teaching my students to take responsibility for their own learning. I explained that they were to pick up an answer key, place it alongside their homework, and check the process as well as the answer. For the first few days, I modeled what using a Working Answer Key tool looked and sounded like and what it did not look or sound like. I tried to infuse humor, and it definitely got the point across. Because my students were in groups of four, I told them to use each other for clarification along the way. They discussed and shared their thinking behind the homework with one another. If all four students didn't understand a problem, we would bring it up as a whole class. It took some time and patience and an occasional call to the home of any student who basically copied my work verbatim. "Copiers" quickly learned from their group that copying wouldn't be tolerated. Many times I'd hear students say something like, "What's the point of copying? You're not learning anything." By the second month, my classroom looked very different during homework check. I could quickly walk around and see who did or didn't complete the assignment, and the students were doing all the work. Homework was now meaningful, providing opportunities for deep understanding and meaningful feedback, and taking half the time to check. They shared ideas, discussed problems, and celebrated successes. The journey was worth taking. They had learned how to monitor and repair *their own* math understanding.

Increase Mental Math Ability

"A good calculator does not need artificial aids" (Lao Tze, 531 BC). This quote gains in applicability as you provide opportunities for your students to think fast, think hard, and think deep. If you really want your students to have mathematical sense when it comes to problem solving, invest time in improving their mental math skills using quick reasoning in practical situations. Mental math does not mean only rote memorization. However, when it comes to multiplication tables, rote memorization is important. We are referring to quick reasoning in practical situations.

- *Realizing how much we use mental math in real life:* Teach the use of compensation and the distributive property when using mental math. Ask, "Can you multiply 29 × 7 in your head? I bet you can. Try it!" Let them wrestle with it, think about it, discuss it. Explain, "What your brain actually did was multiply (30 × 7) – (1 × 7) = 203. Now try this one. 42 × 6. Did anyone's mind naturally multiply (40 × 6) + (2 × 6) = 252?" Some of your students' minds don't naturally do that. You can open *your* mathematical thinking to them in a think-aloud moment. They will greatly appreciate it. We like to call it "taking the mental out of the mental math."

- *Using "friendly" or compatible numbers to make meaning:* When problem solving, change the problem by rounding the numbers into numbers you are more familiar or comfortable with. Sometimes, if you simply round the numbers, you can see how to solve the problem. This is a great way to monitor your understanding before, during, and after solving a problem. This little trick will open your mind to *how* to solve the problem.

- *Model compatible numbers:* Put the following on the overhead and let the students mentally add the numbers in 10 seconds. Let them in on how their brains search for "friendly numbers"—ones that "your brain just seems to clump together naturally."

$$25 + 73 + 75 + 40 + 30 + 60 + 70$$

Allow your students to have the experience of their brains chunking together the compatible numbers. It is amazing how many students can do the calculations in their heads. Now try others! There is no limit to building a sense of compatible numbers. This practice should continue to be encouraged through high school. Include percentages, calculating a tip in a restaurant, and estimating time and distance when taking trips.

- *Making the implicit explicit:* Model how to solve a problem by doing a think-aloud; in other words, demonstrate to students how to think through a problem. Opening up a teacher's critical thinking habits to the students shows the process of problem solving. Many students don't realize that the teacher uses the same critical thinking habits they are being asked to use.

They simply think the teacher is smarter. The benefits of this method are amazing. It levels the playing field for those students who never knew "the smart kids" are actually processing, too. If you are a risk taker, try doing this "cold." It is scary, because you might not know how to work the problem correctly, but isn't that a powerful lesson as well? How will you make it work? How do you remain positive when things are getting tough? What monitoring and repairing strategies do you apply? Have your students notice what you are doing as a mathematician to *stay in the problem*. Then, let them discuss how this thinking helped *you* succeed as a problem solver. Now let them give it a go with a partner a few times. This works best in mixed ability groups. Students are empowered to learn from each other. It gives the slower processor a chance to hear strategic thinking happening during problem solving.

• *Monitoring and repairing to maintain mental stamina, courtesy of professional baseball:* The best way for students to keep focused through standardized testing is to have them monitor and repair their comprehension. Try this! Find two short video clips of two pitchers during a World Series. One clip should present a pitcher who is beginning to fall apart on the mound, whereas the other clip is of a pitcher who seems flawless. Show the failing pitcher first. Have the students fill in their "thoughts." No matter what is going on with the pitcher, he still has to remain focused, somehow. Let them figure out how. Then show the "superstar." What do they think he is saying to himself to keep focused? Okay, now comes the powerful part: Ask the students how this situation is like taking a test. Push the thinking such that the students realize that monitoring and repairing your comprehension gives you the stamina to remain focused through any problem.

Habit 2

Develop Schema and Activate Background Knowledge

Today's knowledge is tomorrow's background knowledge.

—David Pearson, *Contemporary
Educational Psychology*, 1983

Cognitive psychologists developed *schema theory* to explain how a person's previous experiences, knowledge, emotions, and understandings deeply affect what and how we learn (Anderson & Pearson, 1984).

Jean Piaget (1973) distinguishes two types of knowledge development: *assimilation* and *accommodation*. He describes assimilation as the gradual integration of new knowledge into a learner's existing knowledge base. In general, assimilation links old knowledge and new knowledge. Accommodation is a more radical change in knowledge. It involves changing existing knowledge structures as opposed to simply adding to them.

Assimilation is important because it builds background knowledge, which is the first step to numerate mathematical learning—like a backbone for comprehension. For this reason, we call it Backbone Knowledge. Just as the human backbone is crucial to our skeletal structure, background knowledge is crucial to learning. Think of your daily lessons as a vehicle that drives assimilation in your classroom. To cultivate a student's Backbone Knowledge, craft every lesson so that it provides equal access to the learning for all students, regardless of how weak or strong their schema may be. In a mathematics classroom, what that means is that we need to provide lots of opportunities for students to either activate or build their background knowledge.

Accommodation is where the opportunity for deep numerate thinking lies. When a thinker is given opportunities to actively challenge what they know and is encouraged to interact with new ideas or new ways of thinking, *accommodation* knowledge is gained. When students deem mathematics meaningful, powerful, and interesting, they gain conceptual understanding because they truly understand it and are not just memorizing how to go through the steps. Passive learning usually means shallow learning.

ACTIVATING BACKGROUND KNOWLEDGE

We recognize the power of the "aha" feeling we get after learning something important; it is no small thing. As teachers, we cherish every time that light bulb goes off for a student—that breakthrough of understanding. Increasing the number of aha moments in our classrooms has become a very clear goal for all of us.

Activating a student's background knowledge is powerful because of its potential to pull reluctant mathematicians back in, effectively leveling the thinking playing field so that everyone can play. When a student feels that math is too hard or they can't do it or they don't understand it or everyone else gets it but them, you've lost him or her. Letting students consciously identify what they already know increases confidence and engagement. When we connect our past experiences to new information, we are more apt to engage in the learning as well as to understand it (Harvey & Goudvis, 2007, p. 12).

When the teacher purposefully allows students to identity what they already know about a new concept, fears of "I can't do this," or "This is too hard" are erased. In a math class, this Bridge to new learning ensures that new topics are mathematically linked to previous topics and that the subject is not fragmented. Mathematicians do not invent mathematics out of thin air. Each math concept is built upon previous work; hence, a common thread links all math concepts, no matter how advanced the one being taught. We agree with Arthur Hyde when he says, "Forming the right connections in mathematics, regardless of the grade level, is crucial to establishing global conceptual development" (Hyde, 2009). It is a magical moment when a student realizes, "Hey, this is just like . . . ."

BUILDING BACKGROUND KNOWLEDGE

You need to make a conscious choice to scaffold learning by giving students specific tools that will help them make meaningful connections among topics. To move students from "day-dreams to real-time learning," we may have to create cerebral contexts where there are none (Wormeli, 2009, p. 35). If students don't have the personal background to recognize a connection to the content, we must work to create the context. This practice is not a luxury to be considered only if time allows; providing the context can be the difference between function and dysfunction in the classroom. Very little goes into long-term memory if it's not attached to something already in storage. If we want students to move new ideas and skills into long-term memory—not merely to repeat it for a test and then forget it—then one of our best strategies is to create background knowledge (Sousa, 2001, p. 46).

Key Ideas

Frontload: Explain Unfamiliar (Nonmathematical) Vocabulary in Problem Solving

Students will be better able to solve a problem if it is stated in language they understand. For example, suppose that one story problem on probability refers to a deck of playing cards. Gone are the days when students are familiar with how many cards are in a deck or how many suits there are. Without having had the experience of playing cards, you cannot find the answer, no matter how intelligent you are.

Sometimes simple language gets in the way of the actual math. Even though the meaning of a phrase or word isn't important to solving the math problem, some students, especially English language learners (ELLs), may lack the background knowledge necessary to understand the problem, which only adds to their confusion.

Preteach: Create a "Sentence Frame" or Cloze Activity

We used sentence frames and cloze activities in science and social studies for years with great success. We wondered if they would be just as worthwhile in mathematics. The answer is definitely yes!

Begin with a framed sentence to build on students' ideas. The teacher controls the mathematical concept and the format of the sentences by preplanning them so that they activate background knowledge. Sentences should force students to pull out what they know and bring it to the lesson. Keeping students present and accountable to their learning is the ultimate purpose.

Provide the sentence frame or cloze activity. Challenge the students to use what they already know to fill in the blanks. Then have students share their predictions in small groups, discussing their answers.

For example:

Algebraic _____ can be evaluated when you _____ for the _____.

Every _____ includes an _____ _____ and can be solved.

The critical part of this experience lies in the discussion. A quick vocabulary activity without meaning would be far less powerful. An instantly differentiated experience occurs when the students explain their answers to each other. As they discuss, the teacher purposefully eavesdrops for golden nuggets of information on her students. Who understands the difference between an expression and an equation, and who does not?

Now introduce your Purpose and begin the lesson. Students will either verify or change their initial predictions as they learn. Finally, have students regroup and discuss any revisions they want to make. Reveal the answers and, more importantly, discuss the reason(s) they are correct.

Answers:

Algebraic *expressions* can be evaluated when you *substitute* for the *variable*.

Every *equation* includes an *equal sign* and can be solved.

Build Knowledge From Real-World Examples

Try to reinforce concepts with real-world examples so that students can picture themselves in the problem—that is, make it real to them. This practice removes some of the intimidation for reluctant mathematicians and pushes the higher-level students to an even higher level of thinking. For example, if you need to paint a room, you need to know how much area will be covered so that you know how much paint to buy. Look for other memorable ideas or props that can be used to engage students such as recipes, news stories about the economy, or discussions of personal spending habits.

Use Manipulatives Purposefully

Manipulatives are important at all grade levels. Providing your students the opportunity to "play around" with manipulatives prior to the learning will help familiarize them with the concept to be introduced. Allow them to discover the connections, make predictions, and ask questions. The activity will draw them into the learning.

Demonstrate That Words in a Math Setting May Have Different Meanings

Mathematics uses everyday words, but the meanings are defined in precise mathematical terms; everyday meanings to words simply do not apply. This mismatch can be very confusing to students. Help students understand the different meanings of words such as "angle" and "quarter," as well as how to use them correctly in a mathematical context. Also, expose students to the objects and symbols unique to mathematics.

Challenge Students to Create Representations of the Learning and Make Them Available as a Visual Frame of Reference

Present a problem to the students. Challenge small groups to discover how they might represent a solution. Gather the class and discuss the possible options created. Write ideas on poster board for students to use as a frame of reference. Refer to the posters to help foster math-to-math connections.

Create a Math Word Wall

A math word wall is excellent support for making math connections. Every time you introduce a new vocabulary word, include the following: an "in your own words" definition, a representation of it, and a variety of ways you may use it or see it in real life. At the end of the chapter or unit, have the students use the word wall to review. How might they sort the words? What made them sort the words that way? How would they rate their understanding of the words (1 = could teach it; 2 = kind of know it; 3 = no clue)? This activity can be used as a formative assessment.

Encourage Students to Offer Support to Each Other

When students are encouraged to share their thinking with others who are confused, a few things happen. First, the students sharing their thinking gain a deeper understanding of how they arrived at the answer. Second, the students listening gain insight into the "how" of problem solving. Third, over time, you will develop a community of learners who, together, are involved in making sense of mathematics.

 ## HOW CAN I DO THIS IN MY MATH CLASS . . . TOMORROW?

Early Elementary Ideas

Numbers, Numbers, Where Are They

Challenge students to look for numbers at home. Which room had the most numbers? Why? Draw a picture that includes some of the items that had numbers.

Number Surgery

To introduce the concept of addition, challenge students to take apart numbers in as many ways as they can discover. Begin with manipulatives and an easy number (e.g., 10). Lead students from the concrete (objects) to the representational (drawing) to the abstract (numbers and operation symbols).

Discover Volume Sense

Bring in various containers for students to experiment with (gallon container, margarine tub, mustard jar, etc.). Make water available at a station and allow students to use the container to pour water back and forth. Have students draw which container holds the most and the least and which ones might hold the same amount.

Estimate With Little Ones

How many scoops of beans will fill a coffeepot? How many beads will fill a pill container? Take predictions, then fill the container halfway and see if anyone wants to change his or her estimate. Discuss the reasoning behind decisions. After discovering how many scoops it takes to fill the coffeepot, challenge students to find the total number of beans it takes to fill the container. Have groups come up with an estimate and a plan to solve the problem. Students do the experiment and reflect on the reasonableness of their estimate and plan. To encourage monitoring their understanding, students can change their estimates along the way and share why they did so.

Build Number Sense and Division

Share this problem with your students:

Four children were walking together in the hall at school. They looked down and found a $5.00 bill. They went to their teacher right away and gave it to her. The teacher tried to find who lost the money, but after a week, no one claimed it. The teacher told the four students that they could divide the money up evenly among themselves. How could they do this? Share your plan and draw out how it would work. Be prepared to share with the class.

Throughout the week, offer similar scenarios (e.g., 40¢ for 4 people, 8 cookies for 4 people, 20 oranges and 5 friends, 18 shoes belong to how many people, 20 ears are on how many dogs, 36 eggs is how many dozen, etc.). Then begin working with quotient remainders and have students come to an understanding of a remainder (e.g., 16 marbles and 5 students, etc.).

Jellybean Jar

Start adding jellybeans to a jar each week. Challenge students to estimate how many jellybeans are in the jar. Have students talk about their estimates. They should compare them to each other's and to the actual count. They can predict how many will be in the jar next week and share why they think that.

Counting by 2s, 5s, and 10s

Challenge students to think of things that come in pairs, in 5s, and in 10s. Lead students from the concrete (objects) to the representational (drawing) to the abstract (numbers).

A Half Snack?

What snacks can be shared exactly in half with a friend. Talk about it, and then use raisins to do some experimenting. Lead students from the concrete (objects) to the representational (drawing) to the abstract (numbers).

What I Knew/What Is New T-Chart

This is a quicker, more math-friendly version of the KWL (Know/Want/Learn). The example that follows is a subtraction example for Grades K–1, but the same type of exercise can be performed with older students as well. The activity should be done with the whole class, before the lesson, with the teacher posing this question: "Boys and girls, what do we know about subtraction? Take a minute to think about what you know. Talk at your tables to your friends. Ask each other, 'What do you know about subtraction?' Listen closely to your friends because I'm going to ask for volunteers to share with everyone in a minute or two." Let the students talk it out. Listen carefully and then pull it back to the whole group. This is where the T-Chart poster comes in. Record good thinking on the "What We Knew" side of the chart. After the lesson on subtraction, allow for more table discussion. Again, record good thinking on the "What Is New" side of the chart. This chart can now serve as an anchor chart for the teacher to refer back to whenever necessary.

What We Knew	What Is New

What We Knew	What Is New

Upper Elementary/Middle School Ideas

List-Group Label

This cross-curricular idea works very well in mathematics. Students brainstorm words associated with quadrilaterals, polygons, angles, measurement, and so on. Then, in small groups, they categorize the words and create a title for each category. To deepen their thinking, make sure they are able to defend their categories. This is a great way to begin the year or a unit of study. It can be a valuable preassessment. Repeat the activity at the end of the year or unit and use it as a postassessment.

Circle the Category

Prepare cards ahead of time. Hand one card to each student. Have the students mix around the room and make groups in a way that makes sense to them. Have them create a math title defending their category (Forsten, Grant, & Hollas, 2002a).

Word Sort

This is another cross-curricular idea that is a valuable tool in mathematics. While preparing for standardized testing, give anchor vocabulary cards to groups. Have students categorize the terms and justify their categories. Do a quick formative assessment by asking the groups to present their favorite category to the class for approval. The teacher then redirects, clarifies, or scaffolds the learning if necessary. Now, push it even further: Have students develop their own jump rope chants based on their top category. The power lies in the physical act of jumping and chanting. You just may hear your students whispering their chants during the real standardized testing!

Vote With Your Feet

Students are very familiar with this activity. It is a great engagement tool in any subject. Engagement will be increased and background knowledge activated when teaching critical data analysis and the evaluation of misleading graphs. First, make up some judgment statements about the "hot topics" you are about to provide statistics on. These statements will draw the students' interest. Tell the students that they should move to one side of the room if they are strongly opposed to your statements and move to the opposite side of the room if they strongly agree. Now the rest of the students will fill in somewhere between strongly yes and strongly no. You've formed a human continuum and a strong interest in their learning (Forsten et al., 2002a, p. 26).

Preconcept and Postconcept Checks

Your purpose with this activity is for students to quickly self-rate their understanding of certain vocabulary to be introduced before the lesson. The first check occurs before the learning as a Bridge; then check after the learning as a Debrief. At the Debrief, have the students prove their understanding by creating representations or explanations. In this way, the teacher guides student thinking but still allows for a self-discovery of connections, always bringing missed connection opportunities back to the whole class. This method also helps differentiate the lesson. Quickly circulate the room and see which students might need to touch base during the lesson or which students need to be pushed beyond the original plan (Forget, 2004, p. 230).

Preconcept and Postconcept Checks

Ratings: + = could teach it; √ = kinda know it; — = no clue

Before the Learning		After the Learning
____	prime number	____
____	composite number	____
____	divisible	____
____	prime factorizations	____

Anticipation Guide

An anticipation guide (Forget, 2004, pp. 101–107) works well when you want to get your students excited about a new unit or topic. Create a series of controversial or interesting statements about the new unit or topic. Next to each statement, ask the students to check off whether they think the statements are true or not true (or check off whether they agree or disagree). Then let them read the new chapter or work the new problems. Finally, bring the focus back to small groups and let the students discuss their anticipation guides. Do you see what you've done? You've built instant interest in the new topic and created an atmosphere where activating background knowledge is natural and fun. The U.S. Census provides teachers with an authentic sample of the use of mathematics. See the reproducible anticipation guide on the U.S. Census in Appendix B.

Three Facts and a Fib

Three facts and a fib (Forsten et al., 2002a, p. 63) is a perfect setup for learning math. The students are instantly engaged. You present three facts about what they are about to learn and one fib. They discuss which one is the fib and why. The activity is fun and worthwhile. At the Debrief, I have sometimes asked the students to make up their own three facts and a fib as an exit ticket. They identify the fib on the back and write a reflection on what they learned from the lesson. The exit tickets become the next day's Ignition, and the students did all the work. Very cool.

Frontload

Simply provide the concepts that are going to be presented. Have the students write a few sentences, using the words. You might give each person an index card with an idea of what they will be learning and have them mix around the room sharing ideas about what the lesson will be about. (Other similar tools include "give one, get one," "greet and go," or "word toss" [Forsten et al., 2002a]).

Artwork

M. C. Escher, examples of fractals in art and nature, company logos, and many other connections to art are quite useful to mathematics instruction. When teaching transformations, I always bring in some of the most famous art pieces from M. C. Escher. Challenge the students to make connections to the piece, to try to "hear the artist's voice." This prompt gets them thinking outside the box, and the engagement and discussion are amazing. Then carry the ideas into learning about transformations. When teaching functions, patterns, and fractions, I connect the lesson to fractals. We have taken "nature walks," identifying patterns in nature. After the students discover the patterns, they repeat them mathematically. "The profound study of nature is the most fertile source of mathematical discovery" (Joseph Fourier).

Experiment With Generating a Formula

Place three different-sized boxes at each group of four students (e.g., cereal box, mini raisin box, and a pasta box). Ask, "If you had to write one sentence to someone who needed to find out how to measure the amount of cardboard needed to create the boxes, what would you tell them?" (Do not include any of the overlapping cardboard in a typical box.) They will discover the formula for finding the surface area of a rectangular solid. There is no limit to what you can do here. When your students are generating the formulas, they are reasoning why the formula works, not just how it works. That is powerful!

Formulate a Definition Through Observation of Examples and Nonexamples

Before the students enter the room, write several examples and nonexamples of a particular math concept you are going to teach. Have them discuss and formulate a definition. Then ask them to open their books and let them see if they "nailed it." Happens all the time.

Discover Through Manipulatives

Put a little cup of M&M's on the tables before the students enter. On the board write, "How could you use these to teach ratios, percentages, or equivalent fractions?" Let them discuss and share. Now bring them to the learning. They already own it.

Bring It Back to the Learning

Did you ever look at all the visuals in your math text? Sometimes they have nothing to do with the math at hand and can actually be a distraction. Point this out to your students. Learning how to make meaningful connections in math is important. It is also important to understand that some connections can actually impede the learning. Display an enlarged excerpt from your textbook on the overhead. Have your students make connections. Then ask them to share the connections they made. Now it's time to push the thinking. Ask, "When does making connections help with comprehension? How do you know that? When does making connections impede the comprehension? How do you know that? What can you do to stay on track with your connections?" While you circulate, you may need to scaffold by including the concept of "turning down the volume" of a connection that doesn't help with comprehension. You are looking for an understanding of how to turn down the volume when a connection distracts you from comprehension.

"When Are We Ever Going to Use This?"

Make it real. Whenever possible, make real-life connections to the lesson. When in real life will you add decimals or find percents, volume, measurement, and so on? Bring in an expert to show how math fits into her profession. Math will always be involved. It doesn't matter who comes in, an artist, a musician, a construction worker, or the mayor. Math is real! Make it real to students.

Habit 3

Identify Similarities and Differences, Recognize Patterns, Organize and Categorize Ideas, Investigate Analogies and Metaphors

Analogy plays a significant role in problem solving, decision making, perception, memory, creativity, emotion, explanation and communication.

—Douglas Richard Hofstadter, *Fluid Concepts and Creative Analogies*, 1995

Researchers have found that identifying similarities and differences is basic to human thought (Gentner & Markman, 1994; Medin, Goldstone, & Markman, 1995). What's more, employing the critical thinking habits of identifying similarities and differences, including analogies and metaphors, has been proven to help boost student achievement from 31 to 46 percentile points (Ross, 1987; Stahl & Fairbanks, 1986; Stone, 1983).

If identifying similarities and differences is basic to human thought and boosts student achievement, why, then, are we still content to settle for number crunching and formula writing as the dominant form of instruction? Students are simply going through the motions, punching in the numbers, completely unaware of *how* they get the answer. It is the lack of deep understanding, the failure to own the mathematical thinking, that continues to sabotage true number sense, or numeracy. Therein lies the internal disease of American mathematics, the reason our students have little number sense. Mathematics is not a way of hanging numbers on things so that quantitative answers to ordinary questions can be obtained. It is a language that allows one to think about extraordinary questions. Getting the picture doesn't mean writing out the formula or crunching the numbers. It means grasping the mathematical metaphor (Bullock, 1994).

When you empower your students to compare their before and after actions when solving problems and to identify their "givens" when finding the unknown, you allow them not only to see the big picture but to grasp the mathematical metaphor. Teaching students to think metaphorically sharpens their interpretative skills and helps them reach deeper understanding. In this way, students are taught critical thinking skills that stay with them long after the last lesson of the school year (Gallagher, 2004).

Some researchers, like Robert Marzano (2007), consider identifying similarities and differences to be the core of all learning. Classifying according to features or characteristics helps students develop a scheme, a way to organize objects and ideas. This approach allows the brain to process new information, recall it, and learn by overlaying a known pattern onto an unknown one while finding similarities and differences. Looking for similarities and differences prompts the learner to ask, "What do I already know that will help me understand this new idea?" This question fosters relationships and connections to new understanding.

Analytical thinking helps students chunk information, attaching individual ideas to others in their minds as if they were fitting puzzle pieces together on a table top. Teachers can lead students to these discoveries through intentional instruction that builds meaning through effective comparison.

Marzano, Pickering, and Pollock (2001) recognize four highly effective forms of identifying similarities and differences:

1. *Comparing:* identifying similarities and differences between or among concepts

2. *Classifying:* grouping like things into categories on the basis of their characteristics

3. *Creating metaphors:* identifying a general or basic pattern in a specific topic and then finding another topic that appears to be quite different but that has the same general pattern

4. *Creating analogies:* identifying relationships between pairs of concepts—in other words, identifying relationships between relationships

RESEARCH FINDINGS

- Cognitive research shows that educational programs should challenge students to link, connect, and integrate ideas (Bransford, Brown, & Cocking, 1999).
- Students benefit by having similarities and differences pointed out to them by the teacher in an explicit manner. This identification can include rich discussion and inquiry and allows students to focus on the relationship or bridge to the new ideas (Chen, Yanowitz, & Daehler, 1996; Gholson, Smither, Buhrman, Duncan, & Pierce, 1997; Newby, Ertmer, & Stepich, 1995; Solomon, 1995).
- Combining this strategy with the use of nonlinguistic representation enhances student achievement significantly (Chen, 1999; Cole & McLeod, 1999; Glynn & Takahashi, 1998).

KEY IDEAS

Students benefit by direct instruction and open-ended experiences in identifying similarities and differences. Teachers can increase learning potential with research-based strategies such as the following:

- *Point out similarities and differences.* Identifying similarities and differences can jumpstart students' thinking about big ideas. You may want to state the similarities and differences explicitly. When the learning goal is to engage students in divergent thinking, ask students to identify similarities and differences on their own.
- *Have students create and/or use graphic organizers* of similarities and differences, classification systems, comparisons, examples and counterexamples, and analogies. Suggestions include Venn diagrams, matrixes, comparison tables or charts, hierarchical taxonomies, and linked mind maps. One of the most powerful findings within the general category of instructional strategies is that graphic and symbolic representations of similarities and differences enhance students' understanding of content (Marzano et al., 2001).
- *Identify patterns and parallel relationships* by recognizing the specific variations among two or more attributes in a relationship that yield a reliable or repeated scheme (Singapore math). Math is a science of patterns; it is much more than arithmetic. Probably every concept in mathematics is a pattern of some kind (Hyde, 2006, p. 7). Pattern recognition requires insight and deep thinking—solid learning—and

involves a deep understanding of parallel relationships, which is very significant in mathematics.

- *Help students recognize when they are classifying, comparing, or creating analogies or metaphors.* Have students compare what they know and what they need to know before, during, and after solving problems.

 ## HOW CAN I DO THIS IN MY MATH CLASS . . . TOMORROW?

Early Elementary Ideas

I Spy

Students pick an object they can see in the room. They find a partner and give clues about the shape and size of the mystery object, beginning with the phrase "I spy . . . ." Begin with easy clues, and then make them a little harder. Take turns trying to baffle each other.

Count "Bys" With Your Calculator

Give each student a calculator. Have them count by 5s on their calculator and write the numbers 5, ___, ___, ___, ___, ___, ___. What pattern do they notice in the 1s digit? Talk with a partner. Now try counting by 2s, 4s, and 6s with their calculators.

Pattern Block Art

Give out 4 × 6 index cards and challenge students to fill up the card using the pattern blocks. They may not leave any spaces between the blocks, and they must fill up the card. Have students share and talk about their art with a partner. Count the number of blocks it took to fill the card. Notice the arrangements. Sort the shapes. There are endless ways to follow this activity.

Sort Shapes on a Geoboard

Have students create shapes using a rubberband on a geoboard. Display them at the front of the room, and have groups sort the shapes in different ways. Each group draws how it sorted the shapes and shares with the rest of the class (Burns & Tank, 1988).

Heavier or Lighter?

Have students compare the weight of two objects by holding one in each hand. Lead students from the concrete (objects) to the representational (drawing) to the abstract (numbers and inequality symbols).

Upper Elementary/Middle School Ideas

Venn Diagrams

Use Venn diagrams to compare real numbers and integers, attributes of polygons, probability with overlap, sets and subsets, intersection of sets, angle relationships, similar and congruent shapes, and so on. There are endless ways to make comparisons using Venn diagrams.

Example: When comparing two composite numbers, find common factors, uncommon factors, and the greatest common factor.

You can make this a partner game. Draw a Venn diagram; each player rolls two dice to form a two-digit number (e.g., if you roll a 5 and a 6, you can choose the number 56 or 65; of course, the object is to choose the number with the most factors). Now partners take turns writing in factors where they belong in the Venn. The greatest common factor scores 3 points, common factors score 2 points each, and noncommon factors score 1 point each. The winner would be the player with the most points.

Comparisons in Measurement

- Provide partners with 36 tiles and ask them to make as many rectangles as possible with the same area. Draw them and compare their perimeters. Note any discoveries.
- A medium-sized cat weighs 6 kilograms. Use this information to estimate the weights of other animals (Schuster & Canavan Anderson, 2005, p. 147).

Matrixes in Math

A few favorite ideas involve creating a matrix by identifying the attributes of parallelograms and other geometric properties, transformations, data analyses, and so on.

True Statement?

Ask students to consider whether statements are always true, sometimes but not always true, or never true. Have them explain their reasoning. Then challenge the students to create their own statements. A few examples would be:

- A whole number is _____ an integer. (always)
- The sum of two odd numbers is odd. (never true)
- $x + x$ is greater than x. (sometimes but not always true)

Provide for Flexible Thinking

Try different and invented strategies to solve a problem. Have students compare and contrast different ways to solve a problem. Provide the opportunity to think divergently. Allow them time to reflect on their chosen strategy, and challenge them to defend that choice (promoting ownership). Invented strategies are meaning based and not simply digit based.

Simplify

Simplify a problem by separating the problem into subproblems or parts to be solved individually or in sequence. Identify problems as parts of a whole, creating continuity in problem solving.

Highlight Similar Problems Students Have Solved

Ask students how various problems are the same, and how they are different.

Word Sort

A full description of this activity is given in the chapter on Habit 2. To use it for identifying similarities and differences, do a word sort with attributes of shapes, angles, forms of numbers, properties, and so on. Also, try this little twist to a word sort: Do a "secret sort." Have students create a small collection of about five shapes that fit a secret rule. Now the other students try to find additional pieces that belong to the set and/or to guess the secret rule (Van de Walle & Lovin, 2006).

Create Hierarchies

Hierarchies are a visual proof that there is a natural order to things, even in mathematics. Have students illustrate different types of numbers organized into hierarchies. Examples would be the sets of numbers, the subsets of real numbers, quadrilaterals, and so on. This activity will make the concepts easier to remember and understand.

Recognizing and Continuing Patterns

- Identify patterns all around: Take a nature walk with your students. Look for objects that have patterns. Students choose their favorite pattern to draw. They talk about their patterns with a partner. Show students the first three of fours steps of a pattern with materials or drawings. Provide them with appropriate materials or grid paper, and have them extend the patterns and explain why their extension indeed follows the pattern (Van de Walle & Lovin, 2006).

- Create various "if _____, then _____" mathematical statements. Challenge your students to create their own if/then statements and to explain their reasoning behind their choices.
- Make recognizing patterns a logic problem: Which square numbers are odd? Which are even? Can you describe a pattern demonstrated by consecutive square numbers? Will the 17th square number be odd or even? What about the 18th (Schuster & Canavan Anderson, 2005, p. 23)?

Create a Working Word Wall

Allow students to move words around on a word wall according to whatever challenges you present. Provide opportunities to categorize the concepts and create hierarchies using the words. Have students defend their choices.

Create Metaphors in Mathematics to Deepen Thinking

Begin by creating the metaphors yourself and having the students explain them. Then have the students create their own. When students create their own metaphors regarding math content, they reveal what they understand about that content (e.g., How is area like a hat?).

Habit 4

Represent Mathematics Nonlinguistically

What distinguishes a mathematical model from, say, a poem, a song, a portrait or any other kind of "model," is that the mathematical model is an image or picture of reality painted with logical symbols instead of with words, sounds or watercolors.

—John Casti, *Reality Rules*, 1997

C an creating visual representations have a positive effect on learning? Consider this: Norman Rockwell's Dad read passages from Dickens aloud while his young son sketched.

Most psychologists believe in the dual-coding model of information storage (Pavio, 1971, 1990). This theory proposes that knowledge is stored in two forms: a linguistic form and a nonlinguistic or image form. Robert Marzano (2007) believes that the more we employ both systems of representation, linguistic and nonlinguistic, the better we are at reasoning and recalling knowledge (p. 73).

We're going to assume that Mr. Rockwell Sr. didn't realize that he would be aligned with modern pedagogy or that his actions might have a positive impact on his son's brain. But if Mr. Rockwell Sr. hadn't read those passages from Dickens to his young son as he sketched, would Norman Rockwell's adult talent have been as great? Would he have been able to draw with such detail? Such a creative eye? I guess we'll never know for sure, although we can make an educated guess that the father *did* enhance his son's visual representation.

The explicit teaching of representations is an initiative in many countries where a numeracy agenda prevails (Hyde, 2006, p. 72), and the students in those countries consistently outscore American students in mathematics. The National Council of Teachers of Mathematics (NCTM) confirms that teaching representations is not fully developed in U.S. mathematics instruction.

We'd like to pose a question here: What if American math teachers enhanced their students' mathematical understanding by providing opportunities for them to visually represent their understanding?

Gerlic and Jausovec (1999) argue that when you explicitly engage students in the creation of representations you stimulate and increase activity in the brain. Nonlinguistic representations have the power to expand on students' knowledge base, deepen it, and allow students to own their mathematical understanding. Representations provide visual confirmation of the learning.

Many students believe they understand some aspect of mathematics but actually have only procedural knowledge, a surface or superficial understanding. It is not okay to simply teach procedures and hope students will "pick it up later," that "it will suddenly make sense later." Such is a dangerous assumption. An even more dangerous assumption teachers make is that the optimal order is to use algorithms first, because you cannot understand concepts until you've done a lot of work with algorithms. Working a bunch of similar problems with an algorithm is not the same as working with examples of concepts in a context (Hyde, 2006, p. 99).

Nonlinguistic representations are necessary to students' understanding of mathematical concepts and relationships. Representations allow students to convey mathematical approaches, arguments, and conceptual understandings. They let students recognize connections among related concepts and apply mathematics to real-world problems.

It is, therefore, the recommendation of NCTM (1992) that instructional programs from prekindergarten through Grade 12 prepare all students to do the following:

- Create and use representations to organize, record, and communicate mathematical ideas
- Select, apply, and translate among mathematical representations to solve problems
- Use representations to model and interpret physical, social, and mathematical phenomena

Students of every age need exposure to all types of representations. The time it takes to scaffold students from experimenting with manipulatives, to drawing models, to connecting these experiences to symbolic representations is essential. When scaffolding students from the concrete to the symbolic, it is important to provide plenty of opportunity for discourse and reflection. Students will then be empowered to begin the deep thinking needed to translate between representations.

More often than not, we assume students understand a mathematical concept simply because they can work the algorithm. However, when asked to make meaning of the problem, the depth of understanding is not there. They are simply *doing* the math, not *thinking through* the math. For every symbol that students write, there must be a concrete referent in their heads of what that symbol refers to. Hyde (2006) argues that students must be able to conjure up a mental picture, an image of some sort, and that through this creation, students are constructing meaning that can be used to develop their initial understanding (p. 86).

Lesh and colleagues (2010) suggest that, when students create and share multiple representations of the same problem or situation, they are continuing to keep their thinking alive (pp. 275–286). Multiple representations also provide deeper, more elaborate understandings of the underlying mathematics and fresh insights into the problem. By allowing our students to discover meaning through manipulatives and drawing models, we are providing a tactile frame of reference, adding a depth of understanding that does not come through simply teaching a procedure. Show the students *why* traditional algorithms work. This demonstration empowers students to elaborate on "the what" and guides them to broaden their view of problem solving. Ask students to explain and justify their elaborations (Willoughby, Desmarias, Wood, Sims, & Kalra, 1997).

KEY IDEAS

Make Physical Models Using Manipulatives or Physical Representations

The very act of generating a concrete representation establishes an image of the knowledge in students' minds. The use of manipulatives stimulates the learning environment for the tactile learner. Manipulatives give students a conceptual frame of reference, a physical proof that the mathematical concept makes sense.

Construct Meaning by Generating Mental Images/Visualizing

When we create scenarios or pictures in our minds while learning, our level of engagement increases and our attention does not wane (Harvey & Goudvis, 2007, p. 19). We can compare visualizing to a "movie running in our heads." When the "movie" stops, so does our comprehension. It is important to explicitly teach students to notice when they stop visualizing so that they can immediately get back on track (p. 139).

Teaching children to construct their own mental images when reading nonfiction helps them stop, think about, and understand the information (Harvey & Goudvis, 2007, p. 19). It can be difficult for children to construct *their own* mental images when reading their math textbooks. Math textbooks are sometimes on "visual overload," with photos, examples, tables, charts, and graphs. It is important, however, for students to construct the meaning themselves. It may be helpful to afford students opportunities to picture, predict, or draw a representation of the concept *before* being exposed to the visuals in the textbook.

- Enlarge an excerpt without visuals from the textbook. Place it on the overhead and think aloud about how you are creating mental pictures and making connections to the text. Then continue reading aloud, challenging the students to form images and/or to draw a visual representation. Now open the book and let them see how close they are to the examples, pictures, or data given. This activity is a great way to model how to *actively* read a math textbook.
- Use something other than the math textbook as an anchor lesson on the importance of visualizing. There are many articles in science magazines that are both interesting and relevant to the students and the math curriculum. You do not need to read the whole article. Simply enlarge an excerpt, think aloud about how creating mental images helps you make meaning out of the text, and then give the students ample time to try it themselves. This project may take a whole lesson, but it will become a very important frame of reference on how visualizing is an important critical thinking habit.
- Read aloud from a children's math book while sharing your mental images as you go along. A "math read aloud" is done a little differently from a literature read aloud. Your visualizations will focus on the math concept being taught, not necessarily the characters in the book. This situation is a win-win because the students are relaxed, are in the moment, and are learning without even knowing it.

Draw Pictures or Diagrams

Drawing models, pictures, and diagrams can be the conduit to student engagement and is, therefore, especially important for students who struggle (Keene & Zimmerman, 2007, p. 177). Translating words or information into drawings creates meaningful and personal connections to student learning. Drawing diagrams is a key strategy used in problem solving.

Create Graphic Representations: Make a List, Table, or Pictograph

Graphic representations can be used in all phases of math learning, from generating a formula to creating a table from collected data. They can be used individually, with partners, and as a whole class. For example, you can create a class concept ladder at the beginning of a unit on decimals, or each student can complete a "What I *knew* about decimals/What is *new* about decimals" T-chart as an ongoing way to organize and maintain individual learning. You can also create a "Parking Lot" graphic organizer for the whole class to hold their questions throughout a chapter, or each student can record questions individually on a graphic organizer titled "Questions That Keep Going Around in My Head" (Forsten et al., 2002a).

Graphic representations encourage critical thinking in a purposeful way by maintaining the Focus of the lesson. Every table or graph has a message, and it is up to the students to discover this message in order to critically analyze the data. Students are encouraged to think about the information in new ways because the Focus is on the conceptual connections. They are thus a great tool for reviewing concepts and demonstrating understanding.

Graphic representations provide the big picture in an organized and meaningful way and are great for your visual learners or for those students who may need to practice their visual thinking.

Engage in Kinesthetic Representations of the Content

Kinesthetic activities are those that involve physical movement. Most children find them both a natural and enjoyable way to express their knowledge. Neurologist and middle school teacher Judy Willis (2009) says that, if instruction doesn't change delivery styles every 20 minutes, dopamine levels significantly drop in the brain. The brain needs dopamine to absorb new information. We say, change is good, so why not make the change an active one?

Early Elementary Kinesthetic Ideas

- *The Pattern Dance:* Challenge groups to come up with a movement pattern to show the class. They should identify the pattern and teach it to the rest of the students.
- *Graphing With Your Feet:* Have students create a human bar graph or line plot using the following prompt: How many people live in your house?

Upper Elementary/Middle School Kinesthetic Ideas

- *Acting It Out:* Students have been creating skits and acting things out in every other subject area, so why not try it in math? Have students physically create ways to show their understanding of radius, circumference, chord, diameter, area. The possibilities are endless. Students could present in groups. This activity is fun and makes a visual and physical frame of reference.
- *Human Number Line:* Give students rational numbers and ask them to create a human number line. Then have the other students

"critique" their reasoning, right down to the exact location in which they placed themselves. This activity always brings out a worthwhile discussion.

- *Inside/Outside Circle:* This strategy is actually a great way to conduct a review in any subject. Each student receives a vocabulary word or a problem that can be solved verbally or mentally (the students can make up the problems). The students form two concentric circles. The large circle faces inward, and the smaller circle faces outward such that each student is facing a partner. Now have the students in the outside circle ask their questions to the inner partner, and vise versa. Afterward, call out something like "inner circle move three students left." Students will move accordingly and ask their questions again. Keep it going. This is an instant way to review, and everyone's engaged (Kagan & Kagan, 1992).

- *Mix and Match:* This activity is beneficial in all subject areas. Create matching flash cards (equivalent fractions, fractions converted to percents and decimals, word form to decimal notation, scientific notation to decimal notation, etc.). Give each student a card. Have the students mix around the room. Call "freeze." Tell students to find the student with their matching card and then to form a big circle around the room, holding their matching cards in front of them. You can time this and see if the students can break their own record, or you can compete against other classes. Make sure students can explain the reasoning behind their matches (Kagan & Kagan, 1992).

- *Four Corners:* Four corners is a popular way to get students moving. It also encourages estimation and mental math. Make each corner in your room a value (e.g., corner 1 equals a value less than 5, corner 2 equals a value greater than 5 but less than 10, corner 3 equals a value greater than 10 but less than 15, and corner 4 equals a value greater than 15). Now provide different math situations. Ask students to think quietly about their estimate. No pencils, just good reasoning. Have students go to the corner that represents their conclusions and explain why they chose that corner and how they got that estimate (Kagan & Kagan, 1992).

- *Human Scatterplot:* Create x and y axes on the classroom floor with masking tape. Give each student an ordered pair, and challenge students to locate the point on the scatterplot and stand there. This is a meaningful way to prove trend lines, and the visual that is created sticks with the students for years to come.

- *Greet and Go:* Here's another cross-curricular activity. It provides an interactive way for students to use their background knowledge to make predictions about the vocabulary that will be covered in the day's lesson. First, give each student an index card with a term or phrase from the lesson they are about to have. Ask the students to circulate around the room and to read their cards to each other. After a couple of minutes, call "freeze." While returning to their seats, ask the students to predict in their heads what today's lesson will be about. Have the students return to their small groups and jointly write a prediction on what they will be learning about that day. Revisit their predictions during the Debrief. Have students revise and/or add to the original predictions, and challenge students to use their predictions in writing a summary of the learning (Forsten, Grant, & Hollas, 2002b, p. 46). This is a great activity when the lesson is "loaded" with vocabulary.

- *Voting With Your Feet:* Students have loved this idea in other subjects, yet it is a unique way for them to self-assess in math. Create two cardstock signs that say Yes/No. Hang one sign in the front of your room and one in the back. You have now set up the possibility of a human continuum and can ask your students to get up and "vote with their feet" in response to your well-crafted questions. Here are some ideas: "Who is ready for Friday's test?" "I can teach this lesson." "I have no more questions about the concept of _____." "I feel ready for next week's standardized tests" (Hollas, 2005, p. 18).

Good Questions to Ask When Incorporating Visual Representations

- How do I scaffold experiences to move from concrete to abstract?
- Do the students really understand the concept being taught? If you question whether they do, then quickly assess their understanding by asking them to draw a model, show it using manipulatives, or sketch a diagram of the situation. If they truly get it, this will be no problem for them. If they have no real conceptual understanding, this task will be difficult.
- What manipulatives or physical objects can help students appreciate what is going on? Am I using manipulatives for the sake of using manipulatives, or does using them support the learning? It is all about a purposeful, meaningful, well-crafted lesson. Any such lesson can happen with or without manipulatives.
- Is my graphic organizer a meaningful part of the lesson? Does it guide students toward the Focus and Purpose of the lesson? Does it allow for differentiation?

 ## HOW CAN I DO THIS IN MY MATH CLASS . . . TOMORROW?

Early Elementary Ideas

What If?

To encourage number sense with addition and subtraction, have students imagine they have 6 longs and 5 units. Ask them what they would need to add to get a flat. Have them talk, make a plan, and draw out that plan. Circulate, using this time as a formative assessment. Lead students from the concrete (objects) to the representational (drawing) to the abstract (numbers and operation symbols) (Burns & Tank, 1988).

0–99 Patterns

Give each group a 0–99 chart and the following directions cut into separate strips of paper:

- Color all the even numbers.
- Color all the numbers with double digits.
- Color all the numbers with the digits that add up to 8.
- Color all the numbers that are multiples of 10.

Students pick a strip, follow the directions, and talk to the group about what to do and why.

Fractions With 2-Color Counters

Give each student 9 counters. Have students turn the counters so that they all show the same color. Ask them to break them into 3 equal groups. Talk about how they know they are equal groups and then about what each group contains. Try to draw out the concept of thirds. Now have the students turn one group of 3 over and ask, "What fraction of the counters are that color?" Have students talk shoulder-to-shoulder. Students should draw this scenario. Now continue the concept of fractional parts. Challenge the students by using 12 counters, and allow them to make up their own fraction questions. Move to sketching, then connect the concrete to the representational to the abstract by writing the fractions out in number form.

Does Anyone See a Pattern?

Identify and continue patterns using manipulatives and 2-D models, then take this concrete understanding and craft the lesson to scaffold algebraic thinking. The concrete is very important, but providing the bridge to algebraic understanding is the real purpose of identifying patterns (NCTM, 1992). Can your students generalize what the nth number might be?

Identify Sets of Objects

Identify sets of objects in familiar contexts and describe patterns and relationships as shown in repeated addition. What comes in 2s, 3s, 4s, and so on?

Upper Elementary/Middle School Ideas

- Make a T-chart recording Initial Visualizations/Modified Visualizations after further reading (Zwiers, 2004, p. 66).
- Make available the art work of M. C. Escher. Have students identify tessellations and then create their own tessellation, including their fundamental region.
- Analyze the art work of Paul Signac. Discover the artistic technique of Pointillism.
- Take photos or draw pictures of buildings, identifying the various kinds of polygons you see. Decide why each polygon is placed where it appears; is it for aesthetics or for structure? Explain your reasoning.

What Graphic Organizers Work Well in Math Class?

- Venn diagrams
- A T-chart with calculations on the left and an explanation of each calculation on the right
- Sketch-to-stretch: After reading an excerpt from your textbook or another source, ask students to discuss what they visualized (includes numbers, tables, drawings, maps, etc.). Explain that visualizing deepens the understanding of what they are reading in their text. Sketches should be done quickly. The point of the strategy is to get their interpretations down on paper without using words (McLaughlin & Allen, 2002).
- Concept maps
- Anticipation guides (see example in the chapter on Habit 2)
- Tree diagrams
- What I Knew/What Is New T-Chart (see example in the chapter on Habit 2)
- Matrix and Attribute Chart (see example in Figure 1)

 HOW CAN I USE MANIPULATIVES IN MY LESSON?

Early Elementary Ideas

Race for a Flat

Using flats, longs, and units (base 10 blocks), create placemats identifying place value. Include a picture of a flat representing 100, a long representing 10, and a unit representing 1. Allow time for students to "play" with the base 10 blocks and the placemats for a little while. In groups of four, give each student a mat and manipulatives. Give each group two dice. Students take turns rolling the dice and adding the total to their

Figure 1   Classifying Numbers Matrix

	Prime	Positive	Negative	Whole	Integer	Rational	Odd	Even	Irrational	Real
5										
−1/4										
π										

Hierarchy (see example below)

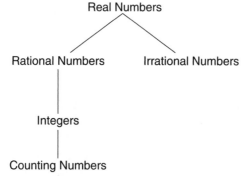

Flow Charts (see example below)

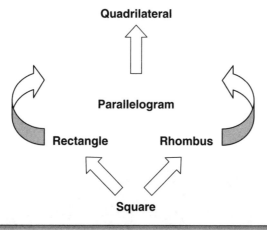

placemats (e.g., a roll of 2 and 5 means that the student adds 7 units to the placemat). Observe groups and encourage replacement (replacing 10 units with 1 long). The winner is the first person to get to a flat (Burns & Tank, 1988). Lead students from the concrete (objects) to the representational (drawing) to the abstract (numbers and operation symbols).

Clear the Board

Using the placemat described above and the base 10 blocks, have students begin with a flat, roll the dice, and take away the total. The winner is the student who clears the board first (Burns & Tank, 1988). Lead students from the concrete (objects) to the representational (drawing) to the abstract (numbers and operation symbols).

How Many Ways?

Using base 10 blocks, challenge students to discover different ways to represent a number (e.g., 106, 212, etc.). Lead students from the concrete (objects) to the representational (drawing) to the abstract (numbers and operation symbols).

Snap It

Give each student 10 interlocking cubes. Students should lock their cubes to make a tower. On the count of three, have students snap apart their tower and hide them behind their backs. Take turns showing the cubes in one hand. Have partners predict how many cubes will be in the second hand (Burns & Tank, 1988). Lead students from the concrete (objects) to the representational (drawing) to the abstract (numbers and operation symbols).

Upper Elementary/Middle School Ideas

Show Multiplication

Use multilink cubes, Unifix cubes, or any small physical objects (beans, chips, etc.).

Experiment With Rates and Scales

- Use bubble gum to discover rates (how many bubbles per minute). Continue with the unit rate, using rate tables to discover how many bubbles that would mean in an hour, day, week, etc. Don't forget to discuss the reasonableness of these rates. What variables are involved? You can also have fun discovering rates taking your heart beat at rest, then after a minute of exercising. Compare and contrast the two rates while climbing the steps, doing jumping jacks, bouncing a beach ball, and so on.

- Use models, maps, blue prints, and AAA Trip Tiks to teach scale.

More Activities With Math Manipulatives

- *Fraction bars and pie pieces* for understanding fractions as equal parts of a whole and for creating equivalent fractions.
- *"Pizza or pie" manipulatives* to show the concept of fractions and to scaffold the concept of equivalent fractions.
- *Base 10 manipulatives* for teaching place value with decimal numbers.
- *Two-sided colored chips* for adding and subtracting whole numbers and integers.
- *String and number cards* to form number lines.
- *A scale and tiles for* solving equations.
- *Pattern blocks* for building patterns, creating and solving critical thinking problems, and exploring geometric shapes. Build compound shapes, explore symmetry, transformations, and explore the relationship between perimeter and area.
- *Straws* of different lengths for experimenting with the triangle inequality property (spaghetti works, too, but can crumble).
- *Compass, straight edge, blue print paper* for introducing constructions.
- *Census results* for analyzing data and making predictions and inferences.
- *Maps* for identifying parallel, intersecting, perpendicular streets and the union and intersection of sets.
- *Antique tiles, Adrinka cloth,* or any handpainted fabric from the Ashanti people in Ghana to show translations and patterns.
- *Things in nature* that show rotational symmetry, Fibonacci sequence, etc.
- *Cardstock samples* of triangles to prove the triangle-sum property.
- *Tangrams and pattern blocks* to create polygons from polygons and to design irregular shapes.

Measurement Manipulatives

- 3-D shapes for identifying shapes and calculating surface area and volume.
- Oranges to let the students discover the relationship between pi and circumference—peel the orange all the way around, then cut a wedge and compare it to the circumference rind. It works every time and establishes a meaningful visual reference.
- Tile blocks for area: Stretch the thinking by discovering the relationship between area and perimeter.
- Pizza for area of a circle: Bring in two small pizzas and one large pizza and ask students to figure out which is the better deal using the area model of a circle. You want them to figure out, keeping the

price in mind, if two small pizzas have more area than one large pizza. What is the best buy? Why?

- Cans with labels for generating formulas on the lateral and surface area of cylinders.
- Different-sized balls to generate formulas and discover the volume and surface area of spheres.
- Different-shaped boxes for generating the formulas for and finding the volume and surface area of a rectangular solid.
- Traditional measuring objects—gallon, quart, pint, cup, tablespoon, teaspoon, ruler, yardstick, tape measure, meter stick, eye dropper, and so on. Having them available to students provides a powerful visual frame of reference.
- Nontraditional measuring objects for estimating. You can use anything: playing cards, your hand, marbles, and so on. This is not only a fun way to discuss estimating and reasonableness in measurement but it can be a quick formative assessment to allow for differentiation.
- Cookies (various-sized circles), rulers, scissors, and string to let the students discover the relationship between pi and circumference:
  - o Distribute one cookie and a piece of string to each student. Make sure each small group has varying sizes.
  - o Ask the groups to observe the materials and predict what they will be doing with everything. Make sure they have mathematical justifications for their predictions. Give them a minute, and circulate about the room.
  - o Gather the students, collect the predictions, and write them on the board. Use these moments to draw math-to-math connections (hopefully someone will bring up perimeter, circumference, diameter, etc.).
  - o Students should understand the concept of perimeter and be familiar with the term *circumference*. Ask groups what they know about finding the circumference of a circle. Give them a minute to brainstorm a list.
  - o As a class, collapse the lists into one list called "What we know about calculating the circumference of a circle." (Many lists will include the word *pi* and may even give you the formula.) Share: We are going to discover the relationship between pi and circumference and will test the formula to see if it works for all circles.
  - o Have students wrap the string around the cookie tightly. Cut the string. Carefully measure the string on the centimeter side of a ruler and round the measurement to the nearest centimeter. Ask the students what they have discovered and have them record this (circumference).
  - o With a new piece of string, find the diameter of the cookie. Measure and record it.

o Place the diameter string alongside the circumference string and challenge students to discover the relationship. Give groups a minute to ponder and discuss. Have students test this relationship, comparing the two strings as well as their measurements.
o Challenge groups to discover a rule for their discovery. You are looking for circumference ÷ diameter = pi for all circles.

READ ALOUDS

Reading aloud children's books is worthwhile in mathematics when it correlates with the concept being taught. Visualization is a way to represent concepts nonlinguistically, and read alouds are the perfect vehicle to make mathematics simple and accessible; the experience also has the capacity to create a solid, visual frame of reference. It's easier for students to visualize with a read aloud because the mathematical content is embedded in a nonthreatening, low-stress format, that is, the book. The read aloud holds a hidden power in that, when students are being read to, it forces *them* to conjure up their own pictures. When they work in their textbook, the visuals are always provided. We would also like to note that read alouds are especially beneficial for English language learners because the math content is delivered in an approachable way. We've listed a few good books here, including some marked with an asterisk that Margie has used with upper elementary and middle school students.

Some Great Books for Read Alouds in Mathematics

On Number Relationships and Number Sense

Aker, Suzanne, *What Comes in 2's, 3's, and 4's?*

Clemens, Andrew, *A Million Dots.*

*Clement, Rod, *Counting on Frank.* (I did this just for fun because our principal's name was Frank. It only takes a couple of minutes to read, and it's funny and helps with reasonableness.)

*Jenkins, Steve, *Actual Size.* (This one really helps create a picture of how big and small some things really are.)

LoPresti, Angelina Sparagna, *A Place for Zero: A Math Adventure.*

McGrath, Barbara Barbieri, *The M & M's Brand Counting Book.*

McMillan, Bruce, *One, Two, One Pair!*

Nolan, Helen, *How Much, How Many, How Far, How Heavy, How Long . . .*

(Continued)

(Continued)

*Pappas, Theoni, *Fractals, Googols, and Other Mathematical Tales.* (Read excerpts when appropriate with the lesson. During a fractal study, read that section, then take the students on a nature walk discovering fractals. Have them sketch one.)

Pinczes, Elinor J., *Inchworm and a Half.*

Pinczes, Elinor J., *One Hundred Hungry Ants.*

Pinczes, Elinor J., *A Remainder of One.*

*Schwartz, David M., *G Is for Googol: A Math Alphabet Book.*

*Schwartz, David M., *How Much Is a Million.* (A great read for number sense for any age.)

*Schwartz, David M., *If You Hopped Like a Frog.*

*Schwartz, David M., *On Beyond a Million: An Amazing Math Journey.*

Tang, Greg, *Grapes of Math.*

Tang, Greg, *Math Fables.*

Tang, Greg, *Math Potatoes: Mind-Stretching Brain Food.*

*Tang, Greg, *Math-terpieces.*

Wells, Robert E., *Can You Count to a Googol?*

Multiplication and Proportional Reasoning

Aker, Suzanne, *What Comes in 2's, 3's, and 4's?*

Anno, Masaichiro, *and* Mitsumasa Anno, *Anno's Mysterious Multiplying Jar.* (This has beautiful illustrations.)

*Calvert, Pam, *Multiplying Menace: The Revenge of Rumpelstiltskin (A Math Adventure).*

*Demi, *One Grain of Rice: A Mathematical Folktale.* (This is a great way to introduce the power of exponential notation. One of my favorites to read.)

Fractions, Decimals, and Percents

Gifford, Scott, *Piece = Part = Portion.*

*Giganti, Paul, *Each Orange Had 8 Slices.* (This one really helps create a visual frame of reference with inclusion classes.)

*Palotta, Jerry, *Apple Fractions.* (This book really creates a visual reference for fractions.)

*Palotta, Jerry, *The Hershey's Milk Chocolate Bar Fraction Book*. (Don't forget to bring in a chocolate bar per group. The students love this book and the activity with the chocolate bar. What a great frame of reference.)

*Palotta, Jerry, *Twizzlers Percentages Book*.

*Silveria, Gordon, *The Greedy Triangle*. (This is a great guest reader choice. Bring in someone you know who can get silly. You can also do this using choral reading.)

Geometry

*Ellis, Julie, *What's Your Angle, Pythagoras? A Math Adventure*. (This is a perfect way to introduce the *Pythagorean theorem. The students love this book.)*

Hoban, Tana, *Cubes, Cones, Cylinders, & Spheres*.

Juster, Norton, *The Dot and the Line: A Romance in Lower Mathematics*.

Neuschwander, Cindy, *Mummy Math: An Adventure in Geometry*.

Tompert, Ann, *Grandfather Tang's Story*.

Algebraic Thinking

Aker, Suzanne, *What Comes in 2's, 3's, and 4's?*

*Demi, *One Grain of Rice: A Mathematical Folktale*.

Neuschwander, Cindy, *Patterns in Peru: An Adventure in Patterning*.

Measurement

*Lasky, Kathyrn, *The Librarian Who Measured the Earth*.

McCallum, Ann, *Beanstalk: The Measure of a Giant (A Math Adventure)*.

*Neuschwander, Cindy, *Sir Cumference and the Dragon of Pi (A Math Adventure)*.

*Neuschwander, Cindy, *Sir Cumference and the Great Knight of Angleland (A Math Adventure)*.

*Neuschwander, Cindy, *Sir Cumference and the Sword in the Cone: A Math Adventure*. (I would have guest readers in to read the Neuschwander books.)

Nolan, Helen, *How Much, How Many, How Far, How Heavy, How Long . . .*

*Schwartz, David M., *Millions to Measure*. (A great read for measurement sense.)

Wells, Robert E., *Is a Blue Whale the Biggest Thing There Is?*

(Continued)

(Continued)

Just Because It's Fun

Hopkins, Lee Bennett, *Marvelous Math: A Book of Poems.*

Hulme, Joy N., *Wild Fibonacci: Nature's Secret Code Revealed.*

*Pappas, Theoni, *Fractals, Googols, and Other Mathematical Tales.*

Reimer, Luetta, *Mathematicians Are People, Too: Stories From the Lives of Great Mathematicians.*

*Scieszka, Jon, and Lane Smith, *Math Curse.*

Tang, Greg, *The Best of Times.*

Tang, Greg, *Math Appeal.*

Tang, Greg, *Math Fables.*

Tang, Greg, *Math for All Seasons.*

Tang, Greg, *Math Potatoes: Mind-Stretching Brain Food.*

*Tang, Greg, *Math-terpieces*.

Habit 5

Predict, Infer, Recognize Trends, Use Patterns, and Generate and Test Hypotheses

And once I had a teacher who understood; he brought with him the beauty of mathematics. He made me create it for myself. He gave me nothing, and it was more than any other teacher has ever dared to give me.

—L. Cochran, *Journal of Mathematical Behavior*, 1991

Life makes more sense when we can interpret our world. Getting a good read on things is apparently part of everyone's profession, even in baseball. Hank Aaron realized this when he admitted to a crowd of fans, "Guessing what the pitcher is going to throw is 80% of being a successful hitter. The other 20% is just execution."

In fact, guessing is a childhood pleasure. Playing Clue or Twenty Questions, reading Nancy Drew, and watching Scooby-Doo were a big part of our childhood memories. Why? Because we became part of the mystery. We collected all the clues, made our predictions, inferred from the implications, and became part of the action. We were reading the situation and actively reading the world.

PREDICTING

Predict: to make known in advance, possible from special knowledge, data or evidence.

—Dictionary.com

Kylene Beers (2003) says that when students make predictions they become active participants, anticipating the direction of the learning (p. 45). Predictions provide students with the motivation to keep learning (Zwiers, 2004, p. 81).

Predicting means you use what you already know to make a guess about what will come next. In mathematics, predictions are best referred to as "forecasting," that is, making an educated guess based on recurring patterns of activity (Steen, 1988). When students read their math text-books, they make predictions about the text, although not about the kinds of things they expect to happen but, rather, about the kinds of things they expect to learn based on what they already know.

Good mathematicians use what is familiar to them to form mathematically grounded predictions and then go back to check their predictions throughout the learning process. It is okay if predictions are wrong. What is important is that the student's mind is working. When students make predictions, they are synthesizing their knowledge by creating different and new conditions. That thought process keeps students engaged in their learning.

As teachers, we need to observe and pinpoint any misconceptions we hear our students making while forming predictions. If students are basing a prediction on a false premise or conceptual misunderstanding, we must create opportunities to challenge that thinking. We need to provide students with a framework for investigating and to scaffold the learning process to maximize the results (Steen, 1988). It is critical to challenge the students to explain their reasoning behind the predictions they make. This explanation will prompt them to clarify their comprehension of underlying concepts, giving you a window into their understanding.

INFERRING

Infer: to reason from premises, circumstances, or evidence.

—Dictionary.com

To infer is to put together the things you read or see with what you already know about the subject. Inferences are ideas lifted out of a situation or text, with your own ideas added to them (Keene & Zimmerman, 2007, p. 154). We make inferences all the time. You figure out when your friend is having a bad day when you see her looking gloomy and teary-eyed. She doesn't need to tell you; you can read it all over her face. That is what we call "reading the world," in other words, making an inference. When you infer, you look for clues, then use the clues and your own experiences to figure out what's not there (Gear, 2008, p. 74). Helping students recognize their own natural ability to infer is a key to deep thinking and later success (Gear, 2008, p. 7).

As we mentioned, your own ideas are added into the text when you make inferences. Often there are things left out of a piece of text. As a good mathematician, you become a math detective and fill in the text with your own thinking (Gear, 2008, p. 28). In mathematics, the equation would look like this: "A dose of schema + a piece of evidence = a solid inference" (McGregor, 2007, p. 55).

Inferring allows students in your math class to make their own discoveries without spoon-feeding the information to them. In this view, understanding cannot be delivered by instructors, no matter how skillful, but must be created by learners in their own minds. True meaning comes when students wrestle with what they see and what they know about what they are seeing, and then learn something new from that process. To infer in a pure sense, then, is to build meaning . . . by doing something with the learning (Keene & Zimmerman, 2007, p. 161). If students don't infer, they will not grasp the deeper essence of the mathematical concepts being introduced.

What is the difference between a prediction and an inference? A prediction is a kind of inference. In fact, you have to infer to be able to make a prediction. A prediction, as stated by Adrienne Gear (2008), is like a level-one inference. It follows a similar process in that you must fill in what is not yet known. A prediction, however, is eventually either verified or not verified. With a prediction, as with a quick question, your thinking stops with the verification or answer. A true inference, on the other hand, is level-two or deep thinking because there is no verification after you have finished reading; hence, your thinking keeps going (Gear, p. 75).

We've learned that we need to add our own thinking to help us understand information better (Gear, 2008, p. 78), and we've discovered that inferring involves drawing a conclusion or making an interpretation that is not explicitly stated in the text (Harvey & Goudvis, 2007, p. 18). In mathematics, predictions lead to inferences, which lead to generalizations, the highest level of mathematical thinking.

GENERATING AND TESTING HYPOTHESES

Hypothesis: an educated, tentative guess.

—Dictionary.com

In mathematics, inquiry in the classroom uses innate curiosity to the student's advantage. Successful teachers craft opportunities to lead students through the process of asking good questions, generating and testing hypotheses, making observations, and finally analyzing and communicating results. Through active learning experiences, students deepen their understanding of key concepts.

Generating and testing hypotheses engages students in complex intellectual structures where they can employ content knowledge in an inquiry-based setting, which enhances their overall understanding of the content. In comparisons of inquiry-based instruction and more traditional teaching methods (such as exclusively lecture-based and textbook-based instruction), researchers have found that inquiry methods help students gain a better understanding of fundamental concepts (White & Frederickson, 1998).

Generating and testing hypotheses can be used in many teaching situations in which students are asked to predict and then investigate the feasibility of their predictions. Generating and testing hypotheses equals predicting results and analyzing data to reach conclusions.

Students are motivated to think when the context of a problem appeals to them. Working in an interesting and meaningful context can help students build an initial understanding of a concept (Hyde, 2006, p. 49). They are inspired by what interests them. When you craft investigative lessons, remember to use your content objective in a manner that intrigues the students. Once you have intrigued them, you have them. As Rick Wormeli (2009) reveals, "You can lead a horse to water, then you do everything you can to make him think he's thirsty." Engagement in the investigation is key.

Once again, teachers should ask students to clearly explain their hypotheses and their conclusions. Research has verified the power of asking students to explain their reasoning behind their hypotheses and conclusions. When the language of reasoning and reflection are used explicitly by the classroom teacher, students are empowered to use the same language in their problem solving (Gawned, 1990, p. 35).

Robert Marzano (2007) recommends three student tasks in generating and testing hypotheses:

1. *Experimental inquiry:* Create activities that promote student use of the scientific method across all disciplines. Understanding increases when students are asked to explain the scientific principles they are working from and the hypotheses they generate from those principles (Lavoie, 1999; Lavoie & Good, 1988; Lawson, 1988).

2. *Problem solving:* Problems involve obstacles and constraints. While engaged in solving problems, students generate and test hypotheses related to the various solutions they predict might work. Using their knowledge of concepts related to the problem, students evaluate different approaches to a solution and then generate and test these approaches to determine what works.

3. *Invention:* Another task that requires students to generate and test hypotheses is the process of invention. Pose an existing problem to students that requires them to develop a solution to the problem. Invention often leads to the generation and testing of multiple hypotheses. In mathematics, generating formulas is a key component of invention tasks (Marzano et al., 2001).

IDENTIFYING PATTERNS

Pattern: a type of theme of recurring events or objects, sometimes referred to as elements of a set. These elements repeat in a predictable manner.

—Dictionary.com

Math is the science of patterns; it is much more than arithmetic. Every strand of math has certain patterns that we look for. Probably every concept in mathematics is a pattern of some kind (Steen, 1990). When we present mathematics as a science of patterns, we bring coherence to a sometimes disconnected curriculum. Every strand of mathematics has its own characteristic patterns. Here are just a few examples:

- *Number sense and numeration:* Search for the relationship between addition and subtraction, multiplication and division. In estimating, we distinguish number relationships and number sense by connecting what is known to what would make the most sense. We recognize and highlight patterns in the findings.
- *Measurement:* In measurement, we discover relationships between area and perimeter, we recognize the correlation between circumference and pi, and so on.
- *Geometry and spatial sense:* In geometry, we see patterns in the properties of polygons and angle relationships.
- *Patterns, functions, algebraic thinking:* We represent information in tables, graphs, and equations, and we find patterns in each of these representations that allow us to form generalizations.
- *Data analysis, probability, and discrete math:* When working with data, we detect patterns and trends that describe the shape of how the data are distributed (Hyde, 2009, p. 24).

One of the finest gifts we can give our students is to facilitate their innate capability to infer patterns and then use these inferences to predict (Hyde, 2006, p. 114). Identifying patterns and making predictions ground students' thinking inside the mathematics, innately connecting them to the problem or new concept. By tapping into students' natural ability to find patterns and think inferentially, the mathematical learning becomes active. Lynn Arthur Steen (1990) challenges us to present mathematics not as "calculations and formulas, but as an open-ended search for patterns. To grow mathematically, children must be exposed to a rich variety of patterns appropriate to their own lives through which they can see variety, regularity, and interconnections" (p. 8).

When students have a hard time with a particular problem, help them identify and use patterns; it will tap into what they already know and build confidence in their math skills. That confidence can shut down the "this is too hard"/"I can't do this" comments and allow for strong mathematical thinking to flourish and deepen. A good way to enhance any lesson in math, then, is to rethink it in terms of patterns (Hyde, 2006, p. 115). Being able to recognize patterns helps us make additional predictions on the data. In mathematics, if a pattern occurs, we should go on to ask, Why does it occur? What does it signify? The answers to these questions bring the deeper understandings we want our students to leave our class with.

 # HOW CAN I DO THIS IN MY MATH CLASS . . . TOMORROW?

Early Elementary Ideas

Making Necklaces

Bring in red and blue beads and yarn. Put each color of bead in two identical containers. Tell the students that they are going to make necklaces using the two colors. Begin modeling the pattern: 1 red, 2 blue, 1 red, 4 blue, 1 red. Describe the pattern as you continue to make the necklace. Have students use choral response to continue the pattern until the necklace is finished. Students should stand side by side while identifying the pattern. Circulate and listen as a formative assessment. Gather the group and share what the pattern is while you write it on the board. Now show students both containers and ask them to predict how full the jars will be after the class is done making a necklace using the same pattern. Have students share predictions shoulder-to-shoulder. Discuss the reasoning behind their predictions. Students create necklaces using the above pattern and draw a representation of it. Lead students from the concrete (objects) to the representational (drawing) to the abstract (numbers and operation symbols).

Riddles

Prepare a mystery bag of marbles (could be 3 blue and 6 yellow). Provide hints until the students can determine what is in the bag.

1. There are yellow and blue marbles.

2. There are less than 12 marbles (have students discuss shoulder-to-shoulder some possible answers while you write them on the board). Make the point that there can't be 12 and there can't be less than 1.

3. There are more yellow than blue marbles. Cross out any options on the board that no longer work.

4. There are twice the yellow marbles than blue ones. Have students discuss their reasoning. Discuss the concept of twice as many.

Continue this idea with different mystery numbers. Have students create bags and hints on their own.

Handfuls #1

How many beans can you pick up in a handful? Predict, experiment, and reflect on the reasonableness of the predictions. Now try popcorn kernels, counters, cubes (Burns & Tank, 1988).

Handfuls #2

Have students take another handful of objects. Challenge them to split the objects in half, thirds, and so on and make discoveries. Lead students from the concrete to the representational to the abstract.

How Many Pockets Is the Class Wearing Today?

Estimate first, then have students place a Unifix cube in each pocket. Collect Unifix cubes, estimate the total, and brainstorm a plan to make the counting easier (i.e., groups of 10). Groups should draw this out and solve the problem. Collect the ideas and scaffold to the abstract by modeling it. Continue this experiment every day and find out how many pockets the class wore over the week. Continue the lesson with beans in a bag. Have groups separate them into groups of 10 and put each group in paper cups. Lead students from the concrete (objects) to the representational (drawing) to the abstract (numbers and operation symbols) (Burns & Tank, 1988).

How Many Stars Can You Draw in a Minute?

Have students predict, try it, and then count the stars (Burns & Tank, 1988).

How Many Popcorn Kernels Can Fill a Cube?

Have students predict, try it, and then count the kernels.

Compare Objects With Nonstandard Units of Measure

Use parts of the body, straws, and so on to compare the length or height of objects.

Penguins and Polar Bears

Share the following (geographically improbable) story problem:

An explorer was traveling to the Arctic. He was hiking one day in a terrible blizzard when, way ahead on the top of an iceberg, he spotted 5 penguins and 3 polar bears. He was curious how many feet and noses there were altogether.

Write the following on the board:

There are 5 penguins.

There are 3 polar bears.

How many feet and noses are there altogether?

Have students share shoulder-to-shoulder what the problem is. They should talk about how to solve the problem. Have manipulatives available to scaffold the thinking. Ask them to draw the problem on paper along with an answer. (You can give the students extra credit if they spot the fact that penguins and polar bears do not co-exist in the wild—penguins are only in the Antarctic, and polar bears are found only in the Arctic.)

Continue prompting similar problems (e.g., tricycles and bicycles—how many wheels altogether?). Challenge the students to make up like problems. If necessary to scaffold this, pull a small group around a table and model how many feet are under the table compared to how many students there are altogether.

Upper Elementary/Middle School Ideas

"Reading the World"

It is empowering when students realize how much they infer every day. It proves to students that they are already experts in making inferences because they do it all the time. I love the following introduction to inferring by Kylene Beers (2003). This statement should be on the board when the students come in:

He put down $10.00 at the window. The woman behind the window gave him $4.00. The person next to him gave him $3.00, but he gave it back to her. So, when they went inside, she bought him a large bag of popcorn.

Ask the students to think about what might be happening. Have them write about it and share. It is amazing the inferences they will make, and it is empowering for them to know they are experts at it. Don't they all know when is the best time to ask their parents for the car, money, a friend to bring along on a vacation? And, more importantly, they also know when *not* to ask for these things. How? By inferring. Transition this realization right into the academic setting. It makes predicting and inferring a lot less intimidating, and the experience proves a perfect anchor lesson to use as a point of reference.

Solving a Good Mystery

There are an endless number of short mysteries that stimulate students to predict and infer their way through to a solution. Here are just a few:

Shannon, George, *Stories to Solve.*

Silverthorne, Sandy, and John Warner, *One-Minute Mysteries and Brain Teasers: Good Clean Puzzles for Kids of All Ages.*

Sobol, Donald J., *Two-Minute Mysteries.*

Treat, Lawrence, *You're the Detective! Twenty-Four Solve-Them-Yourself Picture Mysteries.*

Weber, Ken, *Cleverly Crafty Five-Minute Mysteries.*

Weber, Ken, *Even More Five-Minute Mysteries: 40 New Cases of Murder and Mayhem for You to Solve.*

Monitor and Repair Your Understanding Through Predicting and Inferring

Promote using estimation and number sense to make predictions and to confirm or change these predictions throughout the problem solving. Predicting keeps kids engaged. First, do a think-aloud to reveal how you use estimating to predict and infer.

"Thinking That Keeps Going"

Provide time for reflection. Challenge students to analyze data and make inferences according to the results. Allow students to realize that problem solving is not a set of isolated skills (Gear, 2008, p. 77).

Inference Versus Math Fact

When a student says "I just figured that . . . ," he needs to understand that he has made an inference, not necessarily declared a math fact. It is important for that student to realize what an inference is in math, then to find out how the inference was made and if it, in fact, leads to a better understanding of the math being studied. In other words, students sometimes think that, just because they "figured" something to be true, it is right mathematically. Often, assuming that an inference is a fact is the first mistake students make. Ask students to generate ideas, and then have them decide if the idea is an inference or a math fact. Unrecognized inferences can be dangerous in mathematics. Students need to be able to go back and inspect their inferences, realizing it is in fact an inference and may not necessarily be a math fact. Then students can check their inferences for accuracy (Hyde, 2006, p. 108).

Metacognitive Self-Talk to Maintain Mental Stamina

Ask questions and make predictions and inferences to maintain stamina through problem solving. Model how you actively think through a problem by questioning and predicting, then by verifying predictions, inferring meaning, and making connections. This example will really help students maintain the mental stamina it takes to be a good problem solver, especially during standardized testing.

Generating and Testing Hypotheses Through Discovery and Investigation

Here are just a few ideas, but there are virtually no limits on pushing your students' thinking through discovery and investigation:

1. Why are certain shapes and patterns present in nature and in man-made objects? Have students investigate this throughout the school and in their neighborhood, then have them come up with a conjecture with evidence to support it.

2. How tall is that flagpole? Have students predict all the methods they could use to go about measuring the height of a flagpole. Have students estimate, then investigate.

3. With a predetermined circle, challenge students to predict how many such circles it would take to fit in a standard tennis court. Discuss predictions, estimates, and then investigate.

4. Place a floor plan of your local town center on the overhead. (You make this up ahead of time according to the Purpose of your lesson.) Challenge students to predict how to figure out the area, perimeter, and so on (or whatever your purpose is). Discuss inferences and reasonableness in predictions. Have students work in groups to test their predictions.

5. Have students measure the circumference of a determined circle. Challenge students with the following question, "If you unraveled the circumference of the circle, how many of the circumferences

would be able to fit down the long hall closest to your classroom?" Have groups make predictions, discuss reasonableness, then do the investigation.

6. Draw and measure the sides of three right triangles. Have students complete the following table:

Length of a	Length of b	Length of c	$a^2 + b^2$	c^2

Now give the students three non-right triangles. Include these measurements in the table above. Have students identify patterns and generate a formula for the Pythagorean theorem based on the observations.

Shape Teasers

Draw a series of shapes, extending a pattern. Have students identify the pattern; then continue the pattern to the 10th shape, 30th shape, nth shape.

Use Evidence to Interpret and Apply Ideas

Have students analyze data to notice trends and make inferences.

BDA Predicting and Inferring

(Students are familiar with the BDA format in reading. It is also very effective in math.)

1. **Before Reading: Activating Prior Knowledge**—Read the title, subtitle, and table headings. From this information, have students make a prediction about the text. (Remember that in math the text includes numbers and symbols.)

2. **During Reading: Interacting With the Text**—Students use their schema to help make connections, which leads to inferences.

3. **After Reading Strategy: Reflecting on the Text**—Students will reflect on their predictions. Did they come true? Why? Why not? What inferences can they make from the lesson?

Perform Word Surgery

Word surgery is a tool that can be used across content areas. Show students how to surgically take apart math vocabulary words and identify roots, prefixes, and suffixes. In mathematics, understanding root words will facilitate inferring unfamiliar words. Students can also perform word surgery to help make predictions by dissecting the title of each chapter. This is valuable learning. Pointing out titles in informational texts will lead students directly to the learning, whereas titles in fiction texts often leave a little more room for making inferences. It sometimes takes reading the whole chapter in a fiction book to clearly understand the choice of title. In mathematics, if the students can predict where the learning is going from the title, they have an instant purpose for learning, and it only takes a few minutes (Zwiers, 2004, p. 117).

Scrolling, Skimming, and Scanning

Scrolling, skimming, and scanning is another practical tool that can be used daily in all subject areas.

1. *Scrolling:* To move the eyes quickly over an item to determine what the information is about or if the information is relevant to what you need to find. What supports are there to help you find out what the material is all about?
   - Boldfaced words
   - Headings
   - Photographs
   - Tables, graphs, diagrams, maps
   - Illustrations
   - Examples
   - Captions
   - Sidebars

2. *Skimming:* To read quickly for main ideas or supporting details in a text.
   - What is the topic?
   - What challenges might you get prepared for?
   - Is this a topic that is new to you, or do you know something about it?

3. *Scanning:* To move the eyes quickly over a text to find a specific point or points that answer questions or give a purpose for reading.
   - We scan to look up a phone number, read through the small ads in a newspaper, or check TV schedules.
   - It is also useful when searching quickly for specific information in a book or article when there's not time to read every word (see http://42explore.com/skim.htm).

Object Lessons in Inferring

You can use this tool as an anchor lesson on how to make inferences in any situation and any subject area. It only takes five minutes and sets the stage perfectly for teaching how to infer in mathematics. Anchor lessons also give both the teacher and the students a frame of reference. Tanny McGregor (2007) recommends giving students concrete experiences in inferring. She uses "a brown bag of someone's garbage" for the students to make inferences about "the mysterious garbage owner." She also suggests other concrete examples that encourage making inferences:

1. An old and tethered but interesting shoe

2. A shoehorn

3. A garlic press

4. A brayer

Zoom-In to Nonfiction Text Features

In this lesson, students infer and draw conclusions from informational text using features and text structures (Harvey & Goudvis, 2007, pp. 148–149). Active readers recognize, locate, and are able to interpret and use nonfiction text features such as titles, italics, bold headings, graphs, maps, charts, diagrams, webs, comparisons, captions, visuals, and examples to assist in predicting and determining importance. Teach students to "use their eyes the same way they use a mouse to navigate through the text features to access information" (Gear, 2008, pp. 49–62). This technique is similar to scrolling.

Experimental Inquiry

Inquiry can be used to describe observations, generate hypotheses, make predictions, and test those predictions—in many content areas. The steps for this process are as follows (Marzano et al., 2001, p. 232):

1. Observe something and describe what occurred.

2. Explain what was observed.

3. Based on the explanation, make a prediction.

4. Set up an experiment to test the prediction.

5. Explain the results of the experiment and compare with your earlier explanation.

Inferring Thinking Stems

Create a poster to help students recognize when they are inferring. You can also use the poster to prompt students to infer. This poster can be a great resource for any subject area (McGregor, 2007, p. 51).

My guess is . . .

Maybe . . .

I think . . .

I just figured that . . .

Perhaps . . .

It could be that . . .

This could mean . . .

What if . . .

I predict . . .

I infer . . .

Graphic Organizers

Figure 2 depicts some generic graphic organizers that support predicting and encourage inferring in any subject. They do not fit naturally all the time in mathematics, but teaching how to infer in mathematics is a significant component to a deeper conceptual understanding that leads to generalizations.

Figure 2   Cite Your Evidence T-Chart

Pattern(s) You Notice	Inferences or Generalizations You Can Make From This Pattern

McGregor (2007, p. 53)

Cite the evidence that led you down this path of thinking in the first place.

Inference	Evidence From the Learning That Led to That Inference

A dose of schema	+	a piece of evidence	=	a solid inference
EXAMPLE: This is like going backwards twice.	$-3 + -6 =$			Whenever I add two negatives, my answer will be smaller than each of the addends.

Gear (2008)

O What I Observe From the Learning	W Anything I Wonder From My Observations	I What I Can Infer From Either My Observations or My Wonderings.

I See . . .	I Think . . .

Harvey and Goudvis (2007)

Fact	Inference I Made From This Fact and How I Came Up With This Inference

Background Knowledge:	
Questions	Inferences
I wonder . . .	I think . . .

Background Knowledge (BK) +	Text Clues (TC) =	Inference (I)
What do I know?	What is in the text?	What can I infer?

Facts From Our Observations	Inference/Interpretation From the Facts

Beers (2003)

Predictions ⇨	Inferences ⇨	Generalizations

Habit 6

Question for Understanding

Children enter school as question marks and come out as periods.

—Neil Postman, *Teaching as a Subversive Activity*, 1969

W hat is the disconnect between the skills our students use fluently in comprehension instruction and what they are doing or not doing in mathematics? Why are they okay with wrong answers? How do they *not* realize how unreasonable their answers can be sometimes? Why is questioning so crucial in mathematics? Why do we have so many questions, whereas our students don't seem to have enough questions? We were baffled.

Actually, children are born curious. They look at the world around them and ask why, how? Regrettably, what is second nature to our younger students often dissipates as they move into the intermediate grades (Kelley & Clausen-Grace, 2007). In fact, by the time students are in fourth grade, their problem-solving skills suffer because of a profound lack of thinking and questioning (Hyde, 2006, p. 17).

Questioning is the catalyst of investigation (Buhrow & Upczak Garcia, 2005). If you want to make sense of anything, you often must begin with a question. Albert Einstein attested to this when he said, "I have no special talent; I am only passionately curious." Scientists use questions during the process of discovery all the time. Every invention more than likely began with a question.

Why ask questions in mathematics? To help with understanding, to construct meaning, to discover new information, to clarify what is going on, to check inferences, to facilitate visual representations (Hyde, 2006, p. 16). Questions are the glue of engagement (McGregor, 2007, p. 62). They invite children to linger in the learning, to stick with it. Questions give us a purpose for reading, propelling us forward and moving us from a passive stance to an active stance (Gear, 2008, p. 63). Questions send readers on quests (Keene, 2008, p. 107).

Questions are at the heart of all teaching and learning (Harvey & Goudvis, 2007, p. 18), for they stimulate thinking and reasoning. To maximize problem solving, application, and the development of a variety of thinking skills, it is vital that we pay more attention to improving our questioning in mathematics lessons. We want our students not only to understand *what* they did to solve a problem but also to explain *how* and *why* they came to that mathematical thinking.

TEACHER-GENERATED QUESTIONS: THE IMPORTANCE OF PREPLANNED HIGH-LEVEL QUESTIONING

Research indicates that questions that require students to analyze information produce more learning than questions that simply require students to recall or recognize information (Redfeld & Rousseau, 1981). Known-answer questions are largely unique to school and are rarely used in out-of-school conversation (Allington, 2006, p. 110). As teachers, we need to become less concerned with right answers and more concerned with good questions (Allen, 2000, p. 93). Developing constructive questions can help direct learning toward the process of thinking, while at the same time attend to the study of content (Dantonio & Beisenherz, 2001, p. 60).

It is crucial to plan your high-level questions ahead of time and to write them down. When writing your questions, begin with the end in mind. This method requires us to start with a clear understanding of the desired knowledge, learning, and outcomes (Schuster & Canavan Anderson, 2005, p. 5). Use your Focus or objective, and create your questions from that. What do you want the students to know when they leave your classroom? Preplanned higher-level questions preserve the Focus of the lesson and propel students toward the intended Purpose.

RESEARCH FINDINGS

There are three main features of highly effective questions in mathematics:

1. Highly effective questions push students to elaborate on information, establish number sense, and scaffold understanding (Marzano et al., 2001).

- Highly effective questions require more than remembering a fact or reproducing a skill or procedure.
- Highly effective questions help students make sense of the mathematics (Schuster & Canavan Anderson, 2005, p. 3).
- Highly effective questions push students to elaborate on information, create number sense, and support understanding (Marzano et al., 2001).
- Highly effective questions may, in fact, have several acceptable answers (Sullivan & Lilburn, 2002, p.3).
- Lingering questions extend understanding beyond the text (Harvey & Goudvis, 2007, p. 123).
  - Unanswered questions motivate students to keep searching. Isn't that what we really want, that is, lifelong learners?
  - Unanswered questions stimulate the most stirring discussions (Harvey & Goudvis, 2007, p. 113).
  - Remember that sometimes there is no need for answers . . . even in school (Gelb, 1998).

2. Highly effective questions require students to monitor and repair their understanding, and they support metacognition.
   - Plan high-level questions ahead of time to assess the progress of your students. Make this purposeful and focused.
   - Fill in the gaps from the new to the known by including questions that review content and relate what students have learned to what they already know.
   - Encourage making predictions through questioning the text. Read with a question in mind (Harvey & Goudvis, 2007, p. 117).
   - Use questions that focus on helping students discover importance.
   - Using higher-level questioning is a great formative assessment. Who gets it? Who doesn't? Using your students' answers, where do you go now with your lesson?
   - Some students have learned to answer routine exercise questions without fully understanding the concepts (Sullivan & Lilburn, 2002, p. 4). Higher-level questions will scaffold students to deeper meaning.
   - Think-aloud how you use questioning to self-assess. Encourage students to self-assess throughout the lesson.
   - High-level questions facilitate metacognition.
     - How did using the strategy of questioning help you make meaning of the concept or text?
     - Thinking about the exercises can sometimes be as valuable as sitting down to do them (Harwayne, 1992, p. 201).

3. Highly effective questions elicit, engage, and challenge each student's thinking.

- They are questions that empower students to find real meaning and to defend their process. Provide moments of silence for questions to linger, allowing students the opportunity to wrestle with the concepts a little.
- Highly effective questions keep up the engagement; students want to learn because they are interested.
- Highly effective questions are student centered. The questions are questions students care about (Tovani, 2004, p. 2).
- They require students to think deeply about the mathematics.
- Highly effective questions require students to think about the *why* of a given procedure, going beyond the *what* of that procedure.

KEY IDEAS

The following are possible questions to encourage deep thinking in your math class. We suggest you keep this list near your plans so you can choose the best questions based on your Purpose for the lesson.

Questions to Encourage Deep Thinking

As a Bridge to the Learning

(See Component 3 for more on the Bridge to the Learning.)

- Using the text structure, what do you think we will be learning about today? What makes you say that?
- What do you remember about [title of today's lesson]?
- What is this similar to? What makes you say that?
- If you had to guess, what do you think the answer will be, approximately? How do you know? Does this sound reasonable? If not, what will you do about that?
- What are your givens in the problem? What do you need to find out? How do you know that?
- How is [today's lesson] the same as yesterday's lesson? How is it different?
- How might you picture that? Explain.
- Why do you think that?
- What patterns do you notice? Explain.
- What do you predict will be the most important information in this passage? Why?

During the Learning

- How are you solving the problem? Why?
- How did you know to try that strategy?

(Continued)

(Continued)

- What could you do differently?
- Does what you are doing so far make sense? How do you know? If what you are doing so far doesn't make sense, what will you do next? Why?
- At what point did you get off track? What will you do about it?
- Does this part of the answer make sense so far? How do you know? If not, what will you do next? Why?
- Does what you are doing so far align with your estimate? Why? Why not?
- Why did you choose that strategy? Explain.
- What other strategies do you know that you can use? How do you know that will also work?
- How is your procedure different than [name of another student] strategy?
- How do you know [name of other student] is right? Explain.
- Do you notice anything that could trip you up in the problem solving? What is it? What are you going to do about it? Why?
- What patterns do you notice? Explain.
- Can you show me a part of the text where you have a question? What were you wondering when you read this part?
- Can you show me a part where you were confused? What was confusing about it?

As Part of the Debrief

(See Component 5 for more on the Debrief.)

- How does your answer relate to your guesstimate?
- Is your answer a reasonable one? Why? Why not? If not, what is your plan now?
- Can you show me a part where you were confused? What was confusing about it?
- Does this answer make sense? Why do you think that?
- How do you know you are right?
- What strategy will not work in this instance? How do you know?
- At what point did you get off track? What did you do about it?
- What could you have done differently?
- Will this work all the time? Some of the time? Never? How do you know this?
- Will this process work for every number? Why? Why not?
- What is another example that might work? How do you know that? What is a counterexample? How do you know that?
- What else would work? What wouldn't work?
- Were all of the groups' solutions the same? How were they different? Why do you think there was a difference between your groups' answers?

- From today's lesson, what might you be learning about tomorrow? What makes you say that?
- How is this used in real life? Explain.
- Looking at all of your work, how would you state the problem?
- What can you infer from . . . ? How did you make that inference?
- How might you explain that to a little child?
- How did you work together to solve this problem?
- How did your thinking change? Explain.
- What do you now understand that you didn't understand yesterday?
- How do you know you know?
- How do you know you don't know?
- What do you see that is new to you? Provide clear and vivid examples.
- How is this similar to . . . ? How is it different?
- What strategy would you prefer? Why?
- How would you describe the most important idea you learned today in one sentence?
- What was the main point of the lesson? What makes you say that?
- What are some new questions you generated from what you did in class today?
- In the context of data analysis, questions will arise naturally and meaningfully.

    o What are "they" trying to sell you? What made you think that?
    o How could they be misleading you? How do you know?
    o Who would want this data? Why?
    o Who would want to publicize this data? Why?
    o Who definitely would *not* want this data publicized? Why?
    o What would make an appropriate title for this data? Why?
    o Using the solutions we discovered, how can you organize the data?
    o What type of graph would be most meaningful to represent the data? Explain.
    o Using the graph, what would make an appropriate title for each axis? Why?
    o What would happen to the appearance of the data if you changed the interval? Why would someone do that?
    o What inferences can you make from the data? Explain.
    o What conclusions can you make from this data? Explain.
    o What would you change about this representation? Why?
    o What trends do you notice? Explain.
    o What does this trend mean to your future? Explain.
    o What effect do you think this data could have on society? Explain.

- What is something you would like me to know about your problem solving today?

STUDENT-GENERATED QUESTIONS

Although many of our students become relatively proficient at answering teacher-generated questions, they sometimes forget the most important questions—their own (Kelley & Clausen-Grace, 2007). When students have questions, they are less likely to abandon the learning (Harvey & Goudvis, 2007, p. 82); therefore, it only makes sense to nudge our students toward the habit of asking questions.

Proficient readers spontaneously and purposefully ask questions before, during, and after reading. A proficient mathematician also knows that asking questions brings clarity, focus, and meaning to the learning. Asking questions, in any learning, is a signal that you are constructing meaning. Proficient learners asks questions to clarify meaning, connect prior and new information, set a purpose, speculate about text yet to be read, show skepticism, locate a specific answer, and continue to wonder whether or not their questions can be answered (Harvey & Goudvis, 2007, p. 109). If you ask questions as you learn, you are awake. You are thinking.

How can we encourage children to ask questions in math class? We can create an atmosphere of acceptance where mistakes are a natural part of learning, where successive approximation is valued (Hyde, 2006, p. 17). When students learn that their own questions have value, their confidence soars, and their thinking grows exponentially (McGregor, 2007, p. 62).

 ## HOW CAN I DO THIS IN MY MATH CLASS . . . TOMORROW?

All of the following ideas can be tweaked to fit any grade level.

Skittles and Graphing

Give each student a cup of Skittles. Have them predict how many are in the cup and which color occurs most frequently. Count the Skittles and separate them by color. Students will create a bar graph using the Skittles. They draw an example of their bar graphs and think of questions they can ask a partner. They should switch graphs with a partner and ask the questions.

Bring Any Important Questions You Have to the Table

It is important for students to understand that *their* questions guide the learning process and make learning personal. Encourage them to come to any part of the lesson with questions. Bring the questions up to the whole group. Facilitate the discussion, but try not to answer the questions. The students need to arrive at their understanding themselves, and when we deliver the answers too quickly, we are not giving them a chance to own the learning. The teacher should not be the processor of the knowledge. If a student asks a question and the teacher responds to it by stating the correct answer, the teacher might learn something, but the picture is all wrong. Let's make sure that students are responding to students and that the teachers are just the directors (Wormeli, 2009, p. 142).

Questions to Monitor and Repair Understanding

Students ask questions to clarify confusion (Harvey & Goudvis, 2007, p. 125). Encourage students to monitor their comprehension throughout the problem-solving process. Some question stems are useful to scaffold the thinking. Post the following in the class for students to use as a reference:

Questions to Keep in Mind While Problem Solving

Before Solving

- First, make a guesstimate by asking, What would be a reasonable answer? How do I know that is reasonable? Do my thoughts make mathematical sense?
- What visual representations can I make to help me understand the problem better?
- Have I solved a similar problem? If so, what strategies did I use to solve that problem? If not, what connections can I make to help make this problem easier to understand?
- What are my givens?
- What do I need to find out?
- What are my constraints in the problem? How do I know?
- How is today's lesson similar to yesterday's lesson? How will that help me solve the problem?
- How might I get started? Does this make sense?
- What inferences can I make about . . . ? Explain your inference.

During Solving

- Is what I am doing so far making sense with my original estimate? Why? Why not? If not, what will I do differently, and why?

After Solving

- Does my answer make sense?
- Are my strategy and answer reasonable?
- Does my answer align with my original estimate? If so, how? If not, what do I need to do differently? Why?
- How do I know I am right?
- Is there another way I could have solved this problem? How? Why did I choose the method I did?
- What questions might I still have about . . . ?

Think-Aloud

Using the monitoring and repairing questions above, model explicitly how *you* would use these questions to solve problems. Open your thoughts and your processing to the students. Use the questions to direct your learning. It is powerful for students to see and hear what a good mathematician does to be successful. Some of your students don't know you ask questions while working mathematically. They may just think you're smarter because you are the teacher. Make your math thoughts explicit. It definitely levels the "mathematical playing field" and takes the mystery out of problem solving for your struggling math students (see Component 4, Gradual Release in Mathematics, for a think-aloud example).

Exploratory Questions

Give students plenty of opportunity to investigate before the whole-class instruction. Ask students to create questions from the investigation. Use the questions to lead the learning and the discussion. Here are some great examples of questions for your students to explore. These, and many more excellent questions, are found in *Good Questions for Math Teaching: Why Ask Them and What to Ask, K–6* by Peter Sullivan and Pat Lilburn (2002):

1. What would be a reasonable rounding policy for a supermarket? Why do you think that?

2. How many different ways can you show 2/3? Explain your reasoning.

3. An easy way to add 9 is to add 10 and take away 1. Using a similar strategy, what other numbers might I add or subtract in this way? Explain your reasoning.

4. Two numbers multiply to give 36,000. What might the two numbers be? Explain your reasoning.

5. I am thinking of a number. If I divide by 3, there is a remainder of 1. If I divide by 4, there is a remainder of 1. What might my number be? Explain your reasoning.

The following excellent questions come from *Good Questions for Math Teaching: Why Ask Them and What to Ask, Grades 5–8* by Lainie Schuster and Nancy Canavan Anderson (2005):

1. I am thinking of four odd numbers. They are divisible by 5. The sums of the digits of each number create a consecutive number sequence. My first number is a square number. What are my four numbers? Explain your reasoning.

2. Zach looked at an integer subtraction computation and said, "You can find the difference between these two integers by doubling the

first integer." What might the computation have been? Explain your reasoning.

3. A vase holds red and white roses only. For every 3 red roses, there are 2 white roses. How many flowers might be in the vase? Explain your reasoning.

4. How can you use a calculator to solve $4.58 \div 0.2$ without pressing the decimal point button? Explain your reasoning.

5. A ball of dough is rolled out into a circle with a 12-inch diameter. How many cookies with a diameter of 2.5 inches can be made from this dough? Explain your reasoning.

6. A television screen measures 46 inches along its diagonal. What might be the approximate length and width of the screen? Explain your reasoning.

Central Question

Have students preview the text and then generate and record a focus question they think will be answered by the end of the lesson. While learning, have them revise their question, answer it, or continue with the question. During the Debrief, discuss strategies and answers. Make sure to share those questions that were not answered. If the question cannot be answered at that point, record it, and revisit it for the whole class to answer at some point.

T-Chart of Fact/Page Number and Things I Wonder

This simple T-chart is an uncomplicated way for students to internalize their math textbook. It forces students to record important or confusing facts and the textbook page numbers where they are addressed, which is a lifelong-learner skill, and then deepens thinking by asking for their wonderings or questions, both of which are strong numeracy skills (Tovanni, 2004, p. 85).

I Learned/I Wonder Two-Column Notes

This method works in any subject and has the power to naturally connect students to their learning. By asking students to acknowledge what they learned and to record the questions they still have, you can anchor them to both the lesson and their understanding (Harvey & Goudvis, 2007, p. 111). A modification of this idea is to have students fill out two columns titled "Notes" and "Thinking and Questions I Still Have" (Harvey & Goudvis, 2007, p. 118).

Hot Seat

Have students work in small groups, with one volunteer in the "hot seat" per group. During the learning, the other group members will think of questions they would like to be answered. The student in the hot seat answers the questions. Differentiate using sentence stems or preplanned questions (Zwiers, 2004, p. 102).

Stump the Teacher

This idea is a familiar and popular one in any subject. It is basically the same as the previous activity, but this time the teacher is on the hot seat, and students prepare questions to stump you. The students really love this (Forget, 2004).

Questions Never End, and That's a Good Thing

Hang a roll of adding machine tape in your classroom as a reminder of how questioning goes on and on and on. Encourage students to jot down anything they wonder about, without worrying about finding the answers. Soon it will be filled with the curiosities of your students (McGregor, 2007, p. 62).

"What We Wonder" Poster, "The Parking Lot of Questions" Poster, or "Questions That Keep Going Around in My Head" Poster

Students must reflect on lingering questions to expand their thinking (Harvey & Goudvis, 2007, p. 125). Make a poster using one of these catchy phrases, and encourage students to record unanswered questions on sticky notes that they can attach to the poster. In this way, students feel safe asking questions that they may be a little nervous about asking out loud. You can also make a poster per student and have the students keep track of their own questions and answers along the way. This activity encourages self-efficacy (Forsten et al., 2002a).

To Wonder Out Loud

Take time to "wonder out loud" at different points in the lesson. Encourage the students to share their "wonderings" with a partner. Then circulate around the room and use the questions you hear to either scaffold the learning or facilitate a discussion (Harvey & Goudvis, 2007, p.100).

Questions on Sticky Notes

Have students learn to read actively by responding to the text. Provide Post-its and challenge students to question, visualize, and connect during their reading. They should write responses on Post-its and place them directly in the text. If questions are answered, encourage students to place the original question where the answer is found. If there are still questions to be answered, have students save them to discuss during the Debrief, or place them on a "questions that still need to be answered" poster in the room.

Habit 7

Summarize, Determine Importance, Synthesize

Using Note Taking and Journaling

Learning is a matter of sifting, sorting, selecting, ingesting, and then digesting the most important morsel.

—Maya Angelou

D etermining importance, summarizing, and synthesizing are related acts that together comprise one of the most crucial of the nine critical thinking habits. By instilling this habit, a teacher can push her students' thinking far across the line from simply doing mathematics to deeply thinking through mathematics. These thinking acts have the power to force students to own their mathematical thinking and be able to take it with them into the real world.

Determining importance is the act that gets most directly to the heart of learning. Stephanie Harvey writes, "Determining Importance means picking out the most important information when you read, to highlight essential ideas, to isolate supporting details, and to read for specific information. Teachers need to help readers sift and sort information, and make decisions about what information they need to remember and what information they can disregard" (Harvey, 1998, p. 117).

A significant part of understanding is the ability to separate the nonessential from the essential (Zimmerman & Hutchins, 2003, p. 123), to discriminate what is important from what is not. Harvey suggests that readers have to decide and consider what is essential in the learning if, in fact, they are going to learn anything at all from the experience (Harvey, 1998, p. 118).

We often introduce the strategy of determining importance when teaching nonfiction. After all, they go together since nonfiction reading is reading to learn, and, as mentioned, readers need to decide and remember what is important in the texts they read if they are going to learn anything from them (Harvey & Goudvis, 2007, p. 118). To determine what is important and worth remembering in mathematics reading, students first need to be familiar with the organization of their math textbooks.

There are comprehensive text structures common to all informational texts: a table of contents, chapter titles, lesson headings, a glossary, and an index. Students need experience in how to use these structures to *locate* important ideas. It is helpful to begin the year with an activity to help students navigate through these structures. One such activity could be a textbook scavenger hunt (see box below). While competing to find the items in the scavenger hunt, students become familiar with the overall organization of their math textbooks.

Sample Textbook Scavenger Hunt

Getting Familiar With Your Textbook

Math is all around you. Having good math skills can help solve everyday problems. What kinds of problems can you solve using mathematics? Through the use of your textbook, you will be introduced this year to many of these exciting challenges in mathematics.

The Challenge

With a partner and your textbooks, solve the following scavenger hunt. As soon as you think you have all the right answers, raise your hands. You are allowed to receive one hint from the teacher, which you may use at any time. Be careful—once you have used your hint, you may not ask for help again. *GOOD LUCK!*

The Hunt

1. Where is the safest place to swim when you are in shark-infested waters?

2. On what pages can you find out about Venn diagrams?

3. What website is available for getting assistance and support at home?

4. How many chapters does your book have?

5. In what section of your book can you find a graphic organizer for all the material taught in each chapter?

6. In which chapter will you learn about decimals? Name two ways you discovered this.

7. What is the Chapter Project for Chapter 4?

8. What tool is available to use if you want to check your answers to see if you understand the concept? What is the most effective way to use this tool? Explain.

9. What resource is available if you want to locate the pages in your textbook related to probability? On what page does this resource begin?

10. Which section of your textbook contains a list of important terms and their meanings? Where does this section begin?

11. Where could you find information on Euler's formula?

12. Turn to page 187. What interesting fact is recorded in the "Did You Know" rectangle?

13. On what pages will you find the Measurement Conversion Factors?

14. What text structures are provided in each lesson to help you determine what information is most important?

How could this scavenger hunt be helpful to you?

There are also lesson-specific text structures in most math textbooks. For example, math lessons might include a title, an introductory paragraph, photos with captions, a short investigation to introduce the concept, vocabulary words in bold, sample problems, drawings, graphs or diagrams, and practice exercises. Students need to understand that these organizational aides are built-in clues as to what is important in the lesson. They should learn how to use text structures to predict the objective, to maintain the focus, to validate comprehension, and to reflect on the Purpose of the lesson. They may also need to learn how to "turn down the volume" on distracting visuals that do not support the learning. There is an abundance of information on a typical page of any math textbook that can be described as "input overload." Learning how to navigate through the information given, organize it, and then determine what is most important is a skill that must be modeled by the teacher. The students need to see and hear how you, the teacher, sort through all that is presented and how you organize it, make meaning out of it, and then determine what is most important.

All math textbooks also include hierarchical clues to help students navigate through the pages. Students should be aware of these textual features and how to make use of them when determining importance. There is a hierarchical relationship in the way information is presented for each lesson: The most important ideas are at the top level with a large and bold font, the next level supports these ideas, usually with a smaller but still bolded font, and the bottom level provides the supporting details for each idea, including sample problems. Students need to recognize this structure to determine what is important, and we need to model and facilitate employment of these text features to help students locate, comprehend, and retain the material they are expected to learn.

Summarizing is restating the essence of a lesson in as few words as possible in a new, yet succinct way. When summarizing, students identify key elements and condense important information into their own words during and after learning to solidify meaning (Keene & Zimmerman, 2007, p. 231). Summarizing has been defined as "covering the main points succinctly. A summary is a statement of the main idea of the learning, its very foundation, its core—in just a sentence or two" (Harvey & Goudvis, 2007, p. 118). A summary captures the gist of a lesson.

Summarizing requires students to determine what is important by analyzing the information, organizing it in a way that captures the essential ideas and supporting details, and finally stating it in their own words. One must thus *synthesize* the information to summarize it. A synthesis occurs as students summarize the learning and appreciate what it means to them (Zimmerman & Hutchins, 2003, p. 130).

A summary has the following characteristics (Harvey, 1998):

- It is a short and organized analysis of the learning.
- It is to the point, containing the big idea of the text.
- It omits trivial information.
- It is not a retelling or a "photocopy" of the text but is a synthesis of the learning.

As students practice these strategies, their ability to understand specific content increases. When asked to give a summary, students must scrutinize information at a fairly deep level to decide what information to delete, what to substitute, and what to keep (Anderson & Hidi, 1988/1989; Hidi & Anderson, 1987).

Effective summarizing is one of the most powerful skills students can cultivate. It provides students with tools for identifying the most important aspects of what they are learning (Marzano et al., 2001). Instruction in summarizing helps students

- make the learning manageable;
- identify or generate main ideas;

- prioritize information from essential to nonessential—sifting and sorting information;
- connect the main or central ideas;
- eliminate unnecessary information; and
- capture the meaning and remember what is learned (Zimmerman & Hutchins, 2003, pp. 119–145).

Synthesizing information is when you combine what you already know with what you have learned to make something new. Thinking evolves through a process; it changes and grows as students gather more information. New information makes the learner re-evaluate their schema to form new schema, thus creating original insights, perspectives, and understandings by reflecting on the text(s) and merging elements from it with existing schema. Students put the pieces together to see them in a new way (see http://reading.ecb.org/teacher/synthesizing/index.html).

Synthesizing goes beyond restating and becomes rethinking. It is closely linked to determining importance. Essentially, as students identify what's important, they interweave their thoughts to form a comprehensive perspective to make the whole greater than just the sum of its parts (Zimmerman & Hutchins, 2003, p. 129). Through the process of synthesizing, student thinking deepens and understanding grows.

Synthesizing information requires a student to process and interact with information rather than simply copy information. When educator Debbie Miller (2002) was asked how she began to understand synthesis, she replied,

> It's the ripple, . . . the simple elements of thought transformed into a complex whole. Synthesis is like throwing a rock into a pond: first there's the splash, and then the water ripples out, making little waves that get bigger and bigger. As you read, your thinking evolves as you encounter new information, and the meaning gets bigger and bigger, just like the ripples in the pond. (p. 164)

Giving students the opportunity to synthesize generates a deeper understanding of what they are learning. We, as teachers, need to explicitly teach our students to take stock of meaning while they read and use it to help their thinking evolve, perhaps leading them to new insights but at least enhancing understanding in the process (Harvey & Goudvis, 2007, pp. 144–145).

The most effective lessons (and the experiences students cite years later) involve some kind of reinterpretation of content (Wormeli, 2009, p. 144). We need to set the stage for synthesis by providing lots of opportunities for students to challenge their existing schemata. In mathematics, this process can be a slow one built from many connections. It may seem like one magical moment when a student understands a math concept for the very first time, but, although it may seem that the "light bulb suddenly went on," in mathematics, it often takes time for a concept to crystallize (Hyde, 2006, p. 155).

NOTE TAKING (TO DETERMINE IMPORTANCE, TO SUMMARIZE, AND TO SYNTHESIZE)

Note taking is a strategy for making information meaningful and valuable. Note taking is only effective to the extent that students paraphrase, organize, and make sense of the information while taking notes.

Taking notes requires students to differentiate between information that is considered important and information that is considered supplemental to the topic. These differentiation habits need to be taught and modeled, then re-taught and re-modeled, because of the complexity of thought involved.

Notes can include both linguistic and nonlinguistic forms, for example, idea webs, sketches, informal outlines, and combinations of words and schematics (Nye, Crooks, Powlie, & Tripp, 1984). When students use note-taking strategies, they are better able to understand what they are reading, can identify key information, and can provide a summary that helps them retain the information (Armbruster, Anderson, & Ostertag, 1987).

Effective note taking is not simply moving information from text to notebook; it has to be more than that. Successful note taking is one of the most significant skills students can develop, providing students with tools for recognizing and comprehending the most important aspects of what they are learning (Marzano et al., 2001, p. 48). Students need to learn how to decide what is important and what is not. Creating the time to demonstrate the act of determining importance when taking notes is critical, as is providing ample time for students to practice.

Research Findings

Below are three key points on note taking from Marzano, Pickering, and Pollock's *Classroom Instruction That Works* (2001, pp. 43–44). We've added our thinking as bulleted points below each item.

1. Verbatim note taking is, perhaps, the least effective way to take notes.
   - When students are busy recording everything they hear or see, they cannot possibly be synthesizing the information, which is the primary purpose of taking notes.
   - Students must delete some information, substitute some information, and keep some information when taking notes.
   - To effectively delete, substitute, and keep information, students must analyze the information at a fairly deep level.

2. Notes should be considered a work in progress.
   - Students should be encouraged to add and revise their notes as their knowledge of the content expands.
   - Teachers need to provide chunks of time for students to review and revise their notes.
   - When students review and revise their own notes, the notes become more meaningful and useful (Einstein, Morris, & Smith, 1985).

3. Notes should be used as study guides for tests.
   - Notes have been proven to be a powerful method of reviewing for tests.
   - Students should review their notes as soon as possible after class. The longer the period of time before review, the greater the loss of recall.
   - Review each week's notes at the end of the week.

Benefits of Taking Notes

- Taking notes develops a sense of listening, allowing the student to recognize main ideas and to understand the organization of the material.
- Taking notes provides the clearest and best indication of what the student should encounter on the exam.
- Taking notes in class keeps the student's attention focused, thereby increasing concentration, retention, and understanding.
- Taking notes in class makes the student an active participant in the learning process rather than a passive listener or daydreamer.
- Taking notes helps the student sort out important information by determining importance, summarizing, and synthesizing. This process empowers the student, making the material his own.
- Reviewing notes helps with recall. Recall remains significant immediately after a learning period, such as a lecture, then declines rapidly until, after about 24 hours, recall has diminished by about 80%. However, the decline in recall can be dramatically reduced if one reinforces the learning by a short review within 1 hour.

KEY IDEAS

There are a number of different note-taking systems that have been shown to be effective in educational contexts. Here is an introduction to a few methods: Cornell, cloze, SQ3R, concept maps, and two- and three-column notes.

The Cornell Note-Taking System

The Cornell method is one of the most useful and successful methods for note taking. It was devised 40 years ago by Walter Pauk, a professor at Cornell University. It was meant to be used as an easy study guide for tests. It is now adopted as the preferred method for note taking by most major law schools across the nation. The Cornell method provides a systematic format for condensing and organizing notes.

For this method, the paper is divided into two columns. The first column is used to enter key or cue words, whereas the second is the notes column (for recording ideas and facts).

Notes from the teaching/reading are written in the note-taking column on the right; notes usually consist of the main ideas of the text or lecture, and long ideas are paraphrased. Long sentences are avoided; symbols or abbreviations are used instead. The system lets the students interact with the learning so that they not only understand the topics well but can also see how the ideas are interrelated, which prepares them for taking the tests and exams.

Relevant questions, connections, cues, or keywords are written in the left recall column.

After the notes have been taken, the student writes a brief summary at the bottom of the page. Summarizing helps increase understanding of the topic. When studying for either a test or a quiz, the student can use the summary to review previous lessons.

Cornell notes are a great study tool. The student covers up the note-taking (right) column and answers the questions/keywords in the cue (left) column. The student is encouraged to reflect on the material and review the notes regularly. Students can also revise the notes, adding clarification and connections. If students spend time reviewing their notes, they will not only retain the new information but they will also have a deeper understanding. They are also able to study and test themselves effectively from the notes.

Interactive Cloze System

1. Select a paragraph from the text that is about to be taught or assigned.

2. Delete important keywords from the paragraph and duplicate worksheet copies for students. You can also create your own worksheet. *Important*: Make sure keywords are deleted and not words such as *is, the, and.*

3. Have students predict what they think the missing words might be. Have them justify their choices.

4. Ask students to read the selection quietly.

The Cornell Note-Taking System for Grades 4–8

Name: _____ Topic: _____

Date: _____ Class/Subject: _____

Recall/Cue Column (2½ inches wide)	Note-Taking Column (6 inches wide)

Keywords/Cues/Connections
 	
Reduce ideas and facts to concise phrases and summaries as cues for reciting, reviewing, and reflecting:
 	
    Categories/headings
    Questions
    Review/test alerts!
    Cues/connections
    Reminders
 	
Note: Leave space so you can add notes and test review questions later on when studying
	Record the main ideas of the reading or whole-class instruction as fully and as meaningfully as possible.
	
	Write down only important information.
	
	Look for:
	
	✓ bold, underlined, or italicized words
	✓ properties, principles, and formulas
	✓ process
	✓ nonlinguistic representations—drawings, diagrams, tables, charts
	✓ graphic representation
	✓ information in boxes
	✓ algorithms
	✓ patterns identified
	✓ information the book or teacher repeats
	✓ words, big ideas, or events that might be on a test
	✓ example problems—working the problems out yourself before checking the given solutions. If you are correct, move on. If you are not correct, do not move on until you understand how to solve the problem.
	✓ details you might be able to use later in a paper or presentation or that you see as important to the lesson
	
	Abbreviate familiar words; use symbols $(+, -, >, \#)$
	
	Take notes in bullets and indents; not formal outlines
	
	Cut unnecessary words
	
	Use telegraphic sentences

Summary	
Write one of the following: a summary of what you read/heard; the three most important points of the article/chapter/lecture; questions you still need to answer.	

The Cornell Note-Taking System for Grades K–3

My Connections (2½ inches wide)	My Notes (6 inches wide)

Students draw when they make a personal connection to something in their math textbook.
 	
Grades 2–3
Show them how to record the textbook page number where they made their connection.
	Students draw an example of the main idea.
	
	Grades 2–3 can even include captions of the main idea.
	
	SHOW your students what to do when they come across the following things in their textbook.
	  ✓ bold, underlined, or italicized words
	  ✓ real life examples
	  ✓ drawings, diagrams, tables, charts
	  ✓ graphic representation
	  ✓ information in boxes
	  ✓ patterns
	  ✓ the big ideas
	  ✓ example problems

My Summary	
Draw the most important thing you learned today in math.	

Example of Cornell Note Page (Upper Elementary/Middle School)

Cues and Connections	Lesson 1.1, Numbers Are Everywhere	
	NOTES	
WOW—remember other systems like base 5 or 4 or 3	DECIMAL SYSTEM (AKA the base 10 system): A system of writing numbers based on the number 10.	
	DECIMAL NOTATION: a number written in the decimal system. Example: 35 or 32.8	
A whole number is still in decimal notation.	WHOLE NUMBERS: 0, 1, 2, 3 . . . infinity (no negative numbers here)	
*Remember the word "and" represents the decimal point!	WORD NOTATION	DECIMAL NOTATION
	Nine million, four hundred fifty-two thousand, six hundred seventy	9,452,670
	Two billion, seven hundred thousand, six hundred fifty	2,000,700,650

Cues and Connections	Lesson 1.1, Numbers Are Everywhere
	SOME USES OF NUMBERS
Give examples of each use of numbers in real life	*Counts + counting units: 9,452,670 people. Count = 9,452,670 counting unit = people
	*Identifications + codes: like bar codes, football jersey numbers
	*Ordering—ordinal numbers
	*Locations—addresses
	SUMMARY
Numbers are found in our everyday lives: newspapers, addresses, sporting events, and so on. Most people use the decimal system. We can express numbers in words and decimal form.	

5. Ask students to complete the cloze activity on their own or with a partner.

6. Allow them to discuss their answers with a partner.

7. Students can then reread the actual text to find out if their answers are correct.

SQ3R Method

The SQ3R approach to note taking allows for active elaboration of the material read or presented in the whole-class instruction. It consists of five steps.

1. *Survey:* Flip through the lesson and note the layout, first and last paragraphs, the headings used; familiarize yourself with the reading.

2. *Question:* Ask questions about the way the reading is structured and think about the questions you will need to keep in mind while reading. Think about how this lesson might connect to something you learned yesterday, last week, last year.

3. *Read:* Read actively but quickly, looking for the main points of the reading. Don't take any notes. You might want to read through it twice quickly.

4. *Recall:* Write down the main points of the reading and any really important facts and opinions that help support the main points.

5. *Review:* Repeat the first three steps and make sure you haven't missed anything. At this point, you might like to reread and revise your notes or write down how the material you've just covered relates to your original questions or task. Reflect on how this lesson connects to what you learned previously. Now consider where you think the learning might go tomorrow. Explain how you reached your thoughts (Robinson, 1970).

Concept Maps

Concept maps are visual representations of a complex concept. A concept map presents the relationships among a set of connected concepts and ideas. Concept maps are used to stimulate the generation of ideas in a cohesive and creative way. For example, concept mapping is sometimes used for brainstorming as a way to integrate old and new knowledge. See the example below:

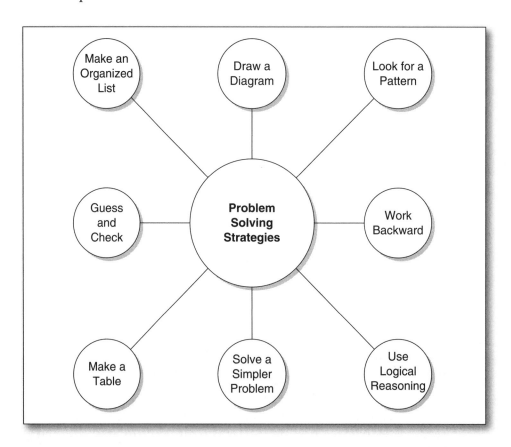

Two-Column and Three-Column Note Taking

Many nonfiction texts are written with headings. These headings usually reflect the main idea, and the text supplies the details that flesh out the main idea. With this note-taking system, students write the main idea in the "Heading" or "Main Idea" column. Next, they read the designated text and list the details that support or explain that topic or idea.

Emphasize to students that *support* and *explain* are keywords to keep in mind. Details that support or explain are important details. Below are some examples of two- and three-column notes:

Open-ended Math Prompt		
Calculations: Mostly numbers with appropriate labels and units. Include each step of the process.	Explanation: Mostly words—the *what* and the *why*. Include a written explanation of each step.	
Topic, Title of Lesson, or Objective		
Main idea	Notes (important details): Explanation and support	
Topic, Title of Lesson, or Objective		
Information/concepts	Nonlinguistic representation of that information or concept in some visual way	
Topic, Title of Lesson, or Objective		
Content	Process	
Topic, Title of Lesson, or Objective		
Key Terms	Examples	
Topic, Title of Lesson, or Objective		
Main points	Responses: Questions, connections, visualizations, inferences	
Title of Lesson or Objective		
Topic	Details	Responses
Title of Lesson or Objective		
Facts	Questions	Responses

Online Note-Taking Resources

- Digital Index Card: http://landmark-project.com/evaluation/dic1.php
- NoteStar from 4teachers (tools for teachers and students): http://notestar.4teachers.org
- NoteTaker: http://interactives.mped.org/view_interactive.aspx?id=722&title=

JOURNALING (TO DETERMINE IMPORTANCE, TO SUMMARIZE, AND TO SYNTHESIZE)

In his book *Writing to Learn* (1988), William Zinsser states, "Writing is how we think our way into a subject and make it our own." Writing is a concrete way to show students' thinking so that they can look at it and analyze it. In mathematics, it focuses thought and enhances critical thinking. Writing sometimes leads to more questions and to the discovery of mathematical connections. Students in math write to clarify their thinking, and as they write, they expand their knowledge of the math.

Writing shifts the responsibility for learning away from the teacher and toward the students by encouraging personal learning. When writing in mathematics, students not only gather knowledge but they also determine which facts to keep, which to discard, and how to represent them.

A math journal is an easy but worthwhile way to introduce writing into your math class. Math journals help students clarify and stretch their thinking. Processing thought with a math journal helps students make sense of confusing problems as they reflect during the writing. For younger students, writing is often in the form of pictures, and part of the processing can be verbal as they share their thinking with a partner. A math journal is the perfect venue for students to move from the concrete to the representational to the abstract.

Through math journals, mathematical facts, personal experience, and visual representations merge as students make mathematical ideas their own. During the writing, ideas become clear, and students are more apt to discover and own the concepts being presented. Writing facilitates synthesis.

Math Journals

Writing in mathematics will help students to:

- Organize their ideas
- Communicate mathematically (early elementary students would do this verbally)
- Draw or sketch out mathematical thinking (drawing allows younger students to access the deep thinking that a journal provides)
- Become more creative mathematically
- Demonstrate their mathematical thinking through a different venue
- Evaluate both process and procedure
- Elaborate on the reasoning behind the math
- Increase confidence in math
- Stay engaged in the learning
- Make math relevant

- Explain and justify their thinking about both process and procedure
- Deepen the meaning
- Think and respond metacognitively
- Modify their thinking
- Examine alternative strategies
- Reflect on their learning
- Cultivate numeracy through the nine critical thinking habits

How to Implement a Math Journal

The biggest stumbling block for teachers when considering journaling is their concern about class time and covering and meeting all content and curriculum requirements. Generally, however, proponents agree that when teachers incorporate writing in their content areas the need for review and reteaching is significantly reduced (Worsley & Mayer, 1989).

Finding the time for your students to write will take some experimenting. How you use math journals will depend on the Focus of the lesson, your preferences, and the particular age and needs of your students. This decision is a personal one, but here are some suggestions that we have found to be beneficial and purposeful for the students and not taxing on our time:

1. *While the students are walking into the classroom, Ignite them with a thought-provoking journal prompt.* This writing task settles the class, sets the tone for learning to begin immediately, and engages all the students. It also gives you a couple of minutes to take attendance and check homework. This journal prompt can perform the following purposes:

- Connect the previous lesson(s). For example:
  - Write a nominating speech for the formula that you feel is most important. Make sure you support your decision with mathematical reasoning (this idea comes from a former teaching colleague, Maria Cuozzo).
  - Create a dialogue between two mathematical items or concepts (for example, between a positive and a negative number, between a multiplication sign and a division sign, etc.). Be imaginative, but be sure the content of the dialogue is of a mathematical nature (this idea comes from a former teaching colleague, Maria Cuozzo).
  - Summarize last night's homework assignment.

- Activate background knowledge. For example:
  - Do you think it makes sense to split a day into 24 hours? Would another number have been a better choice? Why or why not (Schuster & Canavan Anderson, 2005)?

- o We are beginning a study of . . . . Write everything you already know about it, write questions that you might have about it, and tell what you might want to know about it.
- o Write everything you remember about yesterday's class. Share it with a partner.
- o Write everything you know about a square, an expression, etc.

- Cultivate making predictions. For example:
  - o Using what you learned yesterday, what do you think we might be learning about today? What makes you say that? Include mathematical justification.
  - o Skim and scan the lesson. What do you think you will learn after today that you didn't know yesterday?

- Lead them into a discovery moment. For example:
  - o How do you know that $4/6 = 2/3$? Think of at least two different explanations.
  - o What if tomorrow everything was 10 (100, 1,000, 1/10, etc.) times more? Write a journal entry about how that would affect your day.

- Challenge their thinking. For example:
  - o What do you think of when you think of numbers? Draw a picture.
  - o 4 bananas and 1 grapefruit weigh just as much as 14 apples; 2 bananas and 3 apples weigh just as much as 2 grapefruit. How many apples weigh just as much as a grapefruit? Explain your process in writing.
  - o There are 290 red and blue marbles in the bag. There are 120 more red marbles. How many blue marbles are there? Set up an equation that led you to the answer and explain your reasoning (Singapore math).
  - o The answer is 2/3. What might the question be?

- Capture students' attention. For example:
  - o (Remove the main title and the titles for each axis on any type of graph and present it to the students.) Create titles for this graph that make sense with the data presented. Explain your reasoning. (You can do this at any grade level. It really encourages critical thinking because it pushes student thinking to analysis and evaluation.)
  - o (Present a misleading graph to the students.) Identify and explain all the ways this graph is misleading.

- Pinpoint a confusing or easily misunderstood mathematical idea. For example:
  - (Display any type of graph.) Analyze the data in this graph with a critical eye. What if you were the owner of "the business" this graph represents? What does the data represent? How might it affect the business? How can you possibly change the appearance to benefit the business? Who might want this data? Why? Who might want to "hide" this information? Why? What could be missing from the data? Why? (It is difficult for students to evaluate a graph. Frequent exposure will make it much easier for them.)

2. *When you get a room full of blank stares, stop for a moment and have the students write in their journals.* They can

- rephrase what the teacher just taught;
- define it, draw it, explain it;
- list the steps they used to solve the problem;
- explain what they know about . . . ;
- write an explanation they might share with a younger student;
- use drawings and graphs to explain their thinking;
- explain their thinking so far;
- pinpoint where they may have gotten confused and what they can do about it;
- use one of the generic sentence starters and math prompts listed on page 96 to describe their learning; and/or
- include questions they still might have about the lesson.

After the writing, have students share with a partner while you circulate around the room. This gives you an opportunity to assess the understanding and differentiate the learning.

3. *Writing is a way to differentiate the lesson and a perfect transition opportunity.* Giving students a chance to reflect on the learning allows for differentiation and shakes things up a little. Writing is another path to the learning, and we, as teachers, need to provide a variety of approaches for students to achieve the learning purpose.

4. *Writing is a valuable way to Debrief a lesson.* Writing encourages students to synthesize their thinking. Have students reflect on their participation in the class that day and assess their own understanding of the lesson. Again, you do not have to grade these journals; instead, students can share with a partner while you circulate. You can quickly pick up from the discussions who needs further assistance. If you hear the same mistake being repeated, it is important to take the time to clarify and redirect.

Sentence Starters

Here are some useful sentence starters to use:

- I learned that I . . . .
- I still have questions about . . . .
- This lesson was just like . . .because . . . .
- This lesson was different than . . . because . . . .
- I know I understand . . . because . . . .
- What I know about . . .so far is . . . . What I'm still not sure about is . . . .
- I noticed that I . . . .
- The most important information about . . . is . . . . I think this because . . . .
- In what ways are . . . important?
- How would you use what you learned today in your life?
- The main idea of today's lesson was . . . .
- I learned . . . strategies to . . . today. My favorite method is . . . because . . . .
- How and where would you use what you learned today outside the classroom?
- I was thinking metacognitively today when . . . .
- I was pleased that I . . . .
- Where else could you use this type of problem solving?
- What would happen if you missed a step? Why?
- Write and solve a word problem whose solution involves . . . .
- What other strategies could you use to solve this problem?
- Compare and contrast the terms . . . .
- What patterns do you notice in . . . .
- You know several ways to . . . . Which method is your favorite? Why?
- I know what I'm doing makes sense because . . . .
- I used estimating in class today when . . . .
- Explain in your own words what . . . means.
- Explain what is most important to understand about . . . .

5. *Exit tickets are a perfect way for you to formatively assess the learning.* Exit tickets can include calculations, but they must require students to analyze those calculations through writing as well. In other words, make sure students include reasoning that supports their solution. You may want the students to represent the learning visually along with an explanation. You can also use any of the journal prompts above. Collect the tickets as the students leave the room. Assess number sense, estimation, and reasonableness. You could grade the tickets, or you may want to formatively assess the general understanding of the lesson, pulling out the concepts that clearly need review and revisiting.

Exit tickets provide feedback for you and give you the opportunity to give meaningful feedback to the students. Don't feel you have to give individual comments on all entries. When you do decide to give individual responses, avoid general comments such as "good job," which don't provide any genuine feedback. Try to give responses that address what the students wrote. Focus on the mathematics and the reasoning behind the mathematics. Offer suggestions for further thinking.

One idea is to formally grade several exit tickets per quarter without letting the students know which ones will be graded. That method may help with accountability and make your work manageable.

6. *Have students revisit and revise an old journal entry.* This activity helps emphasize that journal writing is a work in progress and that the emphasis is on critical thinking. It is important for students to understand that their thinking is always evolving. Some students will use this time to rethink the math concept; others will work on writing more clearly. Whatever their focus, revision tells students that their ideas are valuable and worth developing.

7. *Have students reflect on their learning.* Giving students ample time to reflect on their own learning empowers them to become lifelong learners. Provide moments for students to dwell in ideas in silence. We completely agree with Ellin Keene (2008) when she says, "To take time in silence, to hold an idea in our mind, to reflect over time. This is how understanding happens in our lives."

Journal Prompts

Here are some possible journal prompts:

- Write a math autobiography. Include math milestones in your life, your favorite memories in math, the aha math moments of the past, and some of the toughest math times. Share how this affected what kind of math student you are today.
- How do you feel you performed on the assessment? Explain in detail.
- How did you study for the assessment? Would you change the way you prepared for future assessments? If "no," why not? If "yes," state specifically how you would change your study strategy.
- Looking back over the marking period, describe your best aha moment. Describe a topic about which you were confused and then later reached an understanding of? What was confusing you, and how did you come to understand it? Include an example of a problem from this section and write directions on how to solve it to someone who has not seen it before. (Examples from the reading are not acceptable.)

☛ HOW CAN I DO THIS IN MY MATH CLASS . . . TOMORROW?

The following ideas have been used successfully in all subject areas and are a welcome addition to the math class. They are effective tools for determining importance, summarizing, and synthesizing.

3-2-1 Journal Entry

The 3-2-1 strategy requires students to summarize key ideas from the lesson and encourages them to think independently. First, students write about 3 things they discovered. Next, they write about 2 things they found interesting. Last, they write 1 question they still have. This strategy can be used as a journal entry during the Debrief or as an exit ticket. The 3-2-1 journal has endless options. You can be flexible with what you want the students to write about; 3 examples of the learning, 2 nonexamples, 1 way you can tell the difference, and so on.

Say Something

Students work in pairs. Each student reads his or her textbook silently to a designated stopping point. When each partner is ready, stop and "say something" to summarize the learning thus far. Continue this process until you have completed the selection. You may want to ask students to record the most important ideas.

Skits or Acting It Out

Have students synthesize their learning by "acting it out" or creating skits that represent the learning. Skits are always fun in problem solving. Another idea is to have groups represent the parts of a circle kinesthetically, a great way to create a visual frame of reference. Be creative with this one. The students love it, and the learning that takes place is amazing.

The Cross-Out Strategy

The cross-out strategy teaches students to focus on the essential words because they cross out the unessential ones. Once they are eliminated, students are asked to write a summary using the important words.

Summaries in Headline Fashion

Challenge students to write summaries in headline fashion, limiting the students to three to six words. Don't even worry about sentences.

Compose Problems

Have students compose their own problems. This is a great way to assess their understanding. If they can create an appropriate problem for the learning, they more than likely get the lesson.

Create a Jingle, Rap, or a Double-Dutch Chant

A great way to differentiate the lesson is to have students create a song, poem, or rhyme from the learning. They will need to think critically to come up with a creative piece.

Overviewing

Overviewing is a form of skimming. Students need to look over the text before they read. They need to pay attention to the headings and sub-headings, examples, text boxes, bold print, photos, graphs, and drawings. From the quick overview, they should predict what they will be learning about and what they think the important ideas might be. They should do this independently in their journals and share it with a partner. Overviewing should be a brief activity.

Sum It Up

Students imagine they are placing a classified ad or sending a telegram where every word used costs them money. Tell them each word costs 10 cents and that they can only spend $2.00; hence, they will have to write a summary that has no more than 20 words. You can adjust the amount they have to spend and, therefore, the length of the summary according to the text they are summarizing (Gear, 2008, p. 99).

Consensus

In this activity, students identify the main ideas in a series of "coming-to-a-consensus" process (Beers, 2003).

- Have students identify individually the three most important things (three main ideas) they learned from the text they read. They should list them on a piece of paper.
- Pair students to share their most important information (main ideas) and come to a consensus about the three most important pieces of learning (main ideas), again listing them.
- Then have each pair join with another pair to form a group to discuss their findings and again come to a consensus about the three most important pieces of learning (main idea).

- Finally, ask the groups to come together as a class, have them exchange ideas, and ask them to come to a class consensus about the three most important main ideas. As they do, list the class's main ideas on the board.

Silent Conversation

Present a problem. Students should be in pairs with only one piece of paper. One student begins the conversation by writing down how he or she would start solving the problem. The other student responds in writing and continues the problem solving. They continue the written conversation until the problem is solved. Then they discuss the process.

Problem-Based Learning

Whenever you create an authentic problem-based learning situation for the students to solve, you have set the stage for critical thinking. The students are interested and involved in finding a solution. It is synthesis at its best!

Four to Six Word Summary

Form a four to six word summary of the lesson or topic. Each student or pair should share their summary as well as why they chose it.

What's the Question?

Give the students "the answer," and they must come up with an appropriate question. This activity is similar to the Jeopardy game format.

What's the Title?

Display an excerpt from your math textbook but remove the title and headings. Give students the chance to determine the main idea by inserting the missing section headings. They can predict the headings before the learning, or synthesize the lesson by creating them after the reading.

GIST

The GIST (acronym for Generating Interactions Between Schemata and Texts) of something is the main idea. Each group or student will write a summary in 20 words (Cunningham & Hentges, 1982; Forget, 2004, pp. 156–162).

Procedure:

- Draw 20 word-sized blanks on the chalkboard.
- After reading a short section of the math text, the students will assist the teacher in writing a 20-word summary to give the gist of what they read.
- Now read an additional section of text. Information from both sections must be incorporated into a new 20 word summary.
- It is possible to read a third section and condense the summary one more time.

You can also use a GIST statement as an exit ticket or journal prompt as part of the Debrief.

Habit 8

Develop Vocabulary

Students' word knowledge is linked strongly to academic success.

—J. F. Baumann, E. J. Kam'eenui, and G. Ash, in *Handbook of Research on Teaching the English Language Arts*, 2003

Any good teacher wants his or her students to be academically successful. After all, when our students are academically successful, we feel like we're doing a good job.

If word knowledge is strongly linked to academic success, then we need to look at developing vocabulary in mathematics. Words are the tools we use to access our background knowledge, to express ideas, and to learn about new concepts. The more words you know, the easier it is to learn more words. The more you focus on words, the more language, the more knowledge, and the more understanding of words your students will acquire (Stahl & Nagy, 2006). Learning new words or new vocabulary is crucial to deepening mathematical understanding. Without a solid understanding of the vocabulary, a mathematician could be seriously confused or, at the very least, stuck. Understanding the language of math gives students the proficiency they need to think about, confer, and integrate new math concepts as they are presented.

"Mathematics presents challenging reading because this content area has more concepts per sentence and per paragraph than any other area" (Harmon, 1999). Mathematics has its own language, and to be fluent in that language, students must be able to use and understand the vocabulary with confidence. With the pressures of standardized testing, we, as teachers, realize that students need to be given appropriate time for vocabulary instruction that reinforces the mathematical concepts being assessed. Making certain that students learn, review, and apply anchor vocabulary is essential for ensuring that students can successfully achieve problem solving on high-stakes assessments. More importantly, when students truly understand the language of mathematics, they have a much greater chance of truly understanding mathematical concepts, which can only lead to more math-making sense.

Research shows that reading is probably the most important mechanism for vocabulary growth throughout a student's school-aged years and beyond (Baker, Simmons, & Kam'eenui, 1995). Let's break that statement apart. "Reading is probably the most important mechanism for vocabulary growth." Your mathematics textbook involves reading—lots of technical reading—and isn't that what American students struggle with? When we ask our students to navigate informational text, we are encouraging what benefits students most—reading. Critical vocabulary lives inside your textbook. Your students are faced with countless words that they must understand to think through the mathematics. That's what we want you to focus on here—those words.

The work of Beck, McKeown, and Kucan (2002) explains that effective vocabulary instruction does not rely simply on definitions. When vocabulary instruction is effective, students learn the words, use the words, remember the words, and can ultimately apply the words fluently in different contexts. No real learning has occurred if words are remembered only for test day. If deep, authentic vocabulary learning is to occur, a numeracy-rich math curriculum must be adopted. The power of numeracy lies in the empowerment of students; that is, students are given opportunities to use academic vocabulary in a natural setting and to recognize the words' relevance in the world outside the math class.

Research shows that when vocabulary instruction is direct and purposeful it is effective. So what does effective vocabulary instruction rely on? We'd like to call the behaviors associated with effective vocabulary instruction Vocabulary Habits.

Vocabulary Habits need to be formed within a mathematics classroom. Your students must be purposefully guided into making these Vocabulary Habits just that—habits. We all know a habit occurs without a tremendous amount of forethought. It's a habit. We just do it. Vocabulary Habits need to happen when you're not "with" your students, for instance, when they're thinking independently.

KEY VOCABULARY HABITS

The three key Vocabulary Habits are as follows:

1. Identifying when understanding breaks down due to an unknown vocabulary word and then trying out the next two habits.

2. Looking at a new word, tapping into your existing knowledge of that word, and making a connection to convey meaning. Have you ever heard this word before? What did it mean? When did you see it before? What were you learning? What connections can you make? What could the word mean here (Zwiers, 2004, p. 116)?

3. Looking at a new word and asking, "Do I see a familiar word hidden or embedded in the larger word?" or "What is the prefix here? Or the suffix?" "Can I figure out the meaning now?" (Zwiers, 2004, p. 117).

When a teacher shows his students via a well-planned think-aloud how *he* identifies a breakdown of *his* understanding due to difficult vocabulary, and how *he* repairs it, he demonstrates the pathway to true understanding. When he allows his students to try out that metacognitive process and encourages consistent Vocabulary Habit use, the teacher has empowered the class. Student thinking is pushed deeper, and the tools they need to successfully navigate any mathematical reading have been handed over.

Indeed, the vocabulary problems of students who enter school with poor or limited vocabularies only worsen over time (White, Graves, & Slater, 1990). Consider this: Poor readers often lack adequate vocabulary to induce meaning from what they read. Consequently, reading is difficult and tedious for them, and they are unable (and often unwilling) to do the large amount of reading they must do if they are to encounter unknown words often enough to learn them. This situation contributes to what is called the "Matthew Effect"—that is, interactions with the environment that exaggerate individual differences over time and result in "the rich get richer, the poor get poorer" consequences. Good readers read more, become even better readers, and learn more words; poor readers read less, become poorer readers, and learn fewer words (Stahl, 1999).

What if we changed that last sentence to read, "Good *thinkers* think more, become even better *thinkers*, and learn more words; poor *thinkers* think less, become poorer *thinkers*, and learn fewer words"? Can you see the impact vocabulary development has in the mathematics classroom? Vocabulary instruction must be an integral part of our daily instruction (see Table 1) for students to fully participate in this highly quantitative society in which we live.

KEY IDEAS

The authors of *Bringing Words to Life* (Beck, McKeown, Kucan, 2002) suggest that a robust approach to vocabulary requires directly explaining the meanings of words along with thought-provoking, playful, and interactive follow-up. In this way, vocabulary is more rooted to a text and dealt with in a way that both teaches the words and brings enriched understanding to the text.

| Table 1 | Vocabulary Instruction |

What Students Need to Learn	How to Teach It
• The meanings for most of the words in a text so they can understand what they read. • How to apply a variety of strategies to learn word meanings. How to make connections among words and concepts. • How to accurately use words in oral and written language.	• Provide direct, explicit instruction to help students learn word meanings. • Maintain high expectations. Use academic vocabulary as part of your daily language and expect students to do the same. • Introduce new vocabulary in multiple contexts. • Engage children in daily interactions that promote using new vocabulary in both oral and written language. • Enrich and expand the vocabulary knowledge of English language learners. • Actively involve students in connecting concepts and words.

Source: Vocabulary Instruction: What Students Need to Learn and How to Teach It, published by the North Carolina Department of Public Instruction. Reprinted with permission of the North Carolina Department of Public Instruction.

• *Be choosy about the words you teach.* In mathematics, the words being taught should be words that will greatly affect students' mathematical thinking or reasoning. Children learn best when what they are learning has relevance for them and when new information connects to information they already know (Akhavan, 2007, p. 13).

• *Point out that mathematics uses words with specific applications in a given context* that have very different meanings in other settings (e.g., odd, radical, rational, etc.). It is important to bring this aspect to the forefront. Using these terms in different contexts allows students to recognize how mathematics has its own language.

• *Perform word surgery* (Zwiers, 2004, p. 117). Show students how to surgically take apart vocabulary words and identify roots, prefixes, and suffixes. In mathematics, understanding root words will make it easier to form mathematical connections.

• *Use graphic organizers.* They can facilitate understanding mathematical vocabulary and words' relations to one another.

• *Use thinking maps.* You can use this visual language (see Table 2) to support you in meaningful vocabulary instruction. (Training and support are available at http://www.thinkingmaps.com.)

Table 2   Thinking Maps

Questions From Texts, Teachers, and Tests	Thinking Processes	Thinking Maps as Tools
How are you defining this thing or idea? What is the context? What is your frame of reference?	Defining in Context	Circle Map
How are you describing this thing? Which adjectives would best describe this thing?	Describing Qualities	Bubble Map
What are the similar and different qualities of these things? Which qualities do you value most? Why?	Comparing and Contrasting	Double Bubble Map
What are the main ideas, supporting ideas, and details in this information?	Classifying	Tree Map
What are the component parts and subparts of this whole physical object?	Part-Whole	Brace Map
What happened? What is the sequence of events? What are the substages?	Sequencing	Flow Map
What are the causes and effects of this event? What might happen next?	Cause and Effect	Multi-Flow Map
What is the analogy being used? What is the guiding metaphor?	Seeing Analogies	Bridge Map

Source: http://www.thinkingmaps.com. Used with permission from Thinking Maps, Inc.

- *Conduct a word hunt* (Beers, 2003, p. 190). Using your mathematics textbook, allow the students to hunt through the book with a partner, identifying unknown vocabulary words and known vocabulary words.

- *Hold high expectations.* Use appropriate mathematical terms in your daily language. Watering down the language in math can make it more difficult for students to come to grips with concepts, thereby stifling the opportunity for mastery. *Expect* students to use correct academic language in their math conversations and written work.

• *Shape word meaning through the process of creating metaphors.* As Marzano (2007) states, "Research indicates that metaphor activities can help students better understand the abstract features of information. . . . In terms of vocabulary instruction, a teacher might present students with metaphors or ask them to create their own metaphors."

• *Be innovative in your vocabulary instruction.*
   o Remember, the key to vocabulary learning and retention is exposure, exposure, exposure.
   o Use the words in your own speech.
   o Preview content vocabulary.
   o Increase opportunities for students to use new words and be exposed to new words in and out of class; repetition and multiple exposures to vocabulary are important.
   o Read aloud and model fluency.
   o Include think-alouds (see Component 4, Gradual Release in Mathematics).
   o Teach word meanings, especially before reading; this practice has been found to be effective for text comprehension.
   o Use children's literature whenever possible (the academic vocabulary is present without the constraints of more advanced vocabulary).
   o Have students collect math words they like, don't understand, sound funny, look funny, or invoke a particular memory.
   o Allow for student negotiation of meaning through collaboration.
   o Focus on a conceptual understanding of vocabulary.
   o Use strategies for predicting and inferring meaning from text.
   o Find root words, that is, word surgery; teach common prefixes, suffixes, and roots.
   o Participate in activities outside the classroom to deepen word meanings.
   o Bring realia into the classroom.
   o Use object lessons to connect vocabulary to meaning.
   o Increase the use of visuals.
   o Use graphic organizers to represent knowledge.
   o Use symbolic representations such as pictures, pictographs, maps, and diagrams.
   o Generate mental pictures.
   o Use explicit cues to access prior knowledge; connect new words to students' background knowledge.
   o Use multimodal/multiple intelligences approaches for understanding and remembering vocabulary (drawing, symbols, movement, music, cooperative learning).

- o Use comparisons of similarities and differences: Venn diagrams, 4-square word maps, semantic mapping, word sorts, category sorts, Frayer model, matrixes, and so on.
- o Ask students to discuss the vocabulary with one another.
- o Involve students in games that allow them to play with mathematics vocabulary ($100,000 pyramid, talk a mile a minute, Pictionary, etc.) (Marzano & Pickering, 2005).
- o Ask questions that elicit inferences.
- o Generate definitions through the use of examples and nonexamples.
- o Use advanced organizers to activate background knowledge and to set a purpose for learning (Marzano & Pickering, 2005).
- o Classify by identifying differences and similarities. Marzano, Pickering, and Pollock (2001) list classifying as one way to provide students with multiple exposures to words to help shape word meanings (see also Marzano & Pickering, 2005).
- o Play vocabulary charades: Describe radius, diameter, circumference, and area using your body—no talking.
- o Use word webs and concept maps.
- o Try nonlinguistic representations: Have students draw word meanings (Marzano & Pickering, 2005) or act out word meanings.
- o Invite students to wonder about a word's use, purpose, and meaning.
- o Try vocabulary cartoons (see below.)

• *Vocabulary cartoons* work on the principle of mnemonics. A mnemonic device helps you remember something by associating it with something you already know. A mnemonic device could be in many different forms: rhymes, songs, or pictures, to name a few. For example, "Columbus sailed the ocean blue in fourteen hundred ninety-two" is a classic mnemonic rhyme that helps you remember when Columbus discovered America. Following the mnemonic principle of association, vocabulary cartoons link an auditory (rhyming) word with a visual in the form of a humorous cartoon. These powerful mnemonics help students retain the meanings of words longer and with less effort than by trying to memorize definitions out of a dictionary.

In the example in Figure 3, the new word *chord* is associated (linked with) the rhyming word *bored*, which in turn is presented visually as a humorous cartoon. The more outrageous and bizarre the cartoon, the easier it is to remember.

Marzano and Pickering's (2005) approach for effectively teaching vocabulary consists of six steps (see Table 3). They encourage nonlinguistic representations to build vocabulary—not just mental pictures but also associated sounds, smells, and sensations of touch or movement.

Figure 3   A Vocabulary Cartoon

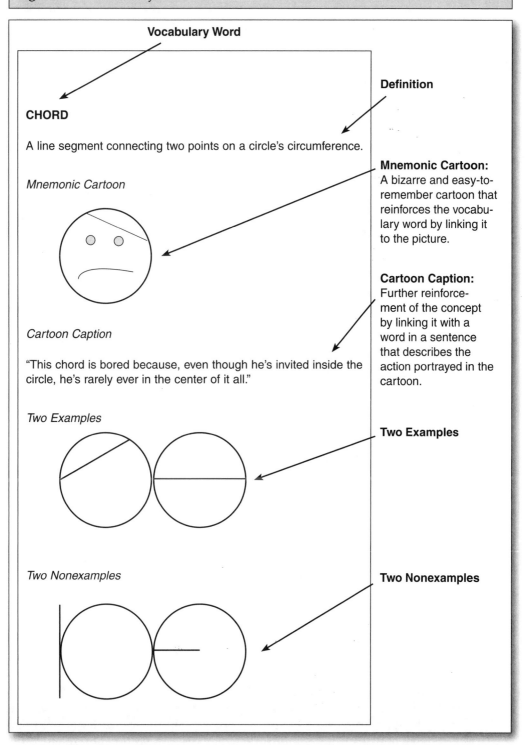

Table 3	Marzano and Pickering's Six-Step Vocabulary Approach
Step 1	Provide a description, explanation, or example of the new terms.
Step 2	Ask students to restate the description, explanation, or example in their own words.
Step 3	Ask students to construct a picture, symbol, or graphic representing the term.
Step 4	Engage students periodically in activities that help them add to their knowledge of the terms in their notebooks.
Step 5	Periodically ask students to discuss the terms with one another.
Step 6	Involve students periodically in games that allow them to play with terms.

Source: Building Academic Vocabulary: Teacher's Manual (pp. 14–15), by Robert J. Marzano and Debra J. Pickering. Alexandria, VA: ASCD. © 2008 by ASCD. Used with permission. Learn more about ASCD at www.ascd.org.

 ## HOW CAN I DO THIS IN MY MATH CLASS . . . TOMORROW?

The following ideas are both easy to implement and worthwhile tools for vocabulary instruction across the curriculum. They are also highly effective for incorporating vocabulary development in math class.

Word Wizard

Have students become "word wizards" by challenging them to discover their math vocabulary used somewhere outside the school setting. Of course, they will need to bring "proof," which could be a news article, a quote from a relative, a TV quote, and so on. This activity raises their awareness of how academic vocabulary is used in the everyday world (Allen, 2000).

List-Group-Label, Word Sort, or Circle the Category

See a full explanation of this activity in Habit 2, Develop Schema and Activate Background Knowledge. Classifying or sorting vocabulary words can be done as an *open* or *closed* sort. In a closed sort, students organize vocabulary words into predetermined categories developed by the teacher. In an open sort, students determine the categories.

Double-Dutch Chants

Start with a word sort of your vocabulary, then read aloud an excerpt from *Double Dutch: A Celebration of Jump Rope, Rhyme, and Sisterhood* by Veronica Chambers (2002). Push the thinking by having students develop their own jump rope chants based on their favorite category. The power lies in the physical act of jumping and chanting. You just may hear your students whispering their chants during the real standardized testing!

Talk a Mile a Minute

This is another great way (from Marzano & Pickering, 2005) to incorporate highly effective Vocabulary Habits in your classroom. Teams of students are given a list of terms that have been organized by categories. Include a category title and six or seven words that fit under that category. To play, designate a "talker." The talker tries to get the team to say each of the words quickly by describing them without mentioning the word in the description. The talker moves down the list until all the words are discovered. Then the group attempts to uncover the category.

**Things Associated
With a Circle**
radius
circumference
diameter
chord
area
sector
pi

Name That Category

This idea also comes from Marzano and Pickering's book, *Building Academic Vocabulary: Teacher's Manual* (2005). This game involves associating and connecting concepts by looking at what they have in common. It is modeled after the television game show The $100,000 Pyramid. You will need a game board per group in the shape of a pyramid (see example). The object of the game is for one player, who can see the categories, to list words that describe or fit into that

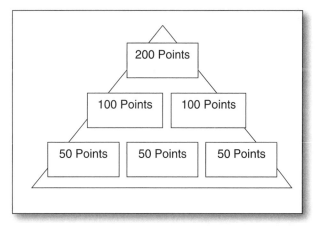

Source: *Building Academic Vocabulary: Teacher's Manual* (pp. 14–15), by Robert J. Marzano and Debra J. Pickering. Alexandria, VA: ASCD. © 2008 by ASCD. Used with permission. Learn more about ASCD at www.ascd.org.

category without saying its name until the other player can name the category. This activity is really fun if you limit the time.

Concept Circles

Concept circles are circles with words placed in the sectors (Vaca, Vaca, & Gove, 1987). Ask students to discuss and write about the connections they see between the words (see one version here). A variation is for students to write the words and challenge other students to find connections. You could also write three words and challenge students to identify the connection, then add a fourth word that would also fit into the category. Another variation is to write three words that "belong" and one word that doesn't and challenge students to find the word that doesn't "fit in." Make sure students can justify their decisions (Allen, 1999).

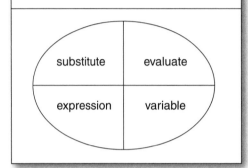

Concept Circle

Look at the terms in each of the sections below. Think about your understanding of the terms by highlighting the connections between them. Discuss this connection with your group and write about how they fit together.

substitute | evaluate

expression | variable

Greet and Go

This is an interactive way to get students to use their background knowledge to make predictions about the vocabulary that will be covered in the day's lesson. First, give each student an index card with a term or phrase from the lesson they are about to learn. Ask the students to circulate the room and read their cards to each other. After a couple of minutes, call "freeze." As the students return to their seats, ask them to think about what they predict today's lesson will be about. Have students return to small groups and jointly write a prediction on what they will be learning. This is a great activity when the lesson is "loaded" with vocabulary (Forsten et al., 2002b, p. 46).

Matrix and Attribute Charts

(See example in Habit 4, Represent Mathematics Nonlinguistically.)

Vocabulary Objects

Grab a dollar-store coloring book; the simpler the drawings, the better. In small groups, have the students logically and creatively label the coloring book drawing with their mathematical vocabulary words. Make sure your students have logical explanations for their labeling. This activity gives the brain a location on the page and a visual now associated with the word. It also puts the mathematical vocabulary word into a new context. Powerful.

Alike but Different

Janet Allen (2004) offers wonderful and practical ways to incorporate highly effective Vocabulary Habits in daily instruction. Begin by writing three terms in three boxes. Have students discuss their similarities, writing what they have in common. Now have students share what is unique about the terms. Let groups brainstorm ways to remember their similarities and differences. To push the thinking, let the students create the words.

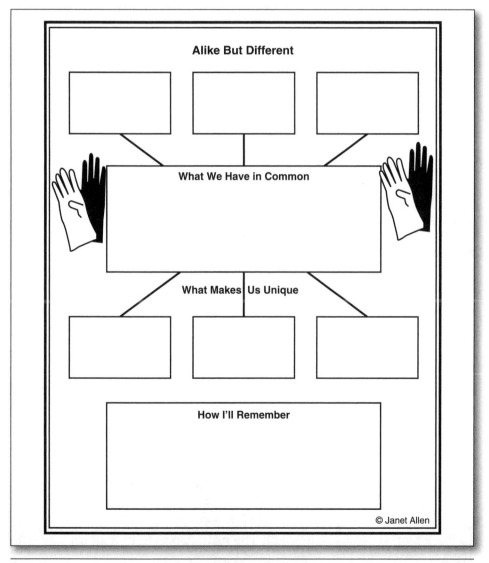

Frayer Model

Students really grasp the meaning of a mathematical concept from the examples and counterexamples. Have them generate their own definition.

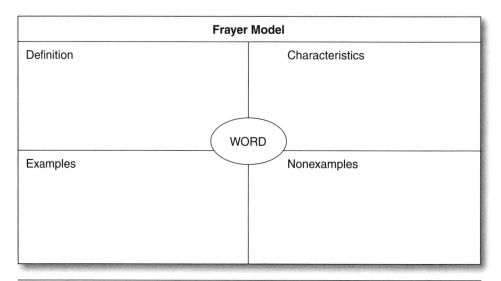

Source: *A Schema for Testing the Level of Concept Mastery* (Working Paper No. 16), by D. J. Frayer, W. C. Frederick, and H. J. Klausmeier, copyright © 1969, reproduced with permission of the Wisconsin Research and Development Center for Cognitive Learning, Madison, Wisconsin.

Pass the Plate

Get a package of sturdy plastic plates and overhead markers. You can put a mathematical term in the center, a problem in the center, and so on. In small groups, the students pass the plate and marker around their table and add synonyms, antonyms, the next step in the problem, and so on. It is fun to turn the activity into a low-pressure competition among the groups by assigning points and time restrictions.

Concept Ladder

This great idea also comes from Janet Allen (2004). It works very well to introduce a unit of study. A concept ladder is a chart that's used to show an idea and its subtypes. Concept ladders work well when teaching how to branch off from a single point. The next step is to branch off into subtypes. Now continue breaking down the subtypes.

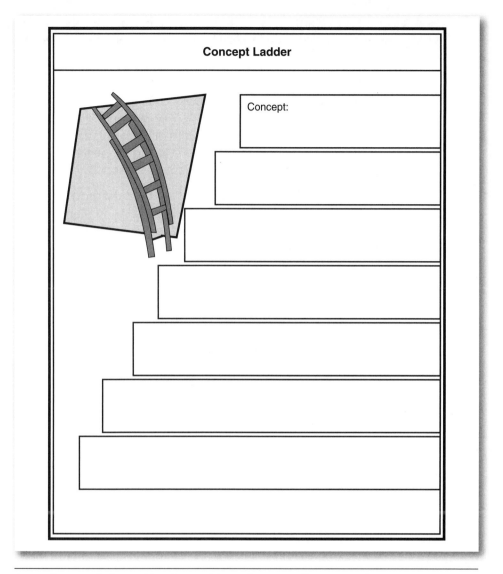

Preconcept and Postconcept Checks

This tool for vocabulary development takes just a minute to prepare, and the payoff is big for students. If the objective for your lesson can only be achieved with a clear understanding of certain terms, or if your lesson is heavy on vocabulary, this is a great entry point.

1. Pull out whatever vocabulary will be presented in the lesson and create something similar to the sample on p. 116. You can pass it out

as a handout, have students write it in their math journals, or provide index cards for students to use that you will collect as a possible exit ticket.

2. Have students quickly self-rate their understanding of the vocabulary before the lesson using the rating shown. Circulate the room using this as a formative assessment. Do you see any class trends? If so, adapt accordingly. Which students might need to work in a small group with you during the lesson, or which students need to be pushed beyond the original plan? This will help differentiate the lesson.

3. At the Debrief, have students re-rate their understanding and prove this rating by creating representations or writing an explanation on the back of the card. Again, use this as a formative assessment. Who has it? Who needs support? How will this affect your instruction the next day (Forget, 2004, p. 230)?

Ratings: + = could teach it; √ = kinda know it; — = no clue

Before the Learning		After the Learning
_____	denominator	_____
_____	numerator	_____
_____	equivalent fraction	_____

Habit 9

Collaborate to Learn

Alone we can do so little; together we can do so much.

—Helen Keller

Arguments in favor of cooperative learning and teamwork come from two rather different sources: from those in education who view collaboration as an effective strategy for learning, and from those in business who view cooperative activities as essential for productive employees (Secretary's Commission on Achieving Necessary Skills [SCANS], 1991). Education advocates envision mathematics classes as communities where students engage in collaborative mathematical practice both with each other and with their teachers (Silver, Kilpatrick, & Schlesinger, 1990). In such classes, students would regularly engage in authentic forms of mathematical *discourse* by inventing strategies, arguing about approaches, and justifying their work. Sounds a lot like numeracy to us.

A crucial numeracy initiative in many countries focuses on making sense out of mathematics. Collaborating makes math accessible to all students. Unfortunately, right now in the United States, when you ask your average student their opinion of mathematics, you'll most likely hear something like "Math is hard." You may even hear "I hate math." We'd like to challenge those two statements with a little hope.

What if we leveled the mathematical playing field in our classrooms? What if we planned for, modeled, fostered, and embedded collaboration into nearly every lesson we teach? How would that level the mathematical playing field?

There is evidence that opportunities to engage in discussion are related to improved achievement (Allington, 2006, p. 117). Further evidence shows that group interaction facilitates knowledge development (McVee, Dunsmore, & Gavelek, 2005). When students are partnered or grouped by their teacher, thereby working together and thinking through the mathematics together, a few incredible things can happen (see Component 4 on Gradual Release in Mathematics for partnering and grouping techniques).

First, mathematics anxiety is quieted, because when a confused student shares her thinking, frustration, or confusion with a fellow student, she's not sitting alone, silently stressing out over the mathematics. It is that internal, silent stress that voraciously devours mathematics confidence. Each silently confused moment gobbles up understanding and thinking, as well as confidence, leading some students to say, "I hate math." Why not instead encourage what Allington (2006) calls "real conversations about learning" or sophisticated, thinking-driven conversations that end such silent confusion?

Next, when one student who "gets it" shares her thinking with a fellow student, complex learning occurs for both students. Receiving language from another is not simply a matter of hearing what the other person is saying. Listening is a metacognitive process, similar to reading: When one listens, one is processing information (Gear, 2008, p. 17). At the same time, the speaker is processing thinking, that is, talking through the mathematical processes, or reasoning. Talking through the math forces the quick processor to slow down and own her thinking. It forces the slow processor to engage and think it through with the other student. It forces the nonprocessor to engage as well, and affords him the opportunity to hear another student's thinking, effectively wiping away the myth, "Oh, they're just smart; they always know the answer. I'm dumb; I never understand it." Cooperative interactions thus facilitate learning complex procedures (O'Donnell, 2006, pp. 781–802).

Let's think about it. Imagine I am a student who struggles in mathematics, and I constantly say things like "I don't get it. Math is too hard. I hate math." If I am partnered with a student who can share how *he* successfully thought through the mathematics task at hand, then, logically, my chances of coming to my own understanding increase dramatically. I have been given another mathematical thinker's perspective—someone other than my teacher. One of the greatest benefits of collaboration is that it allows students to experience content from multiple perspectives (McVee, Dunsmore, & Gavelek, 2005).

True collaboration is not what some consider to be "group work," and it is more than cooperative learning; it is a mindset. Collaboration is purposeful and has a distinct intent. It should happen at consistent times during every math lesson, for instance, when students are given opportunities to brainstorm, share strategies for problem solving, think-aloud through a problem, create a visual representation, discover a depth of understanding, experiment with manipulatives, or collaborate on a plan. Sometimes collaboration is as simple as "turn and talk" or "think-pair-share." Turn and talk provides an opportunity for students to practice their thinking out loud before they begin to write, as well as a chance to hear the ideas of others (Gear, 2008, p. 130). It should last just a few minutes, but the payoff is huge.

When collaborative moments are built into your lessons, your students will learn to appreciate each other's thinking; those moments will begin to build a classroom of trust, with students who are more willing to take mathematical risks. With time and practice, your students will enter into mathematical discussions without you, for students have the potential to respect each other's thinking. Then, the questions are generated by the students and are directed toward each another. To witness this is a rewarding moment in any math teacher's life.

Collaboration

- Increases student engagement
- Deepens thinking skills
- Levels the playing field, allowing all learners to have access to the learning
- Builds curiosity and discovery
- Creates opportunity for individual growth and development
- Broadens individual student's perspective
- Promotes good listening skills
- Fosters a safe learning environment (modeling is crucial for this to happen)
- Strengthens communication skills

It is crucial for students to construct their own meaning, but they do not do this in isolation. Collaboration gives rise to valuable learning opportunities. Collaboration involves much more than combining solution procedures to develop a joint solution. It involves developing reasoning that is meaningful and interpreting and making sense of another's ideas and solution attempts as they evolve (National Council of Teachers of Mathematics, 2002, pp. 41–43). As students attempt to verbalize and interpret mathematical ideas, they engage in what Douglas Barnes (1976) calls exploratory talk as opposed to final-draft talk; this process is an important component in empowering students to become critical thinkers.

Let us be clear: We are not advocating that students simply give answers away, although we know this can happen; we've been there. Instead, we're promoting a "think tank," so to speak, and building this takes time. Success is all in the setup. When we rushed into collaboration, without proper modeling, we didn't see much more than an exchange of answers. When we took the time to patiently develop what it means to communicate effectively in a math class, *all* students proved to be more than capable. Ideally, we want our classrooms to be places where all members learn, take risks, and learn to trust each other. This comes through providing opportunities for discourse and reflection.

RESEARCH FINDINGS

Marzano, Pickering, and Pollock's (2001) four generalizations to guide cooperative learning read as follows:

1. Organizing groups based on ability levels should be done sparingly.

2. Cooperative groups should be kept rather small in size.

3. Cooperative learning should be applied consistently and systematically, but not overused.

4. Use a variety of criteria for grouping students—informal, formal, base groups.

David and Robert Johnson (1984) say that the purpose of cooperative learning is to make each group member a stronger individual in his or her own right. There should be a pattern and flow to classroom learning—learn it together; perform it alone. The same applies to collaboration. Like cooperative learning, true collaboration differs from traditional classroom groupings in that it requires that teachers carefully structure the group so that students believe that they

1. sink or swim together;

2. can assist and encourage others to achieve;

3. are individually accountable for doing their part of the group's work;

4. have to master the required interpersonal and small-group skills to be an effective group member; and

5. should discuss how well the group is working and what could be done to improve the group work.

Unless these five essential elements are included, small groups are not collaborating.

KEY IDEAS

Here are a few simple starting points for shifting from a traditional teacher-centered classroom to one that promotes collaboration and discourse (Kenney, 2005, pp. 75–86):

- Arrange desks so that students can easily talk and listen to each other. We have used partners and groups of three or four successfully.
- Encourage students to generate questions and to direct their questions to the rest of the class, not simply to the teacher. This promotes a sense of community.
- Maintain an atmosphere of acceptance and freedom. When students feel safe, they are more willing to take risks.
- Take the time to model how to be a good listener. Listening is a key component in collaboration. An anchor lesson in "what it looks like and sounds like to be a good listener" will give the students a great frame of reference. A "fishbowl" on the topic of listening works well, too. Plus, you can "ham it up" when it comes to role playing what a good listener *doesn't* do or say. This will definitely get the students' attention.
- Try not to always stand in the front of the room. The simple act of standing in various spots in the room will redirect the conversation from a teacher-student discourse to a student-centered discussion.
- When in doubt, remain silent. Give students a chance to wrestle with the problem. Try not to come to their rescue too quickly.
- Stop and write. Allow brief writing moments to promote deep thinking and meaningful conversation.
- Come prepared with high-level questions as a springboard to conversation.
- Create lessons that promote collaborative thought, ones that foster interdependence, accountability, and justification from each member of the group.
- Involve students in engaging and thought-provoking problem solving.
- Take risks. Show students you are willing to challenge yourself in front of them. Let them see you squirm a little. When you make a mistake, admit it. It provides a safe haven for intellectual risk taking.
- Encourage mathematical "arguments." Argument is a key component in making conjectures and attempting to convince others of validity and reasonableness.
- Ask high-level questions to stimulate the conversation. Allow time to think before the conversation begins.
- Honor diverse thinking. It is tempting to ignore a solution when you believe it might take the learning in another direction, but considering alternative strategies to problem solving can generate critical thinking.
- Let confusion linger for a while. Learning occurs in what Rick Wormeli (2009) calls "compelling disequilibrium." When you hear from your students, "This is hard," or "This is confusing," don't be discouraged. Simply reassure them by saying something like, "Great, now I have you exactly where I need you."

- Allow time for the conversation to get rich in mathematical discourse.
- Train students to recognize when they are getting off track and encourage them to support each other when it happens. Model how to prompt someone back to understanding. You may need to model this many times.
- Allow students to "get you off track" once in a while, mathematically speaking. You are honoring their interests and their needs when you take the time to step back a little to clear up something or give them the opportunity to redirect the learning according to their questions.
- When students ask questions, try not to answer quickly. Redirect questions back to the students by asking follow-up questions. ("What's another strategy that will work?" "Who knows why that is right?" "What if . . . ?" "What do you think about that?")

Classrooms become exciting places when students are encouraged to use critical thinking components in collaborative conversation. Research has shown that students learn better when they are actively involved through collaboration and conversation. Knowing this, the National Teachers of Mathematics (NCTM) provides the following summary on teachers' and students' roles in classrooms that promote collaboration and discourse.

NCTM Professional Standards for Teaching Mathematics

Teacher's Role	Student's Role
Poses questions and tasks that elicit, engage, and challenge each student's thinking.	Listens to, responds to, and questions the teacher and one another.
Listens carefully to students' ideas.	Uses a variety of tools to reason, make connections, solve problems, and communicate.
Asks students to clarify and justify their ideas orally and in writing.	Initiates problems and questions.
Decides which of the ideas students bring up to pursue in depth.	Makes conjectures and presents problems.
Decides when and how to attach math notation or language to students' ideas.	Explores examples and counterexamples to investigate conjectures.

Teacher's Role	Student's Role
Decides when to provide information, when to clarify an issue, when to model, when to lead, and when to let different students struggle with a problem.	Tries to convince himself/herself and one another of the validity of particular representations, solutions, conjectures, and answers.
Monitors student participation in discussions and decides when and how to encourage each student to participate.	Relies on mathematical evidence and argument to determine validity.

Source: Professional Standards for Teaching Mathematics (1991). Reprinted with permission of the National Council of Teachers of Mathematics, Reston, Virginia.

PART II

THE 5 ESSENTIAL COMPONENTS OF A
NUMERACY-BASED MATHEMATICS LESSON

In the first half of this book, we focused on the *what*. We tackled these questions:

- What is numeracy?
- What are the critical thinking habits students need for deep, numerate thinking?

In Part II, we'd like to focus on the *how*. In other words, how do you make numeracy thrive in your instructional practices? Part II shines the light on our style of lesson planning.

We've all planned lessons. In fact, we've all planned many, many lessons. Lesson planning can sometimes feel like an untamed beast, devouring our time, wreaking havoc in our brains, and sometimes achieving nothing more than a pile of tests to grade.

Numeracy comes from classroom discourse that promotes active engagement with mathematical ideas. We've developed five essential components of a numeracy-based mathematics lesson. Each component possesses a common essential characteristic: It stimulates students to purposefully interact with the content in various ways such that they will own their mathematical thinking.

Essential Components of a Numeracy-Based Mathematics Lesson

1. Purpose and Focus (before the lesson): State exactly what you'd like your students to accomplish.

2. Ignition (first 5 minutes): Plan an activity to get your students interested and thinking.

3. Bridge to the Learning (5–7 minutes): Decide exactly how you will Bridge students' interest and thinking generated in your Ignition into your lesson and, equally as important, build and activate background knowledge.

4. Gradual Release in Mathematics (20–30 minutes): Plan how you will allow your students to discover and own their mathematical thinking.

5. Debrief: Tying It All Together (5–7 minutes): Provide an opportunity for students to settle in with the learning and to reflect and benefit from the lesson Focus.

Component 1

Purpose and Focus

Not only do students learn more effectively when they know what they're supposed to be learning and why that learning is important to them, but teachers teach more effectively when they have the same information.

—Madeline Hunter, in *Using What We Know About Teaching*, 1984

How can you craft a numeracy-rich lesson to make every student own his or her mathematical thinking? The answer is, by having Purpose and Focus built into each lesson you plan. These two elements are crucial to a well-crafted lesson. When a teacher has a distinct and well thought-out Purpose to each lesson and knows exactly what she wants her students to learn by the end of every lesson, that teacher can hold herself accountable. When Purpose is clear, the teacher knows when the lesson was realized effectively.

We'd like to offer our *recipe* for well-crafted, numeracy-rich lessons that will induce deep, numerate thinking in your mathematics class.

KEY *INGREDIENTS* OF PURPOSE AND FOCUS

1. *What?* What new understanding do I want my students to walk away with after the lesson? Using your answer, write one to three Focus questions or goals for your lesson. This is what you want the

students to understand by the end of the lesson. Again, this is not what you want them to do; this is what you want them to understand. The Focus questions should be conceptual, and the students should have to think and act to own the knowledge. The point is not about the doing; it is all about thinking through a process mathematically. We definitely understand the pressures and importance of a standards-based curriculum, but the Purpose of any lesson should go deeper than simply naming the standard. It should naturally be based upon a standard or content objective. After all, this is mathematics, and we challenge you to push the focus toward understanding. What do you want the students to understand as a result of your lesson?

2. *Why?* Ask yourself, why am I doing this lesson, and how will it help students think more thoughtfully and critically as mathematicians? Is it designed to be authentic? Would a mathematician think in ways I am asking of my students (Tovani, 2004, p. 20)? Will this lesson work toward making a more numerate individual?

3. What critical thinking components will be necessary for my students to use while they are coming to the new understanding or thinking? How will I implement them into my lesson to encourage deep thinking and genuine understanding? Which components will most effectively empower the students to capture my Focus and run with it?

4. What high-level questions will I purposely and systematically plan to ask throughout the lesson? How can I use these high-level questions to promote thoughtful and purposeful conversation?

5. How am I going to instantly engage or Ignite the students? How will I set the tone for learning and promote deep thinking through the Ignition? Is the Ignition meaningful? Is it engaging enough to interest the students?

6. How am I going to Bridge their learning from the Ignition into the lesson? How can I facilitate making connections between the new and the known? How can I provide opportunities to test and generate hypotheses to make the learning personal?

7. How will I assess the students? How will I know who has a solid understanding? How will I know who may need some help? How will I know who is completely lost? What will I do with that information?

8. How will I provide a Debriefing experience? Will the Debrief afford the students an opportunity to appreciate the learning focus? Will I allow for silent reflection?

Early Elementary Purpose and Focus Statement Examples

Students will understand the relationship between multiplication and addition.

Students will begin to develop an understanding of fractional concepts.

Students will begin to develop a one-to-one relationship for numbers 1 through 10.

Students will begin to understand the concept of probability.

Students will begin to understand how subtraction relates to addition.

Upper Elementary/Middle School Purpose and Focus Statement Examples

Students will interpret data for trends.

Students will understand appropriate interval choice when representing data.

Students will understand the hierarchy of real numbers.

Students will understand the hierarchy of quadrilaterals.

Students will understand that estimation is an integral part of decimal multiplication.

Students will understand the relationship among different types of angles.

Students will evaluate the cause-and-effect relationship an outlier has on measures of central tendency.

Component 2

Ignition

Teaching should be such that what is offered is perceived as a valuable gift rather than a hard duty.

—Albert Einstein

Ignition is how you snare your students as soon as they enter your classroom. It sets the stage for numerate learning; it also sets the tone for mathematical fervor. There are many titles for this moment of instruction: Jumpstart, Do Now, Bell Ringer, Class Starter, Anticipatory Set, and so on.

The name doesn't matter.

What matters is that Ignition is meaningful, highly engaging, and thought provoking and that it always promotes deep thinking. Well-crafted Ignitions can be rich with numeracy. Research shows that students retain 70 percent of the information presented to them in the first 10 minutes of class but only 20 percent purveyed in the last 10 minutes (Meyers & Jones, 1993). Ignition is your moment to excite your students and get them thinking mathematically, for high energy is a stimulus for engagement. Because Ignition is crucial, it needs to happen every day for every class. We believe that varying instructional practice is a key ingredient in engaging your students and that with engagement comes learning.

We're also believers in easy. We'd like to meet the teacher who says, "Time? Ha, I have so much time on my hands, I never know what to do with it!" Is that laughter we hear? The first comment we typically hear from teachers are versions of "Okay, Ms. Instructional Coach, with your fancy Ignition ideas, are you expecting me to think up something engaging for my kids to do every single day? I don't have time to do extra things! I have curriculum to cover!"

We hear you. We've been there. But after realizing and living the benefits of a good Ignition, we became true believers. The first few minutes of class can sometimes make or break the lesson. We saw that this instructional component was one that offered a huge payoff. It only took a few tries to realize that when the students were instantly engaged they were primed for learning and that the lesson we had planned was easier to teach (not to mention that we had fewer management issues to deal with because the students were busy thinking). A thought-provoking Ignition also allowed for checking homework and taking attendance without that deadly downtime. It was well worth the time invested. We came to realize the power Ignition held, and that realization shifted *our* thinking.

KEY ASPECTS OF IGNITION

- Preplan your Ignition and have it on the board before your students come into the classroom. A beautiful routine will be established in this way. Students will come to expect the Ignition and get right down to it.
- Ignition is an awakening of the brain. It is the initial hook, setting the tone in which your lesson will be received.
- Ignition also helps set the tone for a well-managed classroom. When you see students fully engaged in your Ignition, you should be able to identify the factors that "caused" the students to be on task. Then you will be able to re-create and repeat those factors.
- Ignition creates a culture of rigor and an atmosphere of deep thinking. Students know that thinking begins the second they walk in the door. A well-planned Ignition shows students that you take their learning seriously.
- An Ignition should take 3 to 5 minutes maximum. If the Ignition goes beyond 5 minutes, it is no longer an Ignition, and you run the risk of diluting the true Purpose of your lesson. Mastering a 3–5 minute Ignition takes practice. Don't be discouraged in the beginning if your Ignition goes over the 5-minute mark; it happens to the best of us.
- In mathematics, the Ignition can be independent of your lesson; in other words, the topic of the Ignition doesn't have to match the lesson topic. It can simply be interesting, engaging, competitive, funny, or thought provoking. However, on the flip side, it can be connected and lead into the Bridge; ultimately, it is up to you.
- Students can work on Ignitions independently, with a partner, or even in a small group. We would continuously vary this to keep things fresh.

- An Ignition is enticing and engaging. Students should want to pay attention, not because you said so but because they don't want to miss anything. It wakes students up so that the lesson that follows will be better received and understood.
- Offer variety. Some Ignitions might connect previous lessons, some might offer challenging logic scenarios, and some might facilitate algebraic thinking. The possibilities are unlimited. The purpose is to keep it fresh and hook the students into your lesson. *Mix it up from day to day. Many examples follow to get you started.*
- The Ignition can simply be a question. Take the Focus of the lesson and pose it as a question to provoke deep thinking, then revisit the same Focus question during the Debrief for students to revise and add to their initial thoughts. Very powerful!
- Ignition is active, numerate learning in action and at its best.

Active learning isn't a new idea. It goes back at least as far as Socrates and was a major emphasis among progressive educators like John Dewey. Active learning puts our students in situations that compel them to read, speak, listen, think deeply, and write. While well-delivered lectures are valuable and not uncommon, sometimes the comprehension required while attending a lecture is low level and goes from the ear to the writing hand, leaving the mind untouched. Active learning puts the responsibility of organizing what is to be learned in the hands of the learners themselves and ideally lends itself to a more diverse range of learning styles.

Teaching that emphasizes active engagement helps students process and retain information. It leads to self-questioning, deeper thinking, and problem solving. When learning is active, students do most of the work. They use their brains, studying ideas, solving problems, and applying what they learn. Active learning is fast paced, fun, supportive, and personally engaging. To learn something well, it helps to hear it, see it, ask questions about it, and discuss it with others. Active learning involves providing opportunities for students to meaningfully talk and listen, write, read, and reflect on the content, ideas, issues, and concerns of an academic subject (Meyers & Jones, 1993).

Active learners energetically strive to take a greater responsibility for their own learning. They take a more dynamic role in deciding how and what they need to know, what they should be able to do, and how they are going to do it. Their roles extend to become educational self-management, and self-motivation becomes a greater force behind learning as students engage in inquiry (Glasgow, Cheyne, & Yerrick, 2010).

The Ignition can be used to achieve the following:

Preteach

Example: The sum of two whole numbers is 24.

- What is the greatest their product can be?
- What is the least their product can be?
- Explain your strategy.

Review Prior Skills

Example: Take out your homework. Create a headline that would represent the main idea of your homework. Justify your answer. Now include some vocabulary words that you think would definitely be included in a news article using your headline. Explain your reasoning. Let's see who can come up with the best homework headline. (This Ignition could be done collaboratively or independently.)

Encourage Good Number Sense and Estimation

Example: Choose the most reasonable unit of measure for each of the following and explain why you think it is the most reasonable choice.

1. The distance between New York and Philadelphia
   a. inches   b. feet   c. miles   d. centimeters

2. The amount of gasoline in the tank of an airplane
   a. liters   b. milliliters   c. kiloliters   d. kilograms

3. The weight of a raisin
   a. pounds   b. milligrams   c. kilograms   d. grams

4. The amount of coffee in a coffee mug
   a. ounces   b. liters   c. milliliters d. cups

5. The weight of a dog
   a. milligrams b. grams   c. kilograms   d. tons

6. The amount of medicine in an eyedropper
   a. grams   b. milliliters   c. pounds   d. cup

Hook the Students by Providing a Thought-Provoking Question

Example: A world without numbers? What would it be like if tomorrow we lived in a world without numbers? Reflect on this scenario for a moment and write a diary entry describing such a world. Be prepared to share your ideas.

Reinforce Mental Math Skills

Example: You are at the mall with your friends. You want to buy 2 shirts for $13.10, 1 pair of pants for $24.99, and 3 packs of socks for $2.90 each. What is the cost of your total purchases? You may not write down any calculations. You must use mental math. Now explain how you found your answer. What did your mind do naturally? (This type of Ignition should begin independently, and then have students share the various mental math strategies they used. This is a great introduction to how compensation and the distributive property are useful in mental math.)

"Tease" the Students Into Wanting to Learn What's Coming Up

Example: Find the value of each shape:

$\triangle$ + ☆ + ☆ = 140

$\triangle$ + □ + □ = 70

□ + $\triangle$ = 45 (This is best completed in pairs. Have students share different strategies for solving.)

Connect the Math to a Real-World Application

Example: On the overhead, show an excerpt from the following article: "Everyone Counts" by Jaime Joyce, January 4, 2010 (http://www.time forkids.com/TFK/kids/news/story/0,28277,1951561,00.html). Have students read the excerpt and analyze how they think the results from the 2010 Census will be different from the results of the 2000 Census, the 1960 Census, 1910 Census? Have students predict how it might look different in 2020. Always encourage students to explain their reasoning in writing. Writing promotes synthesis. If you want to take this activity further, ask students to research how their predictions match up to the real Census results.

Facilitate Visualizing

Example: Provide each small group with 36 square tiles. Challenge them to make as many rectangles with the same area as possible. Draw the options in their journal and compare their perimeters. What do they notice? (You can simplify this activity or make it more difficult. It depends upon the needs of your students.)

Challenge the Students to Make Conjectures

Example: Provide groups with several data sets along with the corresponding mean, median, mode, and range. Have students examine each data set and their statistics to make conjectures about the meaning of the data. Encourage students to generate definitions of mean, median, mode, and range from their examination of the data sets (Van de Walle & Lovin, 2006, p. 312).

Dare the Students to Discover Missing Information

Example: ? × ? = 2,280. What might the missing factors be? How did you get started? How many different answers can you find (Sullivan & Lilburn, 2002, p. 44)? (This is a great Ignition prior to a divisibility lesson. You can do similar Ignitions using all operations. It promotes number sense and estimating skills.)

Connect the Art/Music World to the Math World

Example: Examine this piece of art and determine what you think the artist's "voice" is in the piece. (Use the artwork of Cezanne, Seurat, Escher, Dali, or Sandro Del-Prete for this activity. Plenty of mathematics to analyze can be found in these pieces.)

Organize and Classify Concepts

Example: Organize the following math terms into categories. Once you have your categories formed, create a title for each category and be prepared to justify your grouping choices and titles.

intersection of sets	point	angle
counterexample	additive identity	line segment
empty set	null set	vertex set
additive inverse	converse	union of sets
plane	measure (of an angle)	disjoint sets
parallel lines	elements, members	degree

(You can do this Ignition with any of your vocabulary words. It works really well with your anchor vocabulary for standardized tests.)

Analyze and Evaluate a Problem From Different Perspectives

Example: Find a common value for the two unknowns.

$G + G + G + G + G + R + R = 57$ (Hint! There are six possible values for G and R.)

$G + G + R + R + R = 36$ (Hint! There are five possible values for G and R.)

$G =$ ___ $R =$ ___ (Hint! There is only one common value for G and R.)

How did you begin solving this problem? Explain your reasoning for beginning this way. What did you do next? Why? Continue to write your thinking and your process. Share your strategies with a partner until you share your answer. How were your methods different? How were they the same? Which method is your favorite? Why?

Supplement Current Instruction by Challenging the Students to "Think Outside the Mathematics Box" and Infer

A good starter here might be "What if . . . ?" Or "If . . . then . . . ."

Example: Use the digits 0–9 to complete the rule. You may only use each digit once, and you must use all 10 digits for this rule to be true.

$$\boxed{\text{RULE: } \times 2}$$

$$35 \longrightarrow \square\square$$
$$\square\square \longrightarrow 96$$
$$\square 7 \longrightarrow 1\square 4$$
$$2\square \longrightarrow \square 8$$
$$\square 2 \longrightarrow \square 4$$

This activity is best done collaboratively. Have the groups share how they got started. The work supports algebraic thinking. To find more problems like this one, see Marcy Cook's *Try-a-Tile/Logic With Numbers* (1990; see also www.marcycookmath.com).

Generate Questions

Example: (Display a graph created by a well-known business or created by you.) You have an opportunity to ask three questions to this company before it publishes this graph. What three questions would you ask? Explain why these three questions are important.

Component 3

Bridge to the Learning

Water that is too pure has no fish in it.

—Tsai Ken Tans

A Bridge to the Learning? What do we mean? Let's start with the definition of the word *bridge* from dictionary.com: *a connecting, transitional, or intermediate route or phase between two adjacent elements, activities, conditions, or the like.* A bridge simply allows you to get from one place to another safely, directly, and as easily as possible.

For our purpose, the key words in this definition are *connecting* and *transitional.* The Bridge to the Learning, in classroom-speak, is when you take your students from where they are to where they need to be to access the upcoming learning. It is the opportunity to activate and build prior knowledge, present an inquiry moment, frontload vocabulary, make connections, fill some gaps, provide cues, and allow for discovery. These achievements can happen in a variety of ways.

You create a Bridge to the Learning by connecting students' previous learning or perhaps the thinking stimulated by the Ignition to your upcoming lesson. The Bridge, which is ultimately you, effectively guides students' thoughts and ideas into the fresh arena, welcoming those thoughts and making students feel comfortable, ready to stretch and deepen. You are given a unique opportunity during the Bridge to quickly assess student readiness and to use that knowledge to adjust the pace of your lesson.

The Bridge to the Learning is a crucial and powerful moment in your instructional practice, one that *cannot be skipped*. It is during this time that you set up your students' thinking for clear numerate thinking and for clarity—again, readying their brains to stretch.

Let's get to the specifics.

The Bridge to the Learning occurs after Ignition or immediately after the homework check. It should take only 5–8 minutes, but as we said, these are probably the most powerful few minutes in that they afford each student access to the learning. It is similar to an Ignition in that it should interest the students and support numerate thinking. The Ignition, however, is all about instant engagement and setting the tone for learning in your classroom. Conversely, the Bridge is all about opening many pathways to the learning so that all students have equal access to it. The focus of Ignition is immediate engagement, whereas the focus of the Bridge is to transition into your instruction.

The Bridge is exactly that: the Bridge to the Learning that is to come.

WHAT IS THE PURPOSE OF A BRIDGE TO THE LEARNING?

- *To provide guided inquiry and discovery:* When students learn by discovery, they are much more likely to understand, remember, and apply their learning to other situations (Allen, 2000, p. 123). Guided inquiry requires students to work together to solve problems, derive patterns, or generate hypotheses as opposed to the teacher delivering direct instructions on what to do. Guided inquiry fosters a numeracy-rich classroom. The teacher's job in guided inquiry is not to impart knowledge but, instead, to facilitate students' movement along the path of discovering knowledge themselves.

- *To activate and build background knowledge:* During the Bridge, you either activate background knowledge or build necessary knowledge so that students can better understand the upcoming lesson. Students need some background knowledge before they know enough to want to learn more (Allen, 1999, p. 132).

- *To preview:* One highlight of a comprehensive approach to numeracy across the curriculum is that students perform some form of previewing prior to the actual presentation of content. Previewing refers to any activity that starts student thinking about the content they will encounter in the lesson. These activities appear to be particularly useful for students who do not possess a great deal of background knowledge about the topic (Mayer, 1979).

- *To supply cues:* A cue is a trigger to initiate thinking. Cues help bring the learning to mind. With cues, teachers provide students with direct links between new content and content previously taught (Marzano, 2007, p. 32).

- *To facilitate predictions:* Making predictions keeps students engaged in the learning. Students care more about their learning when they make predictions. In mathematics, making predictions empowers students to navigate successfully through the textbook.
- *To build interest and make connections:* Students are motivated to think when the context of a problem interests them. Working in a meaningful context can help students build an initial understanding of a concept. Students' knowledge is generally organized around their experiences, not around the abstract concepts within the discipline of mathematics (Hyde, 2006, p. 49).
- *To scaffold comprehension:* Students build up an understanding of concepts gradually. We can use the innate, pattern-creating, meaning-making, inductive reasoning that students bring to school to good advantage. We can provide many examples of the target concept in a particular situation so that students develop a solid initial, local version of the concept. Then we can deliberately provide experiences with the same concept in different contexts (Hyde, 2006, p. 49).
- *To assess:* You can use the Bridge to judge the readiness of your students. Will you need to adjust the pace of your lesson? Who might need additional scaffolding? Who would benefit from small-group instruction?

KEY IDEAS

Students need lots of help getting started. The Bridge is what scaffolds many students toward understanding the purpose of your lesson. Cris Tovani supports the idea that students depend on opportunities to wrestle with the upcoming learning when she states that "meaning does not arrive, it must be constructed" (Tovani, 2004, p. 104). The Bridge is often the pathway to success for many students; without it, some students do not have access to the learning. Studies have shown that true learning takes place only when students engage with information and structures deeply enough to merge that content into their personal views and understandings of how the world works (Harlen, 2000).

There may have been a time when transferring facts from a math textbook to students was the sole objective of a math lesson. In those days, a cursory understanding of the mathematical concepts was probably considered sufficient. But to succeed in the 21st century, we are well aware that simply possessing a mental bag of facts does not guarantee that a person is truly numerate.

In mathematics especially, simple "telling" does not work. Comprehension comes through integrating knowledge into a meaningful whole, for mathematics is no more simple computation than literature is typing (Paulos, 1992). The Bridge to the Learning offers students the opportunity to merge content with strategic thinking.

We all realize that the role of a teacher is to help students learn. How do students learn? Psychological research suggests that learning is a constructive process. It entails making connections, relating new knowledge to what is already known, and applying knowledge to new contexts. Only by working with content do we internalize it and make it our own. Instructors who understand how learning occurs use active learning techniques in the classroom. The Bridge forces students to manipulate the material to solve problems, answer questions, formulate questions of their own, discuss, explain, debate, or brainstorm (http://gradschool.about .com/cs/teaching/a/teachtip_4.htm).

The Bridge is a key component to active, numerate learning in the mathematics classroom. It is the transition into the learning.

Bridge to the Learning

The Bridge to the Learning is where students:

- Preview new material
- Participate in guided inquiry and guided discovery
- Activate background knowledge
- Build background knowledge
- "Buy into" the learning
- Develop a curiosity
- Generate questions
- Make predictions about the learning to come
- Preview text
- Make a personal investment
- Validate their thinking
- Engage in an interesting activity
- Discover meaning
- Brainstorm ideas
- Experiment with manipulatives
- Connect yesterday's lesson to today's lesson
- Collaborate
- Organize and categorize mathematical concepts
- Formulate a hypothesis
- Generate a formula by discovering how and why it works
- Generate questions they would like answered by the learning to come
- Solve a problem that introduces the lesson
- Make real-life applications to the learning

Rick Wormeli (2009) challenges us to "get out of our students' way and let them soar" (p. 75). Teaching that emphasizes inquiry helps students process and retain information. It leads to self-questioning, deeper thinking, and problem solving. Shelley Harwayne (1992) attests to this when she says, "Students will learn most when the journey is really theirs."

Allow your students to notice their thinking before and after the lesson. Lay down a foundation of thinking, and then help them merge the content with their thinking (Tishman, Jay, & Perkins, 1993). Begin with an activity that invites student questions, and then Bridge those questions to inferences as a way of scaffolding the concepts (Gear, 2008, p. 78).

Students often have to touch, physically manipulate, and if possible, smell and taste new concepts to integrate them into long-term memory (Wormeli, 2009, p. 61), and the Bridge is the perfect time to allow for sensory exploration. Wormeli asserts that there are physics involved in teaching students to become critical thinkers. As he paraphrases Newton's First Law on Inertia: "A student at rest stays at rest unless acted upon by an outside force" (p. 75). We need to be that force; and the Bridge provides the platform upon which we can stand.

HOW CAN I DO THIS IN MY MATH CLASS . . . TOMORROW?

Scrolling and Skimming

Scrolling: To move your eyes quickly over an article to determine what the information is about or if the information is relevant to what you need to find. What supports are there to help you find out what it's all about?

- Boldface words
- Headings
- Photographs
- Illustrations
- Captions
- Sidebars

Skimming: To read quickly for main ideas or supporting details in a text.

- What is the topic?
  _____

- Why might you be learning this (make connections)?
  _____

- What question(s) come to mind from the skimming?
  _____

Interactive Cloze

1. Select a paragraph from the text that is about to be taught or assigned.

2. Delete important keywords and duplicate copies for students. You can also create your own worksheet. Important! Make sure keywords are deleted—not words such as *is, the, and,* and so on.

3. Have students predict what they think the missing words might be. Have them justify their choices.

4. Ask students to read the selection quietly.

5. Have students complete the cloze activity on their own or with a partner.

6. Allow students to discuss their answers with a partner.

7. Students can then reread the actual text to find out if their answers are correct.

Word Toss

- Identify major concepts that will be taught in the lesson. Write 7 to 10 words and "toss" them on the board or overhead.
- Ask students to write a few sentences using some or all of the terms. The sentences should show how the students predict the terms will be related to the lesson they are about to learn.
- Have students share their sentences with partners.
- After the lesson, challenge the students to check on the accuracy of their predictions and make revisions, if necessary. (Hollas, 2005, p. 88)

Focus Question

Determine the Purpose of the lesson. Create a Focus question or two that will help craft the flow of the lesson to suit that Purpose. Present the question(s) to the students at the Bridge. Ask them to think, write, and discuss their responses. Then put up the same Focus question at the Debrief and have the students use their new knowledge to add and revise their original responses. Allow time for quiet conversation. Make the questions about real life rather than simply about the behavioral objective of the lesson. You will get more buy-in this way because the students will find relevance in the learning.

Central Question

Ask students to preview the text and generate and record a Focus question they think will be answered by the end of the lesson. While learning, have them revise their question, answer it, or continue with the question. During the Debrief, discuss strategies and answers. Be sure to share those questions that were not answered. If the question cannot be answered at that point, record it visibly for the class to answer at some point.

Greet and Go

This method is an interactive way for students to use their background knowledge to make predictions about the vocabulary to be covered in the day's lesson. First, give each student an index card with a term or phrase from the lesson they are about to learn. Ask the students to circulate around the room and read their cards to each other. After a couple of minutes, call "freeze." While returning to their seats, ask the students to be thinking about what they predict today's lesson will be about. Have the students return to their small groups and jointly write a prediction on what they will be learning about that day. This activity is a great one when the lesson is "loaded" with vocabulary (Forsten et al., 2002b, p. 46).

Three Facts and a Fib

This activity forms a perfect setup for learning math. The students are instantly engaged. You present three facts about what they are about to learn and one fib (Forsten et al., 2002a, p. 63). They discuss which one is the fib and why. It is fun and worthwhile. Sometimes at the Debrief, have the students make up their own facts and a fib as an exit ticket. They identify the fib on the back and write a reflection on what they learned from the lesson. The exit tickets become the next day's Ignition, and the students did all the work.

Three Facts and a Fib

1. All squares are rectangles.
2. All rectangles are squares.
3. All parallelograms are quadrilaterals.
4. All rhombuses are parallelograms.

Preconcept and Postconcept Checks

Your purpose with this activity is to have students quickly self-rate their understanding of certain vocabulary that will be introduced in the lesson. The first check happens before the learning as a Bridge, then after the learning as a Debrief.

Preconcept and Postconcept Checks

Ratings: + = could teach it; √ = kinda know it; — = no clue		
Before the Learning		*After the Learning*
_____	variable	_____
_____	algebraic expression	_____
_____	evaluate	_____
_____	substituting	_____

At the Debrief, ask the students to prove their understanding by creating representations or explanations. In this way, the teacher guides student thinking but still allows for a self-discovery of connections, always bringing missed connection opportunities back to the whole class. This method also helps differentiate the lesson. Quickly circulate around the room and see which students might need to touch base with you during the lesson or which students need to be pushed beyond the original plan (Forget, 2004, p. 230).

Example and Nonexamples

The idea here is to ask the students to formulate a definition by observing examples and nonexamples. Before the students enter the room, write several examples and nonexamples of a particular math concept you are going to teach. Have them discuss and formulate a definition. Then challenge them to revise and add to that definition during the lesson.

Discovery Through Manipulatives

Put a little cup of M&M's on the tables before the students enter. On the board write, "How could you use the M&M's to teach _____?" (e.g., ratios, percentages, equivalent fractions). Let them discuss and share. Now bring them to the learning. They already have a solid understanding.

Concept Circles

Concept circles are circles with words placed in the sectors (Vaca et al., 1987). Ask students to discuss and write about the connections they see between the words (see one version here). You could also write three of the words and challenge the students to identify the connection, then add a fourth word that would also fit in the category. You can write three words that "belong" and one word that doesn't and ask the students to find the word that doesn't fit. Make sure they can justify their decisions. One variation that is valuable as a Debrief is to have students write the words and challenge other students to find the connections (Allen, 1999).

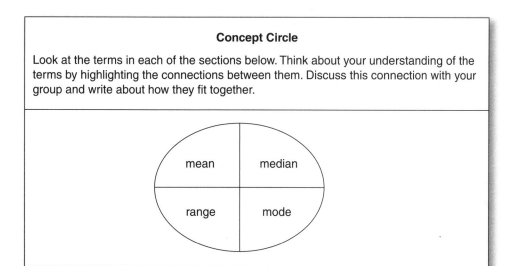

Concept Circle

Look at the terms in each of the sections below. Think about your understanding of the terms by highlighting the connections between them. Discuss this connection with your group and write about how they fit together.

mean | median
range | mode

T.H.I.E.V.E.S.

Here is a great strategy to preview the chapters of any textbook. It is known as T.H.I.E.V.E.S., an acronym for the steps of the strategy. After some practice, you will find this strategy to be easy and very effective in improving your comprehension of what you read. We created bookmarks using the T.H.I.E.V.E.S. acronym, and students used them daily. The best way to introduce this activity is to describe what thieves do when they break into a house: They go in quickly and get out what is most important. Explain that they are to be "thieves" while reading text through this previewing strategy.

T.H.I.E.V.E.S.

T—TITLE

What is the title?

What do I already know about this topic?

What does this topic have to do with the preceding lesson or chapter?

What do I think I will be reading about?

(Continued)

(Continued)

H–HEADINGS/SUBHEADINGS

What does this heading tell me I will be reading about?

What is the topic of the paragraph beneath it?

How can I turn this heading into a question that is likely to be answered in the text?

I–INTRODUCTION

Is there an opening paragraph, perhaps italicized?

Does the first paragraph introduce the chapter?

What does the introduction tell me I will be reading about?

E–EXAMPLES SHOWN (in subjects other than math, E stands for Every first sentence in a paragraph)

Mathematics: What do I think this chapter is going to be about based on the examples provided in the lesson?

Other subjects: What do I think this chapter is going to be about based on the first sentence in each paragraph?

V–VISUALS AND VOCABULARY

Does the chapter include photographs, drawings, maps, charts, or graphs?

What can I learn from the visuals in a chapter?

How do captions help me better understand the meaning?

Is there a list of key vocabulary terms and definitions?

Are there important words in boldfaced type throughout the chapter?

Do I know what the boldfaced words mean?

Can I tell the meanings of the boldfaced words from the sentences in which they are embedded?

E–END-OF-CHAPTER QUESTIONS

What do the questions ask?

What information do I learn from the questions?

Let me keep in mind the end-of-chapter questions so that I can annotate my text where pertinent information is located.

S–SUMMARY

What do I understand and recall about the topics covered in the summary?

Preteach: Create a "Sentence Frame"

Begin with a framed sentence to build on students' ideas. The teacher controls the mathematical concept and the format of the sentence by pre-planning the sentence so that it activates and builds background knowledge before the lesson. The sentence should force students to pull out what they know and bring it to the lesson. The ultimate purpose is to keep students present and accountable to their learning.

The most critical part of this experience is the discussion. Don't make it just a quick vocabulary activity without any meaning. By having them explain their answers to each other, you've instantly differentiated the lesson. While the students are engaged in their discussions, the teacher purposefully eavesdrops for golden nuggets of information on his or her students. Who understands the difference between an expression and an equation, and who doesn't? (See Habit 2, Develop Schema and Activate Background Knowledge, for sentence frame examples.)

Frontload Content-Specific Vocabulary

Many textbooks list vocabulary in sidebars. This layout is to encourage students to activate background knowledge and to help them determine importance. Unfortunately for students with limited prior knowledge, it will be difficult for them to create meaning prior to having a context for their reading.

One effective way to frontload the learning is to bring in realia. If you are teaching about scale, bring in blueprints. If you are teaching fractions, bring in pies, brownies, and so on. Such items give students a visual and meaningful frame of reference.

To frontload vocabulary that cannot be represented easily by something physical, list the important concepts for the lesson. Tell them, "These words all have something to do with [whatever your lesson title is]." Challenge them to work within teams and to discuss how they think the words might be important in a lesson about _____. The discussion may help ground the vocabulary within a context and give the students an opportunity to use the vocabulary in conversation before reading about it. This will also allow students who lack any background knowledge to be privy to what others, with more varied life experiences, may know.

Frontload Nonmathematical Terms

Students will be better able to solve a problem if it is stated in language they understand. For example, one story problem on probability may refer to a deck of playing cards. Many students are now unfamiliar with how many cards are in a deck or how many suits there are. Without prior experience with playing cards, you cannot answer that probability question, no matter how intelligent you are. Sometimes simple language gets in the way of the actual math. Even though the meaning of a phrase or word isn't important to solving a particular math problem, some students, especially ELL students, may lack the background knowledge necessary to understand the problem, which only adds to their confusion.

Frontload Multiple-Meaning Words

Mathematics often uses words with multiple meanings. This can be very confusing for students. It is helpful to present these words prior to the lesson and ask students to brainstorm various meanings. If need be, simply let them know what the math meaning is. This revelation can be a relief to students with limited background knowledge. Some examples of multiple-meaning words in mathematics are *substituting*, *regular*, *angle*, and *chord*.

Component 4

Gradual Release in Mathematics

We should be teaching students how to think. Instead, we are teaching them what to think.

—J. Lochhead and J. Clement, *Cognitive Process Instruction*, 1979

T he National Research Council states, "Research on learning shows that most students cannot learn mathematics effectively by only listening and imitating: yet most teachers teach mathematics this way. Most teachers teach as they were taught, not as they were taught to teach" (*National Research Council Collection*, 1989–1995, p. 6). The NCTM research companion to *Principles and Standards for School Mathematics* (2000) summarized the nature of teaching mathematics that is currently prevalent in the United States: "The most common pattern of classroom practice was extensive teacher-directed explanation followed by student seatwork on paper." A study by the Third International Mathematics and Science Study (TIMSS) in which typical eighth-grade mathematics lessons were videotaped confirmed that teachers gave little attention to helping students develop conceptual ideas.

At one point, we were also guilty of this type of daily instructional delivery. It took intense, honest self-reflection to realize that students were not "getting it" even though we were "saying it," and that students did not truly understand even when they could repeat 20 problems like the one we just presented. We needed to bring the quotation "mathematics is not just a spectator sport" down from the walls of our classrooms and into our daily instructional practice. We realized that true understanding cannot be presented; it needs to be actively sought by the students themselves. They needed to come to their own understanding, and we needed to provide lots of opportunities for that to happen. We researched and, after much effort, finally found the answer to our problem: the Gradual Release of Responsibility.

Gradual Release of Responsibility is a logical approach to teaching developed by literacy scholars Pearson and Gallagher (1983). Gradual Release provides opportunity after opportunity for deep numerate thinking to be strengthened and owned by your students. It also allows teachers to offer more targeted, individualized instruction. Stated another way, the Gradual Release of Responsibility emphasizes instruction that mentors students so that they become capable thinkers and learners through handling tasks for which they have not yet developed expertise (Buehl, 2008). This instructional model requires that the teacher, by design, transition gradually from assuming all the responsibility for performing a task to letting the students assume all the responsibility (Pearson & Gallagher, 1983). The model consists of the following steps:

Gradual Release of Responsibility Model

1. *Modeled:* Model + Think-Aloud Whole-group instruction Approximate time spent: 5–10 minutes	1. ***I do, you watch.*** • Teacher *thinks-aloud* to model the mental processes she uses when she reads/thinks/problem solves. • Teacher *models.* • Teacher focuses the guided inquiry and discovery experience from the Bridge to the learning by connecting to the lesson's Purpose. Students understand the connections. • Students are given the opportunity to experience how a mathematician thinks through a problem.

2. *Shared:* Guided Practice Whole-group instruction (you can go back to step 1 and remodel, if you see a need.) Approximate time spent: 5–10 minutes	2. *We practice together, and I support you by giving tips* • Teacher *gradually* gives the student more responsibility for task completion. • Students self-assess. • Teacher uses *formative assessment* to create flexible groups for guided practice. • Teacher scaffolds the students' attempts and supports student thinking, giving feedback during conferencing and classroom discussions.
3. *Guided:* Guided Practice With Support Small-group instruction Flexible grouping Approximate time spent: 10–15 minutes *In mathematics, Guided Practice often occurs in conjunction with Independent Application. For instance, you may pull a group to work with while the rest of the class works independently.	3. *You do in groups or with a partner, I support.* • Teacher *scaffolds*, supports, and assesses the learning. • Students *self-assess* their understanding so far. • Teacher uses *formative assessment* to determine the effectiveness of his teaching and crafts future lessons accordingly. • Students receive meaningful feedback from the teacher and other students.
4. *Independent:* Independent Application Small-group instruction, as needed Along with Independent Application Approximate time spent: 10–15 minutes *In mathematics, Independent Application often occurs in conjunction with Guided Practice. For instance, while some students are working independently, the teacher may choose to pull a small group as needed, based on the formative assessment.	4. *You do, I assess.* • Students *self-assess* through the Debrief by proving their understanding of the learning. • Teacher uses formative assessment to steer the learning needed by the students.

Source: Reprinted from P. David Pearson and Margaret C. Gallagher, The Instruction of Reading Comprehension, *Contemporary Educational Psychology,* 8(3), 317–344, copyright © 1983, with permission from Elsevier.

RESEARCH FINDINGS

The following list restates the four interactive (or interrelated) components of the Gradual Release of Responsibility model in the previous table (Fisher & Frey, 2008).

1. *Focus Lessons (modeling):* This component allows teachers to model their own metacognitive processes as active readers. Modeled strategies focus on increasing the understanding of content-area texts. Usually brief in nature, focus lessons establish the purposes for reading and clue students into important learning objectives.

2. *Guided Instruction (shared practice):* During guided instruction, teachers prompt, question, facilitate, or lead students through tasks that increase understanding of a particular text.

3. *Collaborative Learning (guided practice):* During the collaborative learning component in the Gradual Release of Responsibility model, students consolidate their understanding of the content and explore opportunities to problem solve, discuss, negotiate, and think with their peers.

4. *Independent Learning (independent application):* This component addresses the most important goal of good instruction—to provide students with practice in applying skills and information in new ways. As students transfer their learning to subsequent tasks, they synthesize information, transform ideas, and solidify their understanding. They become active readers and capable learners.

The Four Teaching Phases of the Gradual Release of Responsibility

Teaching Phases	*Teacher Behaviors*	*Learner Behaviors*
Modeling	• Initiates • Models • Explains • Thinks-aloud • Shows "how to do it"	• Listens • Observes • May participate on a limited basis
Shared Practice	• Demonstrates • Leads • Suggests • Explains • Responds • Acknowledges	• Listens • Interacts • Questions • Collaborates • Responds • Tries out • Approximates • Participates

Teacher Hands Over Responsibility		
Teaching Phases	Teacher Behaviors	Learner Behaviors
Guided Practice	• Scaffolds • Validates • Teaches as needed • Evaluates • Observes • Encourages • Clarifies • Confirms • Coaches	• Applies learning • Takes charge • Practices • Problem solves • Approximates • Self-corrects
Independent Application	• Affirms • Assists as needed • Responds • Acknowledges • Evaluates • Sets goals	• Initiates • Self-monitors • Self-directs • Applies learning • Problem solves • Confirms • Self-evaluates

Source: Better Learning Through Structured Learning (p. 15), by Douglas Fisher and Nancy Frey, Alexandria, VA: ASCD. Copyright © 2008 by ASCD. Reprinted with permission. Learn more about ASCD at www.ascd.org.

MODELED: I DO, YOU WATCH

Teacher modeling is, in other words, your instructional time. We agree with Gear (2008) when she argues that teachers must spend explicit instructional time teaching students *how* to think rather than *what* to think. Teachers cultivate metacognitive experiences for students when they demonstrate how to think in mathematics. Legitimate numeracy experiences can also flourish.

The Gradual Release model allows students to hear their teacher think through the mathematics via the think-aloud. Cris Tovani (2004) says the teacher's first job is to show how he or she is thinking. There is great power in opening up how you, the teacher, process a math problem. Many of your students do not realize you think through the math; they simply think you are smart. When you disclose your thoughts while you are problem solving, students receive the privilege of grasping how you think mathematically. After a think-aloud, one student shared, "I didn't know your brain was doing all that; I just thought you were smarter. I think my brain could do that stuff, too." These moments give your students the confidence to think mathematically and become successful at it.

In addition to showing students how we are thinking through the mathematics, there is power in showing them how to navigate their math textbook as math readers. Students need to be shown how to become strong, numerate math readers. Who will show them? You.

Think-alouds provide ideal platforms for demonstrating how to be a math reader. Think-alouds allow the many complex habits that help us comprehend become visible (Zwiers, 2004, p. 13). They show students how skillful math readers think—how we activate our background knowledge, ask questions, draw conclusions. Teachers model a language of thought that they use for learning new information, asking questions, and making connections (Harvey & Goudvis, 2007, p. 223).

Think-alouds make teachers' thinking public. Public thinking *out loud* does not come easily, contrary to what you might think. Kylene Beers (2003) suggests that think-alouds require constant practice, and we concur. Some educators believe they've been thinking aloud for years when, in fact, they've been teaching aloud. There is a distinct difference, one that bears some further explanation.

Think-alouds let your students directly into your mathematical thinking. When you think-aloud, say, "I am going to show you the thinking that is going on in my head." Then peel back the layers of your thinking to show students how mathematicians approach text, thus making visible how understanding happens in a variety of reading contexts. To demystify the comprehension process, we share our thoughts as we read, surfacing our own inner conversation with the text so that students can learn to do so independently (Harvey & Goudvis, 2007). We must pull out the invisible process of comprehending to reach the visible level (Beers, 2003, p. 105).

It takes practice to keep think-alouds pure and not allow them to morph into *teach* alouds. Again, there is a big difference (see the following example). The teacher's thinking needs to be visible and concrete (Gear, 2008, p. 46). Everything became much clearer for us when we realized that telling students how to do the math doesn't mean we've shown them the more powerful way of how to *think through* the math.

Anchor Think-Aloud: Example Lesson Plan (Grades 6–8)

Purpose

1. Students will observe and notice how I use critical thinking habits while problem solving.

2. Students will identify two reasons to re-read:
   a. to clarify
   b. to redirect focus

3. Students will notice when and how to "turn down the volume" on connections that may distract and impede understanding.

4. Students will practice thinking aloud with a partner.

Bridge to the Learning

Put up the following text (or something just as difficult) on the overhead or Smartboard. (Students should not have a copy of this.)

We now know that we can find equilibria solutions to a differential equation by finding values of the population for which $dP/dt = 0$. But we also observed that the two equilibria solutions for the logistic population model differ: for one equilibrium, nearby trajectories (solutions to the differential equation) are "attracted" to the equilibrium; for the other equilibrium, nearby trajectories are "repelled." We call the first case a stable equilibrium (also called a sink), and we call the second case an unstable equilibrium (also called a source). (Copyright © 1996 by The Geometry Center. All rights reserved.)

Challenge your students to switch roles with you. They are now the teachers, and you are the student. They will be "grading" you in how they think you do as a reader. Make sure you have read this statement ahead of time several times. Really impress the students with your oral reading. Exaggerate your reading so that it sounds like you really understand the piece.

Ask the students to talk to partners and come up with a grade on how you did as a reader. Ask them what grade they gave you, and why they gave you that grade. They will more than likely give you an "A."

Here's the powerful part: Reveal that you have no idea what you read. Tell them about what Cris Tovani calls "fake reading," that is, reading without thinking. Reveal that, if they were to ask you about what you read, you would not be able to answer because you really have no idea. Add that real reading takes both text and thinking.

Let the students know that the same thing often happens in mathematics; we just keep moving along with our problem solving without thinking. When that happens, we aren't getting any true meaning out of the exercise. Sometimes we just underline words, thinking that this alone will help us make meaning out of the text. But without any real connections to what we underline, we rush into strategies that can sometimes lead us astray.

Ask students how many of them have ever faked their way through a math problem—they didn't think, they just kept moving along. Raise your own hand. We've all done it.

(Continued)

(Continued)

Think-Aloud

1. Put the following problem on the overhead or Smartboard (from http://www
.education.state.pa.us/portal/server.pt/community/pennsylvania_system_
of_school_assessment_%28pssa%29/8757/resource_materials/507610-
2008-2009; Grade 7 Mathematics Item and Scoring Sampler). Students
should not have a copy of the problem, which would be distracting. You want
them to pay attention to your think-aloud.

   A total of 8,000 runners started a long-distance race. The results of the
   race are listed below.

   - 3/16 of the runners finished the race in less than 4 hours.
   - 0.65 of the runners finished the race in 4 or more hours.
   - The rest of the runners did not finish the race.

   A. Calculate the number of runners who finished the race in less than 4
   hours. Show and explain all your work, even if you used a calculator.
   B. Calculate the number of runners who did not finish the race. Show all
   your work. Explain why you did each step.

2. Give out the following T-Chart for students to complete during the think-aloud.
   Make a copy on chart paper to use as a reference in future problem solving.

What I notice my teacher doing to help make meaning of the text.	How does this help my teacher understand the text better?

3. Tell students that you are going to think-aloud through this problem. Challenge them to notice and write down anything you did to help you make
   meaning of the text.

   - Read the entire problem through one time (do not read parts A or B
   yet). Then say, "Wow, that's a lot of information. I think I better re-
   read it slowly and take it apart."
   - Start over and read the first sentence. Stop and make a personal
   connection that helps you visualize the scenario, but get off track a
   little. Say something like, "I can make a connection to this. I went to
   a marathon once. I can visualize this many runners beginning a race.
   That was a really hot day. Oh wait, I'm getting off track. That connection is not helping me make meaning of the text. I'm going to
   have to 'turn down the volume' to that and get back to the problem.
   I better re-read it from the beginning to get myself back on track."
   - Continue reading. Make a connection to 3/16 of 8,000. Say something like, "Hmmm, 3/16 of 8,000. Let me make sense of this before
   I move on. I know that 3/16 is really close to 3/15 and that's 1/5.
   Write 1/5 in front of 3/16. I know that 1/5 of 8,000 is 1,600. So
   around 1,600 runners finished the race in less than 4 hours. That's
   not a lot of the runners. That has to be a really good time then.
   (Write all this down to show your active problem solving.)

- Read aloud the next sentence. Round 0.65 to 0.6, then convert that to 3/5. Estimate by rounding and say that 3/5 of the runners would be 4,800, so 0.65 of the 8,000 should be around 4,800 runners. That means most of the runners finished the race in 4 or more hours. (Write all this down to show your active problem solving.)
- Notice that "if 1/5 finished in less than 4 hours, and 3/5 finished in 4 or more hours, then that leaves 1/5 that did not finish." You know this because 1/5 + 3/5 + 1/5 = 1. That means around 1,600 runners did not finish the race. (Write all this down to show your active problem solving.)

4. Stop and have partners share what they noticed you doing. Discuss it with the whole class, and write down what the students noticed on chart paper (as a T-chart) to use as a reference. Lead students in the "noticing." Did they notice you visualizing, making connections, "turning down the volume" on connections that distracted you, making sense of the problem, re-reading to clarify, re-reading to get back on track, and estimating?

5. Challenge the students to discover how critical thinking helped you make meaning of the text.

6. Point out that you haven't even begun answering the questions yet; you have been making sense of the problem first.

7. Share that, even though you did underline words, you did it only when they began to hold meaning to you for solving the problem.

8. Do not solve the problem. It can be a problem they solve later on.

9. Hand out copies of similar problems and have partners use active reading strategies to think through them out loud to each other. While one student thinks aloud, the other student notices what critical thinking habits they use to make meaning of the text.

10. If you have time, students can then solve the problem. Be careful not to rush into this. The focus here is on how to think critically through problem solving.

SHARED PRACTICE: WE DO, I SUPPORT

Shared practice is when students give it a try in a whole-class setting. At this stage, you are gradually giving your students more responsibility by providing them the opportunity to practice. They will practice by thinking through the mathematical concept while you circulate, support, and make decisions. Some aspects of formative assessments enter the lesson at this point. W. James Popham's *Transformative Assessment* (2008) describes a formative assessment (p. 5, used with permission):

- Formative assessment is a *process*, not any particular test.
- It is used not just by teachers but by *both teachers and students*.

- Formative assessment takes place *during instruction.*
- It provides *assessment-based feedback* to teachers and students.
- The function of this feedback is to help teachers and students make *adjustments* that will improve students' achievement of intended curricular aims.

Formative assessment has a long history. In 1967, Michael Scriven coined the terms formative and summative evaluation and emphasized their differences both in what information they seek and how that information is used. The main goal of formative assessment is to improve; the main goal of summative assessment is to prove.

This may be a good time to mention what formative assessments are not. They are not intended to produce grades or to have your students prove what they know. Formative assessments cannot be categorized as quizzes or tests or any other grade-producing assessment. Formative assessments are used to deliver crucial information on where understanding stands before the summative test or quiz is given.

Formative assessments have evolved as a means of adapting instruction to meet student needs. Bell and Cowie (2000) define formative assessment as a bidirectional process between teacher and student to enhance, recognize, and respond to the learning. Black and William (1998) consider an assessment formative when the feedback from learning activities is actually used to adapt the teaching to meet the learner's needs. It is important to note that the feedback must be explanatory and linked to how success can be attained; feedback in formative assessment should be nonpunitive and nonthreatening. This is when you have the opportunity to redirect or guide student thinking back to the original desired outcome. Marzano (2007) shows that major reviews of the research on the effects of formative assessment indicate that it might be one of the most powerful weapons in the teacher's arsenal; we agree.

Why do we agree?

Well, when formative assessments are embedded into your instruction, both you and your students get immediate feedback about their understanding. That is powerful information, information that can be used to scaffold current instruction, decide how to differentiate instruction, and form small groups.

Tovani (2004) thinks that the students' job is to show you that they are thinking. Shared practice occurs when students are afforded that opportunity. During shared practice, formative assessment can be as simple as observing your students as they respond to questions, ask questions, or wrestle through problems with a partner or small group. Because the results are both nonthreatening and immediate, teacher and student can use formative assessment results to make decisions about what should come next to promote further learning. Teachers can see how both individual students and the whole class have performed and how far along understanding has come.

Decisions will need to be made based on the understanding you see in action; those decisions should influence how you proceed.

- Do most of your students need to be shown your thinking again?
- Do you need to change the overall pace of your lesson?
- Are there only a handful of students who need another think-aloud?
- How will you move the rest of your class forward and meet the needs of those few?
- Are there any students who need to be pushed deeper into the mathematics because they're ready?
- Who needs to be in what small group?
- What will the small groups work on?
- What group will you work with? Why?

GUIDED PRACTICE: YOU DO IN GROUPS OR PARTNERSHIPS, I SUPPORT

During guided practice, students are "trying on" the learning in groups while you facilitate. In mathematics, guided practice and independent practice can occur at the same time. Students can work independently while the teacher pulls out groups and works with them.

Why Small-Group Instruction in the Math Class?

There is a natural and necessary sequence in Gradual Release, but there still needs to be a point when the release occurs. Guided practice allows the teacher to craft the start of independent thinking. During small-group instruction, students are provided the opportunity to "try on" the learning focus.

Although whole-class instruction is a key component of the math lesson, students cannot master a skill or concept unless they are given the opportunity to apply it themselves. True understanding does not come during the whole-class instruction. Students need time to wrestle with the learning, either with a group of peers, with a teacher facilitating a small group, by working independently, or with one-on-one student/teacher contact. Janet Allen (2000) testifies to this when she says, "We should expect students to work at meaning making and they should expect that we will be there to support that work at the individual student level" (p. 16). The NCTM *Handbook of Research on Mathematics Teaching and Learning* (1992) states that students must "construct their own mathematical knowledge rather than receive it in finished form from the teacher" (p. 74).

It is very difficult for teachers to assess students' knowledge without spending some time interacting directly with them. Working directly with a small group affords a natural means of performing individual assessment and consequently provides clarification and support where needed.

The typical classroom discourse does not allow for this depth of analysis by the teacher. NCTM maintains that students are too passive and need to become more involved intellectually in the classroom learning. Breaking students into small groups engages more students in the learning process and can lead to a deeper understanding by a greater number of students (National Council of Teachers of Mathematics, 2000, p. 60).

When students collaborate, they often get more out of learning than when working on their own. Students in a group setting must verbalize their thoughts and discoveries, which helps them understand these ideas and use them as steps on the path to a solution (Posamentier & Jaye, 2006, p. 26). When students are isolated from each other, their learning is not as deep, and they have fewer opportunities to improve their thinking.

Students who work cooperatively achieve at higher levels, persist longer when working on difficult tasks, and are more motivated to learn because learning becomes fun and meaningful (Posamentier & Jaye, 2006, p. 27). When the opportunity is provided for active, meaningful participation in the mathematical process, the motivation of most students increases substantially, and many, in fact, become more self-motivated.

25 Key Reasons to Include Small-Group Instruction

1. To improve problem-solving aptitude by engaging students in the following types of mathematical thinking (Posamentier & Jaye, 2006, p. 29):
   - Understanding the problem by (a) making connections, (b) using visual representations, (c) predicting and inferring (estimating), and (d) asking questions to maintain mental stamina
   - Analyzing the problem
   - Planning an approach to solve the problem
   - Monitoring and repairing comprehension
   - Exploring a problem-solving approach to see whether or not it works
   - Implementing the plan for solving the problem
   - Verifying various strategies
   - Confirming the final solutions
   - Listening to and watching other students during the problem-solving process

2. To increase comprehension

3. To facilitate critical thinking—analyze, compare, contrast, investigate, and test problems and solutions

4. To differentiate instruction, forming groups according to ability, interest, and learning profile

5. To provide more student/teacher contact time

6. To assess individual understanding

7. To foster a sense of community

8. To build background knowledge in subsets of students

9. To model and practice how to work effectively as a member of a team

10. To guide individual students according to their individual needs

11. To show that you care about the progress your students are making

12. To open numerous pathways to the learning

13. To give more students access to the mathematical thinking necessary to succeed

14. To learn how to pull together resources to achieve success

15. To enhance motivation and generate greater student involvement

16. To model mathematical thinking

17. To develop positive attitudes toward mathematics

18. To develop skills specific to the lesson purpose

19. To provide practice in the application of mathematical concepts

20. To generate ideas among students concerning ways of applying acquired knowledge

21. To create a stimulating environment

22. To develop student commitment to mathematical thinking and problem solving

23. To emphasize an important mathematical concept

24. To acquire new insights into problems by hearing different viewpoints

25. To provide meaningful feedback

 ## HOW CAN I DO THIS IN MY MATH CLASS . . . TOMORROW?

We have included here several ways to form small groups in your math class. The following ideas work flawlessly for math; all are both low maintenance and highly effective. We use all of them regularly, depending on the level of skill we are teaching and the learning purpose. Choosing different ways to form small groups makes the learning fresh and keeps the students more engaged. Class is more fun, too. We do, however, ask the students to self-assess every day and differentiate how we form groups after the self-assessment.

Before implementing any of the following ideas, it is important to model for students how to work effectively without you. You may want to show what appropriate and inappropriate group behavior looks like and sounds like by doing a "fishbowl" with your students first. To do so, choose two small groups of students to role play both the "good small group" and the "bad small group" while the other students form a large circle around them and take note of how both groups behave. Then lead a discussion that pinpoints criteria for effective group behavior.

You will need some norms, and if students are going to follow the norms, they will need to set them up themselves. You may want to begin by asking the students to remember their past group experiences and to write three things that really bugged them about working in groups and three things that worked well. Their responses will lead you to create "good small group rules."

Self-Rating: 1–2–3, Green Light, Yellow Light, Red Light, or Thumbs Up, Thumbs to the Side, Thumbs Down

This way of grouping is needs based and flexible. You ask the students whether they understand what you just taught, and they put up one finger for good understanding, two fingers for so-so understanding, and three fingers if they need some help. The key to success with this formative self-assessment is in your setup. For your students to be honest with themselves and not just repeatedly put up one finger, they need to understand the power behind the number of fingers they hold up. Take a few weeks to lay the groundwork by repeatedly highlighting how their learning is linked to their self-assessments—their learning and understanding. They have to fully realize that their learning is the issue here. Set up experiences that show how empowering it is for them to be able to quickly assess where they are with their understanding. Such judgments promote self-efficacy on many levels.

This method of grouping arms you with a tremendous bit of information that should affect how you proceed with your small-group instruction.

1. Will you meet with the 1's to push their thinking and have the 2's and 3's partner up and work through something together?

2. Will you meet with the 3's to re-teach and have the 1's and 2's partner up and work through something together?

3. Will you pull the 2's and have the 1's share their thinking with the 3's?

Compass Rose Groups: Teacher-Created Mixed Ability Teams

When you have a clear picture of the abilities of your students (through observing tests scores, problem-solving capabilities, work ethic, learning profile, etc.), create mixed ability groups of four using a compass rose. (We usually wait until October to create these groups.)

After creating the groups, distribute a compass rose sticker (one per student) with the names of each of the group members at one of the directions. If you would like to jigsaw at some point, you can place your most advanced students in the west slot, your lowest in the east, and your two middle-ranged students at north and south. This way, if you supply varied texts or problems, you can have all the norths get together, the wests, and so on. Afterward, the groups reconvene, and each member teaches the rest of his or her compass rose group what he or she discovered.

Compass rose groups are perfect for problem solving. The varied abilities provide an atmosphere where diverse problem-solving methods can flourish. Students who may struggle with the math have a chance to listen to the mathematical reasoning of several others in a low-risk, conversational way. We can attest to the power that collaborative problem solving provides. Mixed ability grouping affords all members a pathway to the learning. Some may lead, some may listen, but all learn.

Random Groups: Our Favorite Way to Form Partnerships

Perfect Partners

Prepare "perfect partner" cards ahead of time on cardstock and laminate them. Distribute one card to each student and ask the students to find their "perfect partner." It is more fun if you do not tell them what the cards' "mates" are. Let them think about it first, make a guess, locate their partners, and then get to the work you planned for them to do. If you have an odd number of students, you can simply add a student to another pair. You can then pull several groups to work with at one time while the others work collaboratively. There are many variations to this way of forming groups.

Perfect Partners

Peanut Butter	Jelly	Spaghetti	Meatballs
Winter	Summer	Bacon	Eggs
Up	Down	Cookies	Milk
Brother	Sister	Hairy	Bald
Chips	Salsa	Sun	Moon
Cheeseburger	Fries	Happy	Sad
Night	Day	Salt	Pepper
Cheese	Crackers	Bread	Butter

Clock Partners

There are two versions of the "clock partners" method: one for daily use without team building, and another that includes a team-building component.

Directions for forming partners without a beginning-of-the-year icebreaker: Each student is given a clock on colored cardstock that has been hole-punched to fit into a binder (see Appendix C). The students "travel" around the room and ask another student to be their one o'clock partner. Both students write their names under the corresponding numbers on both of their clocks. (I use pencils for this so you can change partners when students move in and out of the district.) They then find two o'clock partners, three o'clock partners, and so on until all the clocks have been filled out. We always specify that students can list a particular individual's name only once. According to the makeup of the class, we may insist that the students choose an equal number of boys and girls. We collect and make a copy of each clock before handing them back to the students. The students then insert them as the first page of their binders. We make new clocks twice a year. When you want to use this strategy, you simply say, "Get with your nine o'clock partner and discuss . . . ." You can adapt the "clock" partner strategy for your specific subject area by replacing the clocks with pictures unique to your class. Computer clipart is perfect for customizing your "clock" strategies. I know teachers who use the same concept but with counties of their states, world oceans/seas, and continents. The options are endless.

Directions for getting-to-know-you clock partners: This icebreaker helps students understand that they are not as different from each other as they may think. For this *active* method of group formation, the teacher displays and reads a series of questions, and participants respond by selecting a multiple-choice answer. First, place the letters A–D in the corners of your room. Make a transparency with the following questions, or put one question at a time on your Smartboard.

- If I had to see a movie, I would rather see: (A) *The Time Traveler's Wife*, (B) *Harry Potter and the Half-Blood Prince*, (C) *Star Trek*, (D) *Up*.
- If I could go out to eat, I would eat at: (A) Red Lobster, (B) Olive Garden/Pasta House, (C) McDonalds, (D) Pizza Hut.
- If I could bring a famous person to class today, I would want it to be: (A) Barak Obama, (B) Oprah Winfrey, (C) Lance Armstrong, (D) Mother Teresa.
- My favorite thing about myself is: (A) my personality, (B) my musical/artistic ability, (C) my sports ability, (D) my brain.
- If I had to give up one thing at home, it would be: (A) air conditioning, (B) television, (C) microwave, (D) computer.
- If I could hold one of the four jobs listed, I would be a: (A) pilot, (B) webmaster, (C) teacher, (D) doctor.

When the students go to their chosen corners for each question, ask them to find two partners there to sign their clocks (see above directions). Ask the students to sit down before you go to the next question. After six questions, the clocks are filled. We collect them and make copies before the students place them in their binders.

Line-Ups

Very quickly and silently line up your students according to a certain criteria—alphabetical order according to middle name, numerical order according to number of siblings, and so on. Be conscious of the social nuances of categories—height can sometimes put the spotlight on the smaller boys, which can be a little embarrassing. After the students are lined up, you can form groups any way you choose.

Numbering Off

Asking students to "number off" allows you to form groups of any number—odds and evens makes two teams, counting off by fours forms quads, and so on.

MEANINGFUL FEEDBACK IN MATHEMATICS

The single most powerful modification in instruction to enhance achievement is to provide meaningful feedback (Hattie, Biggs, & Purdie, 1996, p. 9). The NCTM *Professional Standards for Teaching Mathematics* (1991) endorse thoughtful discourse between teachers and students. Studies have shown that improved student performance is connected to the amount of meaningful feedback given to students. Students need to receive specific feedback on the progress of their practice for learning to be valuable. The NCTM *Assessment Standards for School Mathematics* (1995) states that consistent and meaningful feedback "not only facilitates students' learning of mathematics but also enhances confidence in what they understand and communicate" (p. 14). Meaningful feedback allows students to consider their progress, understand what they know and can do, be confident in their learning, and discover what they must still learn. Ultimately, we want students to analyze, evaluate, and reflect on their own progress (Posamentier & Jaye, 2006, p. 106).

Providing useful feedback is an important step in allowing students to identify errors and make appropriate corrections (Posamentier & Jaye, 2006, p. 113). This builds confidence, increases students' self-esteem, and provides valuable information to both the students and the teacher about progress. Teacher feedback should be presented in a way that is supportive and encourages students to take action to apply the intended feedback to achieve improvement.

Marzano, Pickering, and Pollock (2001) have created the following generalizations to guide teachers in providing meaningful feedback (pp. 96–99):

1. *Feedback should be "corrective" in nature.* (In other words, the best feedback involves an explanation as to what is accurate and what is inaccurate.)

2. *Feedback should be timely.* (In general, the more delay in giving feedback, the less improvement in achievement.)

3. *Feedback should be specific to a criterion.* (For feedback to be the most useful, it should reference a specific level of skill or knowledge. Generally, the more specific the feedback, the better.)

4. *Students can effectively provide some of their own feedback.* (Students should simply keep track of their performance as learning occurs. Self-evaluation is strongly advocated.)

What Defines Meaningful Feedback in Mathematics?

The NCTM *Assessment Standards* (1995) ask teachers to reflect on how their feedback creates "opportunities for students to evaluate, reflect on, and improve their own work, that is, to become independent learners" (p. 14). In other words, teachers should be providing feedback that focuses on students' depth of understanding rather than simply checking for right or wrong answers (Posamentier & Jaye, 2006, p. 105).

Paying attention to the items that are incorrect is related to improved achievement. Studies have shown that students benefit more from learning about what they did wrong than what they did right. In addition, for students to improve their future performance, they need to know *why* something is wrong. When students understand why something is wrong, they are more likely to learn appropriate strategies to eliminate their errors (Posamentier & Jaye, 2006, p. 83). Perhaps the best way to ensure that a teacher's feedback is heeded is to have students write about their errors, examining what they did incorrectly, where they went wrong, and what they did to get back on track.

There are several types of errors that occur in mathematics. Errors common to a large portion of the class are one type. These can be attributed to a past misconception or can be the result of the present teaching. Usually, if you find a common error being made by several students, it means there was a miscommunication or a misunderstanding between the teacher and the students during the whole-class instruction. At this point, it is important to clarify and remedy the misconception. It is easiest to gather the class as a whole and repair the learning. This is also a great learning lesson for the students, that is, knowing that you are willing to admit that the misunderstanding is due to something you did to confuse the students. There is power in admitting mistakes in front of your students; it makes you human. It also makes you a fellow learner.

A second type of mathematical error is the conceptual error. Conceptual errors require deeper feedback and support, which is quite different from the feedback needed for careless calculation errors. Teachers should analyze incorrect responses to see if the errors are in reasoning, incorrect interpretations, faulty work with algorithms, or perhaps a simple calculation error. Though these analyses can be quite time consuming, they are extremely worthwhile, for these discoveries can be the keys to helping students sort out their mathematical difficulties (Posamentier & Jaye, 2006, p. 84).

Naturally, a simple calculation error is not usually a cause for big concern (although they drive parents and teachers crazy). The calculation error must be identified, and the student ought to discover a tactic not to repeat it again. The teacher should facilitate this approach to make sure it is accurate and meaningful.

If the mistake comes from a conceptual misunderstanding, the teacher should connect with the student as soon as possible to analyze the misconception and lead the student toward understanding. The teacher, at this point, may need to return to a previous learning before moving forward. The sequential nature of mathematics instruction makes it difficult for the student to continue successfully if incorrect mathematical reasoning is not resolved.

INDEPENDENT: YOU DO, WE ASSESS

Independent application equals student practice, formative self-assessment, and reflection. We should expect students to work at making meaning, and they should expect that we will be there to support that work at the individual student level (Allen, 2000, p. 16). Well-established criteria must be in place and understood by your students for formative self-assessment to be effective. Self-assessment provides decisive feedback to both teacher and student when it shows what has been taught and learned well and what has not been taught and learned well. Again, this information is powerful and is the exact information a numeracy teacher needs to move forward his or her students' thinking. When students formatively assess, they gain ownership of their mathematical thinking because they know what they understand and what they don't. Ownership of mathematical thinking is crucial if one is to think as a numerate mathematician. Learners need these times of independence—times when they make choices and live with the consequences of those choices (Allen, 2000).

Knowing where your students stand mathematically allows you to craft future lessons and think-alouds. You will know who needs what, who is ready to move on, who needs to hear it again, and who needs to be pushed deeper.

Component 5

Debrief

Tying It All Together

Do not confuse recall with understanding.

—Dick Allington, *What Really Matters for*
Struggling Readers, 2006

Debriefing is the time when students dwell on and synthesize the day's work. Allowing students to remember, revise, and reapply *their* learning provides a tremendous opportunity for growth as a numerate thinker—for both you and them. Debriefing or "knowing you know" helps students experience their intellect, discover what they have learned and how they learned it, and then consider what they should do next to stretch and perfect their learning. For the teacher, Allington (2006) explains that the Debrief is his or her chance to have students "identify points of confusion and levels of certainty" (p. 114).

When you afford time for a Debrief, your students get the chance to own their learning and determine where their understanding is and where it isn't. The message that "the greatest reward for learning is the opportunity to learn" is validated during the Debrief moments (Keene, 2008).

If you skip the Debrief, you sacrifice a lot. Why? Because the end of each lesson is priceless and is the perfect time for reflection. The Debrief needs to be treated as such—priceless and perfect. Both of us have been rushed for time on occasion, and the Debrief was the first thing to go. Whenever we succumbed to the clock and skipped those moments of reflection, the cohesiveness crafted during the lesson did not congeal.

Asking students to identify and record their areas of confusion not only enhances their learning but also provides the teacher with valuable diagnostic information (Butler & Winne, 1995; Cross, 1998). A Debrief is an important way to assess, providing you valuable information that can set up the Focus for tomorrow's lesson. Quite often, we have even used the Debrief as either the Ignition or the Bridge for the next day. Doing so works particularly well when students are prompted to create their own problems as an exit ticket to prove their understanding. We then simply collect them and put them out the next day for students to solve.

Arthur Hyde (2006) states that he cannot emphasize too strongly how important Debriefing is, as well as the critical role language plays in Debriefing. Teachers are pressed for time to cover massive amounts of content, but the better the Debriefing, the more complete the crystallization of concepts and the less reteaching will be needed.

We like the idea of less reteaching because, as Hyde states, teachers are being faced with less and less time each school year, yet what they are expected to cover increases. Quite the conundrum. The Debrief is instructional time well spent, providing teachers with a quick yet meaningful snapshot of each student's understanding. Our individual and whole-group assessments each day should inform our teaching and show us where to start again (Allen, 2000, p. 201). Knowing where to start the next day so that every student's needs are met also constitutes differentiation in action.

The Debrief, to be successful and meaningful, should be well crafted. It is the time to determine the importance of the learning, to summarize, and to synthesize. A groundswell of evidence indicates that, when language or reasoning and reflection are used explicitly by the classroom teacher, students are empowered to use the same language—indeed, the same processes—in their problem solving (Gawned, 1990, p. 35).

Harwayne (1992) defines reflection as lingering over a topic and gathering new insight. This lingering during the Debrief doesn't need to take large amounts of time. If you craft your Debrief question or activity with care, the time spent can be minimal yet powerful. New insights *will* occur.

The Debrief occurs during the last 3–5 minutes of the class period. When you end each math lesson with a Debrief, dare we say, a magical transference of power occurs. No longer is the learning something for which you, the teacher, are solely responsible. Shelley Harwayne (1992) argues that students need to "learn to pause, let things in their lives matter, hold their lives in their hands, and reflect upon them" (p. 93).

 # HOW CAN I DO THIS IN MY MATH CLASS . . . TOMORROW?

Exit Tickets

Exit tickets are a simple but very effective technique for promoting application, analysis, and synthesis of the learning. Students complete their exit tickets before leaving the class. You then use the collected exit tickets as a quick formative assessment to gauge the needs of the class. They thus serve as closure for a day's class and as information that can be used for planning (Allen, 2004, p. 201). They can also be used by students at the beginning of the next class to generate common class questions or to form study groups (p. 24). What do exit tickets look like in math? They can be summaries, problems to solve, questions that remain, visual representations, journals, analogies, examples and counterexamples, reflections on the progress of the lesson, sketches, and so on. Basically, an exit ticket can be any way you want the students to demonstrate what they learned from class that day.

Essential Question Revisited

Determine the Purpose of the lesson. From that statement, create an essential question or two that will help students reach an understanding of the lesson's Purpose. Present it to the students at the Bridge. Ask them to think, write, and discuss their responses. Then put up the same essential question at the Debrief and have the students use their new knowledge to add to or otherwise revise their original responses. Allow time for silence. Make the questions conceptually grounded, with a real-life flavor to them, rather than simply address the behavioral objective of the lesson. You will get more buy-in this way because the students will find relevance in the learning.

Evaluation of Today's Learning Objective

Have the students fill out sheets that summarize their understanding and signal their efforts to reach the goals for the day's lesson (see the sample forms that follow).

Student Self-Evaluation of the Learning

Name of student: _____

Date: _____ Period/Block: _____

The mark on the continuum below represents how clearly I understood [*place your learning objective here*].

Did not understand at all				Could teach it tomorrow
1	2	3	4	5

Proof of mastery (examples, illustrations, explanation) or questions you still have:

Evaluation of the Student's Effort in Learning Today's Objective

Name of student: _____

Date: _____   Period/Block: _____

The mark on the continuum below represents how well I succeeded in meeting my math goals today.

Did not do my best				Met my learning goals
1	2	3	4	5

Here is what I accomplished:

_____

_____

_____

Here is my plan for tomorrow:

_____

_____

_____

Source: Hollas, 2005, p. 148.

Human Continuum

Place cards at the front of your classroom labeled along a continuum as follows (Hollas, 2005, p. 78):

I could teach what we learned today!

If I took a test on what we learned today, I would do pretty well!

I still don't get what we learned today and would like to revisit it with help!

On the floor in front of the cards, make a line with masking tape. Ask students to stand on the masking tape, positioning themselves so that they are near the card that best describes their understanding of the content. Ask each student to turn to a neighbor and discuss what he or she knows about the topic and/or why he or she chose to stand at that location.

GIST: "Generating Interactions Between Schemata and Text"

GIST has been proven to effectively improve students' reading comprehension and summary writing (Cunningham, 1982, p. 42–47; Forget, 2004, pp. 156–162). At the Debrief component of the lesson, have students generate a summary of 20 or fewer words. Then ask students to share their GIST statements with a partner. Now challenge the students to come to a consensus for a class GIST summary. By restricting the length of students' GIST summaries, the teacher compels the students to use the three major strategies necessary for comprehension and retention of key ideas in any text: They must delete trivial information, select key ideas, and generalize in their own words.

Before and After the Learning

Return to your "anticipation guide" or "preconcept and postconcept check" to review for accuracies and inaccuracies. (See the full explanations of both the anticipation guide and preconcept and postconcept checks in Habit 2.)

Making Connections

What connections link this learning to the big ideas in mathematics (Hyde, 2006, p. 125)? Encourage the students to make math-to-self, math-to-math, and math-to-world connections.

Whip Around

Have your students make a large circle. You state the Focus, and each student quickly states a connection to that Focus. The connection can be a related concept, an important idea, an example, a strategy for problem solving, a personal connection, a math-to-math connection, or a math-to-real-world connection.

Three Facts and a Fib

This activity is a summative assessment. Ask students to write on an index card four statements about any content the class has just studied (Forsten et al., 2002b, p. 88). Three of the statements (examples, equations, etc.) should be true, and one should be false. Tell students to move about the room, sharing their list of statements with each other. Explain that each student should ask his fellow students to try to pick the false statement. An alternative to this activity is to collect the cards and use them as an Ignition the next day.

Three Facts and a Fib (Sample Card)

1. 23 is a rational number.

2. The square root of 225 is a rational number.

3. 0.678532179 … is a rational number.

4. ¼ is a rational number.

Writing Summaries

Summarizing one's understanding or thinking in writing facilitates deep processing. In short, writing is hard, and the act of writing requires not only deep thinking but also processing your knowledge. Writing summaries is even harder. A written summary is synthesis in action.

3-2-1 Journal Entry

The 3-2-1 strategy requires students to summarize key ideas from the lesson and encourages them to think independently. First, students write about 3 things they discovered. Next, they write about 2 things they found interesting. Last, they write 1 question they still have. This strategy can be used as a journal entry during the Debrief or as an exit ticket. The 3-2-1 journal has endless options. You can be flexible with what you want the students to write about: 3 examples of the learning, 2 nonexamples, and 1 way you can tell the difference, and so on.

Math Journals

Journaling affords time for students to reflect, reconsider, revise, and reapply the learning. A math journal is the ideal place for students to process their mathematical thinking. The math journal can also hold reflections, connections, and syntheses, all of which require skills necessary for success on your state's open-ended math questions. Reflective writing allows students to experience the quietness of their own minds at work, which is a gift.

Teaching an Adult at Home!

After you introduce a new math concept, the students' homework could include "teaching" an adult at home what was learned in class that day. During the Debrief, we practice in class by role playing what they will do at home that evening. Only assign a few problems, with the bottom half of the math page a space for the adult's signature as well as any comments.

This activity allows students to synthesize the learning and provides a worthwhile formative assessment. If the student doesn't truly understand the concept, there is no way he or she will be able to explain it clearly to someone else.

"Leftovers . . . Again!"

Have "leftover" containers available for each small group. Their assignment is to place "leftovers" in the container for someone to "mull over" tomorrow. The leftovers should provide the "main dish" from the learning and some of the "side dishes" that supported it that day. The "dessert" should be their favorite part of the lesson. They can do this with pictures, manipulatives, explanations, and so on. Make sure groups can defend their choice of leftovers. Now use the containers the next day as the Bridge to the Learning.

Representation of the Lesson

Students represent the learning in some visual way: 2-D models, tables, graphs, sketches, graphic organizers, cartoons, Venn diagrams, examples/nonexamples, and so on. This visualization will promote critical thinking. Challenge the students to explain their visual representations.

Stump the Teacher

Students, working in partnerships or small groups, prepare questions or problems to try to "stump their teacher" (Forget, 2004, pp. 221–225). This activity is a high-level way to review just before a test because students need to have a deep understanding of the content to craft difficult and stump-worthy questions.

Journaling

Journaling is a great way to Debrief the lesson. The following prompts are intended for middle/high school students, but they can easily be adapted to fit any age. The younger the students, the less they write and the more they draw out their learning.

Math Journal Prompts for Secondary Students

Problem Solving

1. If a problem can be solved using more than one strategy, what are some questions you ask yourself to decide which strategy to use?

2. When you are "stuck" in the middle of solving a problem, what are some things you think about to help you get "unstuck"?

3. What are some ways you would approach solving a problem in which a plan is not immediately obvious?

Number Patterns and Relationships

1. How could you complete this analogy: "The commutative property is to peanut butter and jelly as the associative property is to _____?" Describe your thinking.

2. $?/? < \frac{3}{4}$ What might the fraction be? How do you know?

3. You have been asked to find all the ways 48 CDs could be packaged. What are some ways you could use number relationships to solve this problem?

4. A friend of mine put these fractions into two groups: 3/4, 2/5, 1/3, 6/10, 1/10. What might the two groups be? Explain your reasoning.

Whole Number and Decimal Place Value

1. What are some of the similarities and differences of terminating and repeating decimals?

2. What are some ways you can represent a number such as 45.37 to someone who has not learned about decimals? Describe what you would say and do.

3. What real-life concepts or items might you use to represent 0.5?

Fraction Concepts

1. It is necessary to find equivalent fractions for many mathematical procedures. What are some real-life instances in which you might need to find equivalent fractions?

2. Items from shoes to tennis rackets to cakes are sold in fractional sizes. What are some items sold only in wholes that you would like to see sold in fractional sizes or parts? Explain your thinking and offer strategies for sizing or pricing.

3. How would you complete this analogy: "Subtracting fractions is to subtracting mixed numbers as _____ is to _____?

(Continued)

(Continued)

Percents

1. The price of a computer game that you have been thinking about buying is reduced by 65%. What might have caused the company to reduce the price so drastically?

2. A bank pays interest on money you deposit and charges interest on money you borrow. The interest rate on deposited money is lower than the interest on borrowed money. What are some things that would happen if the reverse were true?

3. Pollsters predict election results with a leeway of about 3%. What are some of the advantages and disadvantages to these predictions? What is your opinion of publicly announcing these predictions on Election Day? Explain your answer.

Statistics, Data Analysis, and Graphing

1. What conclusion can be drawn about a school or district by examining state or national assessment data?

2. What are some questions you might ask yourself when deciding which graph would best represent data that you have collected?

3. Television shows are paid for by their commercial sponsors. What kinds of data do you think sponsors collect about the show before making a decision to advertise on it?

Algebra: Solving Equations and Inequalities

1. What are some visual representations for equations and inequalities?

2. Learning how to solve math problems gives you insight into solving other problems you encounter in life. Do you agree or disagree? Why?

3. The dictionary definition of an expression is a "word, phrase, look, or intonation that conveys meaning." In what ways is the mathematical meaning for expression an interpretation of the dictionary's definition?

Source: Kagan, Miguel. (2005). *Higher Level Thinking Questions: Secondary Mathematics*. San Clemente, CA: Kagan Publishing. Reprinted with permission.

Conclusion

Our *Debrief*

Keep cleaning the cobwebs from the attic and dusting off the souvenirs in storage. New treasures will emerge.

—Rick Wormeli (2009)

This book is the result of our earnest belief that all children can be successful thinkers in mathematics if we can only figure out how to get them there. Our journey, quite honestly, was born out of frustration. Why were students okay with leaving answers that made no sense at all? How was it that they *didn't* know how to reapply a skill we had taught them just two days earlier? These questions, and many more, drove us to the research. Then, as often happens during research, more questions arose: Why do New Zealand, Australia, Japan, China, Scotland, and England consistently outscore American students in international tests? What do they know that we don't know?

Obviously, it is imperative that students understand the everyday use of numbers conceptually, for them to question, predict and infer, generate formulas, reason with numbers, in short, to discover. Students, in other words, must become numerate thinkers.

We have concluded that teaching numeracy successfully boils down to one thing: true lesson crafting. We need to view teaching as a craft. Given a truly crafted lesson, students can be brought and molded toward the Purpose of the lesson. We thus attempt to prepare our lessons in a way that creates opportunities for students to think through the mathematics and become numerate mathematicians.

We'd like to propose an experiment for you: Think about the teachers in your building. Carefully decide who you think would get the title "Best Teacher I Know." (For this experiment to work, you can't choose yourself!)

Now that you have a specific teacher in mind, ask if she crafts her lessons. By craft we mean—oh, by now you know what we mean by craft.

We're serious. We want you to talk to that teacher. Ask how he sets up his instructional practices. Ask how he knows when he has nailed a lesson. We think every great teacher would agree with Shelley Harwayne (1992) when she says, "We need to keep teaching on the frontiers of our thinking. Our work will always bear the label, 'To be Continued . . .'" (p. 338).

In other words, we challenge you to never be satisfied with good enough, to never settle for just okay. Continue to craft and revisit and to question yourself—every single day. Continue to push yourself out of your comfort zone.

Numeracy needs to run through your mathematical veins, feeding and nourishing your mind and mathematical thinking. We teachers are helpful interpreters and fortunate facilitators, but the genius of our students must be set free (Wormeli, 2009). When embedded and carefully crafted, numerate thinking will run through every lesson, and your instructional practice will feed your students a healthy diet of logic and number sense. Gone will be the empty calories of simply doing the math. Numeracy forces your students to think through the math. Both you and your students will be full and satisfied on the new rich diet—trust us.

Bon appétit!

Appendix A

Sample Numeracy-Based Lesson Plans

In case you are wondering how a highly effective, numeracy-based math lesson plan looks, or how to pull everything together into one real-life document, wonder no more. We've provided here three different grade-level samples so you can see how it works. Try on one of these lessons for size. Spend some time familiarizing yourself with the lesson and the thinking behind the lesson, and then go for it. If it is a raging success, kudos to you. If it fails miserably, don't give up. It took us years of trial and error, planning and practice, to perfect these plans to our satisfaction.

Sample Lesson 1
Introduction to Division (Grades 2–3)

Purpose

- To introduce the concept of division
- To make connections between division and multiplication

Ignition

Place the Ignition that follows on the overhead or Smartboard before the students enter the classroom. Have worksheet copies available for students at their desks. Each student should also receive a baggie filled with 30 M&M's. This Ignition will help engage your students immediately in the learning. They should begin the activity independently, thus allowing each student the opportunity to "wrestle" with the concept a little. And you will be given a few minutes to check homework and attendance. When you see that the students are ready, have them share their answers and reasoning behind those answers with a partner. This sharing should only last 3–5 minutes. You can circulate and listen to the conversations, which will give you a glimpse into the background knowledge students have on long division.

Bridge to the Learning

Display the following Bridge to the Learning on the overhead or Smartboard. Students can have a copy as well. The purpose of this Bridge is for students to realize what actually occurs mathematically in division. This activity increases confidence and allows struggling math students to relax a little before the lesson begins. The Bridge should be quick—only 3–5 minutes.

Gradual Release

I Model—Think-Aloud (5 minutes): Place the think-aloud that follows on the overhead or Smartboard. Students should not have the handout; it may distract them from listening to you navigating through the problem. They can write their "noticings" in their notebooks or journals. As you share your mathematical thinking, make sure to include how you make sense of the problem, how you eliminate answers that don't make sense, and how you predict to stay actively involved in the problem. It is always helpful to write out this think-aloud before trying it. That will allow you to pay attention to your own problem-solving strategies. Challenge the students to pay close attention to "what your brain does to work through the problem." Have them write three things they notice you doing to work through the problem. Then have them "turn and talk," sharing what they noticed and how these critical thinking habits made it easier for you to solve the problem. Have a short discussion.

We Do It Together (5–10 minutes): Now display the division handout provided here. Challenge the class to try out the first problem with a partner. Have them self-reflect, using a 1–2–3, thumbs up/thumbs down/thumbs to the side, or whatever way your students self-reflect. This method will help you form groups. Students who do not understand at all may need to form a small group that you facilitate. To scaffold this learning, you may want to use manipulative blocks for students to "see" how division works concretely. For example, to use base ten blocks, give each table 10 rods of 10 and 1 flat of 100. Let them discover how the 10 rods equal the flat of 100 by manipulating and discussing. You can guide them to discovery by asking them to stack the rods on top of the flat, and then ask how many groups of 10 are really in 100. The single-unit blocks can also be brought out to show smaller groups.

You Try It, I Support–Small-Group Instruction (15 minutes): Form ability or random groups (use whatever fits your purpose best). Have the groups complete the activity while you join or pull groups for clarification.

Debrief

Exit Ticket (5 minutes): Have each student pull a problem from the problem bag (you've created simple division problems earlier and placed them in a bag). Ask students to work through the problem on one side and to explain how they solved the problem on the other side.

Sample Lesson 1: Introduction to Division (Grades 2–3) student handouts follow.

Ignition Into the Learning

Name: _____

Directions: Come right into class, get seated, and get your pencil out and your brain ready to start thinking. This lesson will make you smarter—guaranteed!

Now get to work and complete this problem.

Use the M&M's in your baggie. Count how many you have in your baggie first and record it here: _____

1. Put your M&M's into groups of 6.

    Draw a quick picture of what your M&M groups look like.

    How many groups of 6 were you able to create? _____

2. Now put your M&M's into groups of 5.

    Draw a quick picture of what your M&M groups look like.

    How many groups of 5 were you able to create? _____

Think: How do the two groups look the same? How are they different?

Pair and share: Now talk with a partner about how the groups of 5 look different from the groups of 6. How are they the same?

Bridge to the Learning

[*Whole group*] Let's talk about what you did with your M&M's. What did you notice? Can anyone tell me what you did with your M&M's by using a math word? [*Try to get out the word* division] Well, today we are going to learn about division. But guess what? First, we are going to talk about multiplication. Anyone think they know why? Talk at your tables for a minute. [*Teacher wanders and listens for strong mathematical thinking and refers to it when the class is brought back into the whole group.*]

[*Put on the board:*]

$5 \times 6 = 30$
$6 \times 5 = 30$

Now I want to challenge you. How could you rewrite these two facts using division? Think and write what you think. Then share what you wrote with a partner.

Ahhh! Now you see how multiplication and division are related.

Let's try some more.

1. Take your M&M's and divide them into groups of 10. Create the fact family that represents what you did.

   _____ × _____ = 30   30 ÷ _____ = _____

2. Now divide your M&M's into groups of 3. Create the fact family that represents what you did.

   _____ × _____ = 30   30 ÷ _____ = _____

3. Take your M&M's and divide them into groups of 2. Create the fact family that represents what you did.

   _____ × _____ = 30   30 ÷ _____ = _____

4. Now divide your M&M's into groups of 15. Create the fact family that represents what you did.

   _____ × _____ = 30   30 ÷ _____ = _____

Let's Take a Real-World Break

Think: Before we move on, think of a time when you use division in life. Give one example.

1.

_____

_____

_____

Pair and share: Turn to the person next to you and share how you use division in life.

You are now ready to learn more about division.

Division Think-Aloud

I am going to share my thinking as I solve the following problem. I want you to pay attention to what things I did to try to solve the problem. Be thinking about how my thoughts help me understand the problem better.

The balloon seller sold bags with 6 balloons in each bag. Use the chart below to help the balloon seller figure out how many bags of 6 balloons he has sold.

	Red Balloons Sold	Blue Balloons Sold	Green Balloons Sold
Sunday	30	54	24
Monday	60	42	48

How many bags of blue balloons were sold on Sunday? How did you figure it out?

Write down what you notice me doing while trying to solve the above problem.

Three things I noticed my teacher doing to try to solve the problem:

1. _____

_____

2. _____

_____

3. _____

_____

Share your ideas with the person next to you and discuss how doing these things helped me while I was solving the problem.

These things made the problem easier to solve by:

_____

_____

_____

Let's Do Division . . . Together

Name: _____

The balloon seller sold bags with 6 balloons in each bag. Use the chart below to help the balloon seller figure out how many bags of 6 balloons he has sold.

	Red Balloons Sold	Blue Balloons Sold	Green Balloons Sold
Sunday	30	54	24
Monday	60	42	48

Do this first problem with a partner at your table. Be sure to discuss how you figured out the answer.

1. How many bags of green balloons were sold on Monday? _____

How did you figure it out?

_____

_____

_____

Can you write this information in the form of a division problem? Try it . . .

Can you figure out what two multiplication problems are in the fact family here?

Think about your understanding. Would you give yourself a 1–2–3?

_____ Explain your rating.

Now try this problem on your own:

2. How many bags of red balloons were sold on Sunday? _____

How did you figure it out?

_____

_____

_____

Can you write this information in the form of a division problem? Try it . . .

Can you figure out what two multiplication problems are in the fact family here?

Think about your understanding now. Would you give yourself a 1–2–3?

_____

Sample Lesson 2

Elapsed Time (Grades 5–6)

Purpose

- To make math-to-self connections using elapsed time
- To demonstrate how to actively think through a problem using elapsed time
- To apply elapsed time skills in real-life situations

Ignition

Place the Ignition provided here on the overhead or Smartboard before the students enter the classroom. Have copies available for students at their desks. This activity will help engage your students immediately in the learning. They should begin the work independently, allowing each student the opportunity to "wrestle" with the concept a little. Also, you will be given a few minutes to check homework and attendance. When you see that the students are ready, have them share their answers and reasoning behind those answers with a partner. This sharing should only last 3–5 minutes. You can circulate and listen to the conversations, which will give you a glimpse into the background knowledge students have on elapsed time.

Answers to the Ignition:

1. 2 hours, 10 minutes
2. 7 hours, 30 minutes

Bridge to the Learning

Display the Bridge provided on the overhead or Smartboard. Students can have a copy or they can simply write their responses in their notebooks/journals. The purpose of this Bridge is for students to realize that they calculate elapsed time problems every day. This knowledge increases confidence and allows struggling math students to relax a little before the lesson begins. This activity should be quick (3–5 minutes).

Gradual Release

I Model—Think-Aloud (5 minutes): Place the text for the think-aloud on the overhead or Smartboard. Students should not have the handout; it may distract them from listening to how you navigate through the problem. They can write their "noticings" in their notebooks or journals. As you share your mathematical thinking, make sure to include how you make sense of the problem, how you eliminate answers that don't make sense, and how you predict to stay actively involved in the problem. It is always helpful to write out this think-aloud before trying it. That will allow you to pay attention to your own problem-solving strategies. Challenge the students to pay close attention to "what your brain does to solve the problem." Have them write three things they notice you doing while trying to solve the problem. Then have them "turn and talk" by sharing what they noticed and by coming up with how these critical thinking habits made it easier for you to solve the problem. Have a short discussion.

Answer: a. Sunday at 8:50 p.m.

We Do It Together (5 minutes): Now display the Let's All Go to the Movies handout. You choose a movie you would like to see and model how to solve the first problem. Challenge the class to try an example of this problem together—everyone using the same movie and showing. Let them work through the problem with a partner. Have them self-reflect using a 1–2–3, thumbs up/thumbs down/thumbs to the side, or whatever way your students self-reflect. This method will help you form groups. Students who do not understand at all may need to form a small group that you facilitate. To scaffold this learning, you can bring in small analog clocks whose hands the students can maneuver. The actual movement helps create a sensory image to use as a frame of reference.

You Try It, I Support—Small-Group Instruction (15 minutes): Form ability or random groups (use whatever fits your purpose best). Have the groups complete an activity while you join or pull groups for clarification.

Debrief

Exit Ticket (5 minutes): Display the present time and ask the students how many hours and minutes until lunchtime, the end of the day, tomorrow's beginning of class, whatever. Have students explain in writing and/or pictures how they figured this out.

Sample Lesson 2: Elapsed Time (Grades 5–6) student handouts follow.

_____

Ignition Into the Learning

Name: _____

Directions: Come right into class, get seated, and get your pencil out and your brain ready to start thinking. This lesson will make you smarter—guaranteed!

Now get to work and complete problems 1 and 2.

1. If it is 9:30 a.m. right now, and you have lunch at 11:40 a.m., how long is it until lunchtime? Explain how you figured out your answer.

It is _____ hour(s) and _____ minutes until lunchtime.

I figured this out by

_____

_____

_____

_____

2. It is 9:00 in the morning. You have been invited to the movies with your best friend this afternoon. The movie starts at 4:30 p.m. How long is it until the movie begins? How did you figure this out?

It is _____ hours and _____ minutes until the movie. I figured this out by

_____

_____

_____

_____

Bridge to the Learning

Today we are going to learn about elapsed time. You will be responsible for knowing this concept in PSSA this year, but you already do this every day. Whenever you look at the clock and ask yourself one of these questions, you are solving an elapsed time problem:

- How long until this class is over?
- How long until I go to lunch?

Think: Now think of other times when you solve elapsed time problems. They can be in school or out of school. Give three examples.

1. _____

2. _____

3. _____

Pair and share: Share your examples of elapsed time with the person next to you and then listen to their examples.

You are now ready to learn more about elapsed time.

Elapsed Time and Standardized Testing Think-Aloud

I am going to share my thinking as I solve the following standardized test problem. I want you to pay attention to what things I do to try to solve the problem. Be thinking about how my thoughts help me understand the problem better.

1. Mr. Ennis left for a weekend trip at 3:10 p.m. on Friday. He was gone 2 days, 5 hours, and 40 minutes. When did Mr. Ennis return home?

   a. Sunday at 8:50 p.m.

   b. Saturday at 7:50 a.m.

   c. Sunday at 7:50 p.m.

   d. Saturday at 8:50 p.m.

Write down what you notice me doing while trying to solve the above problem.

Three things I noticed my teacher doing while trying to solve the problem:

1. _____

2. _____

3. _____

Share your ideas with the person next to you and discuss how doing these things helped me while I was solving the problem.

These things made the problem easier to solve by:

_____

_____

Let's All Go to the Movies!

Name: _____

Use the movie listings below to answer the following questions

Flipped (PG)
10:00 a.m.   12:15 p.m.   2:45 p.m.   5:00 p.m.   7:15 p.m.   9:45 p.m.

The Twilight Saga: Eclipse (PG-13)
11:50 a.m.   3:00 p.m.   5:40 p.m.   8:00 p.m.   10:20 p.m.

Toy Story 3 (G)
9:45 a.m.   12:00 p.m.   2:30 p.m.   5:10 p.m.   7:40 p.m.   9:55 p.m.

Harry Potter and the Deathly Hallows: Part I (PG-13)
11:30 a.m.   3:15 p.m.   7:00 p.m.   10:30 p.m.

Tangled (G)
10:20 a.m.   12:45 p.m.   3:15 p.m.   5:35 p.m.

Rango (PG)
8:00 p.m.   10:45 p.m.

1. Choose a movie you would like to see: _____.
Now choose a good showtime for you: _____. Let's say it is
now 11:35 a.m. How many hours and minutes until your movie?

_____ hours, _____ minutes

Now explain to the person next to you how you figured out this problem.
Check out his or her movie and time as well. Help out each other if you
need to.

2. Choose another movie and showtime.

a. Movie: _____

b. Showtime: _____ (Do not choose the last show.)

Pretend that showing is sold out. How many hours and minutes will you have to wait until the next showing? _____ hours _____ minutes

Now explain to the person next to you how you figured out this problem. Check out his or her movie and time as well. Help out each other if you need to.

3. Let's say it is Saturday, and you want to go to the 10:00 a.m. showing of Flipped. You get there at 10:00 to discover that there are no seats left. The manager gives you five complimentary tickets for the showing that is 11 hours and 45 minutes away. What showing is this? _____

Explain how you figured that out.

_____

_____

What movie do you think is the most popular?

_____

_____

What makes you say that?

_____

_____

4. What movie do you think your teacher would most like to see?

_____

_____

What makes you say that?

_____

_____

_____

Sample Lesson 3
Surface Area of a Right Rectangular Prism (Grades 7–8)

Purpose

- To discover the concept of surface area
- To generate a formula for calculating the surface area of a right rectangular prism
- To calculate surface area of a right rectangular prism with accuracy and meaning
- (Optional) To compare and contrast the surface area of right rectangular prisms with the same volume using 24 cubes; to make a conjecture about how the surface area changes according to the dimensions of the box (if you do not have time in your class period, these last ideas could form the next day's Bridge to the Learning)

Ignition

Place the Ignition (see box below) on the overhead or Smartboard before the students enter the classroom. Have students write their answers in their math notebooks or journals. This Ignition will help engage your students immediately in the learning. They should begin the work independently, which will allow each student the opportunity to "wrestle" with the concept a little. Also, you will be given a few minutes to check homework and attendance. When you see that the students are ready, have them share their answers and reasoning behind those answers with a partner. This sharing should only take 3–5 minutes. You can circulate and listen to the conversations, which will give you a glimpse into the background knowledge students have on measurement sense and the concept of a right rectangular prism. (You will need to know the measurements of your classroom before doing this Ignition.)

Ignition

The class in which you are sitting right now is about _____ feet from the floor to the ceiling, _____ feet from the front of the room to the back of the room, and _____ feet from one side of the room to the other.

Think of three reasons anyone might need to know these measurements.

How does this question relate to yesterday's lesson? What do you think you will be learning today? What makes you say that? Explain your reasoning. Share and discuss with a partner.

Assess the reasonableness of the measurement answers. Use formative assessment to direct future Ignitions. Share real-life applications to the Ignition. Discuss connections from the previous lesson to this one. Activate background knowledge to scaffold the necessary connections from the new to the known. Circulate the room, taking note of discussions. (You might bring a clipboard and actually take notes.) This assessment will help you form flexible groups.

Bridge to the Learning

Give each student the Bridge to the Learning handout provided here with the necessary materials. Let them experiment and discover. The purpose is to generate a formula for calculating the surface area of a right rectangular prism. Do not worry about terms or appropriate definitions at this point. Allow the students to come to the understanding themselves; the learning will be much more meaningful that way. A Bridge that focuses on discovery using manipulatives sometimes takes a little longer (10 minutes), but the time is well spent. The students are forming a frame of reference that will help with connections when the learning gets more involved. Two formulas the students will need to use in the future are $S = 2(lw + lh + wh)$ and $S = 2B + Ph$ (B = area of a base, P = perimeter of a base, and h = height). Use what the students generate to craft the Bridge to these formulas, but do not tell the students what they are. They will come up with something very close. Ask questions to lead them to the formulas, then allow them to substitute values for the variables and simplify. You want your students to picture why this formula works, how it all makes sense. Come to a class consensus for the definition of surface area. (The surface area of a polyhedron is the sum of the areas of its faces.) Include a drawing, labeling edges, faces, and vertices. Again, do not give the definition. Draw out the definition from the experiment.

Gradual Release

I Model—Think-Aloud (5–7 minutes): Place the text for the think-aloud (below) on the overhead or Smartboard. Students should not have the handout; it may distract them from listening to how you navigate through the problem. They can write their "noticings" in their notebooks or journals. As you share your mathematical thinking, make sure to include how you made sense of the problem, incorporated a formula to assist you in the problem, predicted to stay actively involved in the problem, and used a visual representation to clarify that every lunch bag has an open top. Include a formula you used to calculate the surface area, and explain why you chose that formula.

It is always helpful to write out this think-aloud before trying it. That will allow you to pay attention to your own problem-solving strategies. Challenge the students to pay close attention to "what your brain does to solve the problem." Have them write three things they notice you doing while trying to solve the problem. Then have them "turn and talk," sharing what they noticed and coming up with how these critical thinking habits made it easier for you to solve the problem. Make sure you monitor and repair your understanding throughout the think-aloud. Ask yourself questions like, "What do I think the answer might be close to?" "Does this answer make sense?" "Why or why not?" Have a short discussion.

Answers:

S = B + Ph (there is only one base in a lunch bag)

S = (15.2 × 10.1) + 32(2 × 15.2 + 2 × 10.1)

S = 153.52 + 32 × 50.6

S = 1772.72 cm²

We Solve Together: Now display another sample problem. You can use a problem from your textbook, or you can use the one provided here. If you use our sample problem, there are two reasonable answers depending on how the students want to paint the file cabinet. It makes sense to (1) paint the front, top, and two sides or (2) paint the front, top, back, and two sides. Bring up this point. Reasonableness is a key component in numeracy. Read the problem aloud. Re-read it, stopping for students to think and share their understanding of the problem so far (turn and talk). Let them work through the problem with a partner. Have them self-reflect using a 1–2–3, thumbs up/thumbs down/thumbs to the side, or whatever way your students self-reflect. This method will help you form groups. Students who do not understand at all may need to form a small group that you facilitate. To scaffold this learning, you may want to come back to the whole class and have students share the different strategies they used to solve the problem (5 minutes).

Answer for painting the front, top, and two sides = 4120 cm² or 28.6 ft² = buy 1 spray can

Answer for painting front, back, top, and two sides = 5360 cm² or 37.2 ft² = buy 2 spray cans

You Try It, I Support—Small-Group Instruction (15 minutes): Form ability or random groups (use whatever fits your purpose best). Have the groups complete whatever problems you would like to assign from your textbook while you join or pull groups for clarification.

Debrief

Exit Ticket: Give each group of four students 24 cubes. Have them create a rectangular prism with the cubes. Calculate the surface area. Then have students quickly visit the prisms made by other groups. Do they look the same? Why? Why not? Now quickly compare each group's surface areas. How are they the same? How are they different? What do you notice? What is the reason for this difference? (Don't worry about accuracy here; you are just exposing them to the effect that changing the dimensions of a right rectangular prism has on surface area, even though the volume is the same.) Ask the students to make a conjecture (5 minutes).

Sample Lesson 3: Surface Area of a Right Rectangular Prism (Grades 7–8) student handouts follow.

Bridge to the Learning

Name: _____

Materials needed:

- Bridge to the Learning handout
- Miniature box of raisins
- Scissors
- Glue stick
- Metric ruler
- Your brain

Directions:

1. Take out the raisins and eat them!

2. Flatten the box by cutting along the *edges*. It should look like a *net* (yesterday's lesson).

3. What do you notice about this net? What is added to the net that was not present in any of the nets you have worked with so far? Why is it there?

4. Okay, now cut off the *overlap* and throw it out.

5. Cut along the *edges* of the net and create separate rectangles. Measure each rectangle to the nearest millimeter. Include your measurements in the table below. Glue the six *faces* in the appropriate rectangle.

Face	Length (mm)	Width (mm)	Area (mm²)
Front			
Back			
Top			
Bottom			
Left Side			
Right Side			

Glue the six faces here.

6. Calculate the total area of all the faces. Show your calculations below (even if you used a calculator). Include labels and units of measure.

7. Can you think of an easier way to find the total area of the raisin box? Explain your thinking below. Then share your thinking with your group and come to a consensus. Generate a possible formula for calculating the total area of a right rectangular prism (the raisin box).

8. Let's gather our information and come to a class consensus. How could we calculate the surface area of a right rectangular prism? Let's think of and agree on at least two formulas we could use.

Class Formula #1:	Class Formula #2:
Reasoning behind this formula:	Reasoning behind this formula:

9. From this experiment, what is the definition of surface area? Write your definition. Share it with a partner. Add to or revise your definition. Be ready to discuss.

Surface Area =

Surface Area of a Right
Rectangular Prism Think-Aloud

I am going to share my thinking as I solve the following problem. I want you to pay attention to what I do to try to solve the problem. Be thinking about how my thoughts help me better understand the problem.

Gloria is trying to convince her Mom to "go green." She bought her own lunch box so her mom doesn't have to use paper bags anymore. To help with the argument, she presented the following problem to her mom:

A paper lunch bag measures approximately 32 cm in height, 15.2 cm in width, and 10.1 cm in depth. Ignoring overlap, how many square centimeters of paper are needed to make the bag? Show and explain all your work, even if you used a calculator.

Write down what you notice me doing while trying to solve the above problem.

Three things I noticed my teacher doing to try to solve the problem:

1. _____

2. _____

3. _____

Share your ideas with the person next to you and discuss how doing these things helped me while I was solving the problem.

These things made the problem easier to solve by:

_____

_____

We Solve Together! Sample Problem

You just purchased a file cabinet in which to store all your great math work. It measures 62 inches high, 20 inches wide, and 20 inches deep.

- What makes sense to paint? Why do you think that?
- How many square inches will you be painting? Show and explain all your work, even if you used a calculator. (Include a formula.)
- A spray paint can uses square feet as a measure of coverage. One spray can covers 30 square feet. How many cans must you buy?

Appendix B

Anticipation Guide: The 2010 Census

Before-Reading Rating Check whether you agree or disagree			After-Reading Rating Check whether you agree or disagree	
Agree	Disagree		Agree	Disagree
		1. The 2010 Census is very important to American citizens.		
		2. The Census determines the number of congressmen that serve in the U.S. government.		
		3. The first Census was taken in 1790.		
		4. Census takers should visit homes whenever the Census is not returned.		
		5. I would want the results of the 2010 Census.		

You can find plenty of reading materials on the 2010 Census with a quick search online. Here's one example: http://www.timeforkids.com/TFK/kids/news/story/0,28277,1972251,00.html.

Appendix C

Clock Reproducible for Clock Partners

Reproduce a clock for each student. See page 164 for detailed directions on creating small groups.

References and Further Reading

Akhavan, N. (2007). *Accelerated vocabulary instruction: Strategies for closing the achievement gap for all students.* New York: Scholastic.

Allen, J. (1999). *Words, words, words: Teaching vocabulary in Grades 4–12.* Portland, ME: Stenhouse Publishing.

Allen, J. (2000). *Yellow brick roads: Shared and guided paths to independent reading 4–12.* Portland, ME: Stenhouse Publishing.

Allen, J. (2004). *Tools for teaching content literacy.* Portland, ME: Stenhouse Publishing.

Allington, R. L. (2006). *What really matters for struggling readers. Designing research-based programs* (2nd ed.). Saddle River, NJ: Pearson Education.

Allsopp, D., Kyger, M. M., & Lovin, L. H. (2007). *Teaching mathematics meaningfully: A solution for struggling learners.* Baltimore, MD: Paul H. Brooks Publishing Co.

Anderson, R. C., & Freebody, P. (1981). Vocabulary knowledge. In J. T. Guthrie (Ed.), *Comprehension and teaching: Research reviews* (pp. 77–117). Newark, DE: International Reading Association.

Anderson, R. C., & Pearson, P. D. (1984). A schema-thematic view of basic processes in reading comprehension. In P. D. Pearson, R. Barr, M. L. Kamil, & P. Mosenthal (Eds.), *Handbook of reading research* (pp. 255–291). White Plains, NY: Longman.

Anderson, V., & Hidi, S. (1988/1989). Teaching students to summarize. *Educational Leadership, 46,* 26–28.

Armbruster, B. B., Anderson, T. H., & Ostertag, J. (1987). Does text structure/summarization instruction facilitate learning from expository text? *Reading Research Quarterly, 22*(3), 331–346.

Baker, S. K., Simmons, D. C., & Kam'eenui, E. J. (1995). *Vocabulary acquisition: Curricular and instructional implications for diverse learners.* Tech. Report No. 13. Eugene, OR: National Center to Improve the Tools for Educators, University of Oregon.

Barnes, D. (1976). *From communication to curriculum.* London: Penguin Press.

Baumann, J. F., Kam'eenui, E. J., & Ash, G. (2003). Research on vocabulary instruction: Voltaire redux. In J. Flood, D. Lapp, J. R. Squire, & J. Jenson (Eds.),

Handbook of research on teaching the English Language Arts (2nd ed.). Mahwah, NJ: Lawrence Erlbaum.

Beck, I. L., McKeown, M. G., & Kucan, L. (2002). *Bringing words to life: Robust vocabulary instruction.* New York: Guilford Press.

Beers, K. (2003). *When kids can't read: What teachers can do.* Portsmouth, NH: Heinemann.

Bell, B., & Cowie, B. (2000). *Formative assessment and science education.* New York: Springer Netherlands.

Best, J. (2001). *Damned lies and statistics: Untangling numbers from the media, politicians, and activists.* Berkeley, CA: University of California Press.

Billmeyer, R. (2004). *Strategic reading in the content areas: Practical applications for creating a thinking environment.* Omaha, NE: Dayspring Printing.

Blachowicz, C. L. Z., & Obrochta, C. (2005). Vocabulary visits: Virtual field trips for content vocabulary development. *The Reading Teacher, 59*(3), 262–268.

Black, P., & William, D. (1998). Inside the black box: Raising standards through classroom assessment. *Phi Delta Kappan, 80,* 139–148.

Block, C. C., & Mangieri, J. N. (2006).*Vocabulary enriched classroom: Practices for improving reading performance for all students in Grades 3 and up.* New York: Scholastic.

Bransford, J., Brown, A., & Cocking, R. (1999). *How people learn: Brain, mind, experience, and school.* Washington, DC: National Academy Press.

Buehl, D. (2008). *Classroom strategies for interactive learning.* Newark, DE: International Reading Association.

Buhrow, B., & Upczak Garcia, A. (2005). *Ladybugs, tornadoes, and swirling galaxies: English language learners discover their world through inquiry.* Portland, ME: Stenhouse Publishers.

Bullock, J. (1994, October). Literacy in the language of mathematics. *American Mathematical Monthly.*

Burchers, S. (2007). *Vocabulary cartoons: SAT word power.* Punta Gorda, FL: New Monic Books.

Burns, M. (2007). *About teaching mathematics: A K–8 resource.* Sausalito, CA: Math Solutions Publications.

Burns, M., & Tank, B. (1988). *A collection of math lessons from Grades 1 through 3.* Sausalito, CA: Math Solutions Publications.

Butler, D. L., & Winne, P. H. (1995). Feedback and self-regulated learning: A theoretical synthesis. *Review of Education Research, 65*(3), 245–281.

Bynner, J., & Parsons, S. (1997). *Does numeracy matter? Evidence from the National Child Development Study on the impact of poor numeracy on adult life.* London: Basic Skills Agency. Available at http://www.eric.ed.gov/ERICWebPortal/search/detailmini.jsp?_nfpb=true&_&ERICExtSearch_SearchValue_0=ED406585&ERICExtSearch_SearchType_0=no&accno=ED406585

Casti, J. (1997). *Reality rules: Picturing the world in mathematics: Vol. 1. The fundamentals.* New York: Wiley.

Chall, J. S., Jacobs, V. A., & Baldwin, L. E. (1990). *The reading crisis: Why poor children fall behind.* Cambridge, MA: Harvard University Press.

Chen, Z. (1996). Children's analogical problem solving: The effects of superficial, structural, and procedural similarities. *Journal of Experimental Child Psychology, 62*(3), 410–431.

Chen, Z. (1999). Schema induction in children's analogical problem solving. *Journal of Educational Psychology, 91*(4), 703–715.

Chen, Z., Yanowitz, K. L., & Daehler, M. W. (1996). Constraints on accessing abstract source information: Instantiation of principles facilitates children's analogical problem solving. *Journal of Educational Psychology, 87*(3), 445–454.

Chuska, K. R. (1995). *Improving classroom questions: A teacher's guide to increasing student motivation, participation, and higher-level thinking.* Bloomington, IN: Phi Delta Kappa Educational Foundation.

Cole, J. C., & McLeod, J. S. (1999). Children's writing ability: The impact of the pictorial stimulus. *Psychology in the Schools, 36*(4), 359–370.

Coles, D., & Copeland, T. (2002). *Numeracy and mathematics across the primary curriculum: Building confidence and understanding.* London: David Fulton Publishers.

Cook, M. (1990). *Try-a-tile/logic with numbers.* Creative Publications.

Cortese, E. E. (2003). The application of Question–Answer Relationship strategies to pictures. *The Reading Teacher, 57*(4), 374–380.

Cross, K. P. (1998). Classroom research: Implementing the scholarship of teaching. In T. Angelo (Ed.), *Classroom assessment and research: An update on uses, approaches, and research findings* (pp. 5–12). San Francisco: Jossey-Bass.

Cunningham, J. (1982). Generating interaction between schemata and text. In J. Niles & L. Harris (Eds.), *New inquiries in reading research and instruction. Thirty-first yearbook of the National Reading Conference.* Washington, DC. National Reading Conference.

Cunningham, L., & Hentges, J. T. (1982). *The American school superintendency, 1982: A summary report.* Arlington, VA: American Association of School Administrators.

Cunningham, P., & Allington, R. (1994). *Classrooms that work: They can all read and write.* Saddle River, NJ: Pearson Education.

Cunningham, P., Hall, D. P., & Cunningham, J. W. (2000). *Guided reading the four blocks way.* Portland, ME: Stenhouse Publishing.

Dantonio, M., & Beisenherz, P. C. (2001). *Learning to question, questioning to learn: Developing effective teacher questioning practices.* Boston: Allyn and Bacon.

Einstein, G. O., Morris, J., & Smith, S. (1985, October). Notetaking, individual differences, and memory for lecture information. *Journal of Educational Psychology, 77*(5), 522–532.

Elliott, P. C. (Ed.). (1996). *Communication in mathematics: K–12 and beyond.* Reston, VA: National Council of Teachers of Mathematics (NCTM).

Fisher, D., & Frey, N. (2008). *Better learning through structured teaching: A framework for the gradual release of responsibility.* Alexandria, VA: Association for Supervision and Curriculum.

Flick, L. (1992). Where concepts meet percepts: Stimulating analogical thought in children. *Science and Education, 75*(2), 215–230.

Forget, M. A. (2004). *Max teaching with reading and writing: Classroom activities for helping students learn new subject matter while acquiring literacy skills.* Victoria, BC, Canada: Trafford Publishing.

Forsten, C., Grant, J., & Hollas, B. (2002a). *Differentiated instruction: Different strategies for different learners.* Peterborough, NH: Crystal Springs Books.

Forsten, C., Grant, J., & Hollas, B. (2002b). *Differentiating textbooks: Strategies to improve student comprehension and motivation.* Peterborough, NH: Crystal Springs Books.

Frayer, D., Frederick, W. C., & Klausmeier, H. J. (1969). *A schema for testing the level of cognitive mastery.* Madison, WI: Wisconsin Center for Education Research.

Gallagher, K. (2004). *Deeper meaning.* Portland, ME: Stenhouse Publishing.

Gawned, S. (1990). The emerging model of language of mathematics. In J. Bickmore-Brand (Ed.), *Language in mathematics.* Portsmouth, NH: Heinemann.

Gear, A. (2008). *Non-fiction reading power: Teaching students how to think while they read all kinds of information.* Portland, ME: Stenhouse Publishing.

Gelb, M. (1998). *How to think like Leonardo da Vinci: Seven steps to genius every day.* New York: Dell Publishing.

Gentner, K., & Markman, A. B. (1994). Structural alignment in comparison: No difference without similarity. *Psychology Science, 5*(3), 152–158.

Gerlic, I., & Jausovec, N. (1999). Multimedia: Differences in cognitive processes observed with EEG. *Education Technology Research and Development, 47*(3), 5–14.

Gholson, B., Smither, D., Buhrman, A., Duncan, M. K., & Pierce, K. A. (1997). Children's development of analogical problem-solving skill. In L. D. English (Ed.), *Mathematical reasoning: Analogies, metaphors, and images.* Mahwah, NJ: Erlbaum.

Glasgow, N. A., Cheyne, M. C., & Yerrick, R. K. (2010). *What successful science teachers do: 75 research-based strategies.* Thousand Oaks, CA: Corwin.

Glynn, S. M., & Takahashi, T. (1998). Learning from analogy-enhanced science text. *Journal of Research in Science Teaching, 35,* 1129–1149.

Groves, S. (2001). Numeracy across the curriculum: Recognizing and responding to the demands and numeracy opportunities inherent in secondary teaching. *Mathematics Teacher Education and Development, 3,* 48–61.

Harlen, W. (2000). *Teaching, learning and assessing science 5–12.* London: Paul Chapman Publishing/Sage.

Harmon, J. M. (1999). Initial encounters with unfamiliar words in independent reading. *Research in the Teaching of English, 33,* 304–338.

Hart, K. M. (Ed.). (1982). *Children's understanding of mathematics: 11–16.* London: John Murray.

Harvey, S. (1998). *Nonfiction matters: Reading, writing, and research in Grades 3–8.* Portland, ME: Stenhouse Publishing.

Harvey, S. (2002, September). Nonfiction inquiry: Using real reading and writing to explore the world. *Language Arts, 80*(1), 12–22.

Harvey, S., & Goudvis, A. (2007). *Strategies that work: Teaching comprehension for understanding and engagement.* Portland, ME: Stenhouse Publishing.

Harwayne, S. (1992). *Lasting impressions.* Portsmouth, NH: Heinemann.

Hattie, J., Biggs, J., & Purdie, N. (1996). Effects of learning skills interventions on student learning. A meta-analysis. *Review of Education Research, 66*(2), 99–136.

Heibert, J., & Carpenter, T. P. (1992). Learning and teaching with understanding. In D. A. Grouws (Ed.), *Handbook of research on mathematics teaching and learning.* New York: Macmillan.

Hellwig, S., Monroe, E. E., & Jacobs, J. S. (2000). Making informed choices: Selecting children's trade books for mathematics instruction. *Teaching Children Mathematics, 7,* 138–143.

Hidi, S., & Anderson, V. (1987). Providing written summaries: Task demands, cognitive operations, and implications for instruction. *Reviewing Educational Research, 52,* 473–493.

Hiebert, E. H., Pearson, P. D., Taylor, B. M., Richardson, V., & Paris, S. G. (1998). *Every child a reader.* Ann Arbor, MI: Center for the Improvement of Early Reading Achievement (CIERA).

Hill, P. W., & Rowe, K. J. (1998). Modeling student progress in studies of educational effectiveness. *School Effectiveness and School Improvement, 9*(3), 310–333.

Hofstadter, D., & Fluid Analogies Research Group. (1995). *Fluid concepts and creative analogies.* New York: Basic Books.

Hollas, B. (2005). *Differentiating instruction in a whole-group setting (Grades 3–8).* Peterborough, NH: Crystal Springs Books.

Hollas, B. (2007). *Differentiating instruction in a whole-group setting, Grades 7–12.* Peterborough, NH: Crystal Springs Books.

Horest, J. (2006). *Primary mathematics 5A: Home instructor guide.* Littleton, CO: Sonlight Curriculum, Ltd.

Hoyt, L. (2002). *Make it real. Strategies for success with informational text.* Portsmouth, NH: Heinemann.

Huat, J. N. C., & Huat, L. K. (2003). *A handbook for mathematics teachers in primary schools.* Singapore: Marshall Cavendish Education.

Hunsader, P. D. (2004). Mathematics trade books: Establishing their value and assessing their quality. *The Reading Teacher, 57*(7), 618–629.

Hunter, M. (1984). Knowing, teaching, and supervising. In P. Hosford (Ed.), *Using what we know about teaching* (pp. 169–192). Alexandria, VA: Association for Supervision and Curriculum Development.

Hyde, A. (2006). *Comprehending math: Adapting reading strategies to teach mathematics, K–6.* Portsmouth, NH: Heinemann.

Hyde, A. (2009). *Understanding middle school math.* Portsmouth, NH: Heinemann.

Hyerle, D., & Yeager, C. (2007). *Thinking maps(R): A language for learning.* Cary, NC: Thinking Maps.

Johnson, D., & Johnson, R. (1984). *Circles of learning.* Washington, DC: Association for Supervision and Curriculum Development.

Kagan, S. (2000, Fall). Kagan structures. Not one more program, a better way to teach any program. *Kagan Online Magazine.*

Kagan, S. (2001, Winter). Kagan structures are brain based. *Kagan Online Magazine.*

Kagan, S., & Kagan, L. (1992). *Cooperative learning course workbook.* San Clemente, CA: Kagan Publishing.

Keene, E. O. (2008). *To understand: New horizons in reading comprehension.* Portsmouth, NH: Heinemann.

Keene, E. O., & Zimmerman, S. (2007). *Mosaic of thought: The power of comprehension strategy instruction* (2nd ed.). Portsmouth, NH: Heinemann.

Kelley, M. J., & Clausen-Grace, N. (2007). *Laying the foundation for the metacognitive teaching framework: Comprehension shouldn't be silent.* Newark, DE: International Reading Association.

Kenney, J. M. (2005). *Literacy strategies for improving mathematics instruction.* Alexandria, VA: Association for Supervision and Curriculum Development (ASCD).

Klingner, J. K., & Vaughn, S. (1999). Promoting reading comprehension, content learning, and English acquisition through Collaborative Strategic Reading (CSR). *The Reading Teacher, 52,* 738–747.

Lavoie, D. R. (1999). Effects of emphasizing hypothetico-predictive reasoning within the science learning cycle on high school students' process skills and conceptual understanding in biology. *Journal of Research in Science Teaching, 36*(10), 334–360.

Lavoie, D. R., & Good, R. (1988). The nature and use of prediction skills in biological computer simulation. *Journal of Research in Science Teaching, 25,* 334–360.

Lawson, A. E. (1988). A better way to teach biology. *The American Biology Teacher, 50,* 266–278.

Lesh, R., Galbraith, P., Haines, C., & Hurford, A. (Eds.). (2010). *Modeling students' mathematical modeling competencies.* London: Springer Science-Business Media.

Lochhead, J., & Clement, J. (Eds.). (1979). *Cognitive process instruction: Research on teaching thinking skills.* Philadelphia: Franklin Institute Press.

Madison, B. L., & Steen, L. A. (Eds.). (2003). *Quantitative literacy: Why numeracy matters for schools and colleges.* Princeton, NJ: National Council on Education and the Disciplines.

Manz, S. L. (2002). A strategy for previewing textbooks: Teaching readers to become THIEVES. *The Reading Teacher, 55,* 434–435.

Martin, H. (2007). *Active learning in the mathematics classroom, Grades 5–8.* Thousand Oaks, CA: Corwin.

Martin, K. (1996, June). Problem-based learning: What is problem based learning? *Issues of Teaching and Learning.* http://help4teachers.com/MarthasResearch.htm

Marzano, R. J. (2007). *The art and science of teaching.* Alexandria, VA: Association for Supervision and Curriculum Development.

Marzano, R. J., Norford, J. S., Paynter, D. E., & Pickering, D. J. (2004). *A handbook for classroom instruction that works.* Alexandria, VA: Association for Supervision and Curriculum Development.

Marzano, R. J., & Pickering, D. J. (2005). *Building academic vocabulary: Teacher's manual.* Alexandria, VA: Association for Supervision and Curriculum Development.

Marzano, R. J., Pickering, D. J., & Pollock, J. E. (2001). *Classroom instruction that works: Research based strategies for increasing student achievement.* Alexandria, VA: Association for Supervision and Curriculum Development.

Mason, L. (1994). Cognitive and metacognitive aspects in conceptual change by analogy. *Instructional Science, 22*(3), 157–187.

Mason, L. (1995). Analogy, meta-conceptual awareness and conceptual change: A classroom study. *Educational Studies, 20*(2), 276–291.

Mason, L., & Sorzio, P. (1996). Analogical reasoning in restructuring scientific knowledge. *European Journal of Psychology of Education, 11*(1), 3–23.

Mayer, R. E. (1979). Twenty years of research on advance organizers: Assimilation theory is still the best predictor of results. *Instructional Science, 8*(2).

McGregor, T. (2007). *Comprehension connections: Bridges to strategic reading.* Portsmouth, NH: Heinemann.

McLaughlin, M., & Allen, M. B. (2002). *Guided comprehension: A teaching model for Grades 3–8.* Newark, DE: International Reading Association.

McVee, M. B., Dunsmore, K., & Gavelek, J. R. (2005). Schema theory revisited. *Review of Educational Research, 75*(4), 531–566.

Medin, D., Goldstone, R. L., & Markman, A. B. (1995). Comparison and choice: Relations between similarity processes and decision process. *Psychonomic Bulletin & Review, 2*(1), 1–19.

Mesmer, H. A. E., & Hutchins, E. J. (2002). Using QARs with charts and graphs. *The Reading Teacher, 56,* 21–27.

Meyers, C., & Jones, T. B. (1993). *Promoting active learning: Strategies for the college classroom.* San Francisco, CA: Jossey-Bass.

Miller, D. (2002). *Reading with meaning.* Portland, ME: Stenhouse Publishing.

National Council of Teachers of Mathematics. (1989). *Curriculum and evaluation standards for school mathematics.* Reston, VA: Author

National Council of Teachers of Mathematics. (1991). *Professional standards for teaching mathematics.* Reston, VA: Author.

National Council of Teachers of Mathematics. (1992). Overview: Learning and teaching with understanding. In *The handbook of research on mathematics teaching and learning* (p. 74). Reston, VA: Author.

National Council of Teachers of Mathematics. (1995). The learning standard. In *Assessment standards for school mathematics.* Reston, VA: Author.

National Council of Teachers of Mathematics. (2000). *Principles and standards for school mathematics.* Reston, VA: Author.

National Council of Teachers of Mathematics. (2002). *Putting research into practice in the elementary grades.* Reston, VA: Author.

National Research Council Collection. (1989–1995). Archives of American Mathematics, Dolph Briscoe Center for American History, University of Texas at Austin.

Newby, T. J., Ertmer, P. A., & Stepich, D. A. (1995). Instructional analogies and the learning of concepts. *Educational Technology Research and Development, 43*(1), 5–18.

New South Wales Department of Education and Training. (2003a). *Quality teaching in NSW public schools: A classroom practice guide.* Ryde, NSW, Australia: Author.

New South Wales Department of Education and Training. (2003b). *Quality teaching in NSW public schools: A discussion paper.* Ryde, NSW, Australia: Author.

Nunley, K. F. (2001). *Layered curriculum.* Kearney, NE: Morris Publishing.

Nye, P., Crooks, T. J., Powlie, M., & Tripp, G. (1984). Students note-taking related to university examination performances. *Higher Education, 13*(1), 85–97.

O'Donnell, A. M. (2006). The role of peers and group learning. In P. Alexander & P. Winne (Eds.), *Handbook of educational psychology* (2nd ed., pp. 781–802). Mahwah, NJ: Erlbaum Group.

Packer, A. (1997). Mathematical competencies that employers expect. In L. A. Steen (Ed.), *Why numbers count: Quantitative literacy for tomorrow's America* (pp. 137–154). New York: The College Board.

Pauk, W. (1989). *How to study in college* (4th ed.). Boston: Houghton Mifflin.

Paulos, J. A. (1992). *Beyond numeracy.* New York: Vintage.

Pavio, A. (1971). *Imagery and verbal processing.* New York: Holt, Rinehart, & Winston.

Pavio, A. (1990). *Mental representations: A dual coding approach.* New York: Oxford University Press.

Pearson, P. D., & Gallagher, M. C. (1983). The instruction of reading comprehension. *Contemporary Educational Psychology, 8*, 317–344.

Piaget, J. (1973). *Main trends in psychology.* London: George Allen & Unwin.

Popham, J. W. (2008). *Transformative assessment.* Alexandria, VA: Association for Supervision and Curriculum Development.

Posamentier, A. S., & Jaye, D. (2006). *What successful math teachers do, Grades 6–12.* Thousand Oaks, CA: Corwin.

Postman, N., & Weingartner, C. (1969). *Teaching as a subversive activity.* New York: Delacorte Press.

Pressley, M. (1998). *Reading instruction that works: The case for balanced teaching.* New York: Guilford Press.

Pressley, M., Symons, S., McDaniel, M., Snyder, B. L., & Turnure, J. E. (1988). Elaborative interrogation facilitates acquisition of confusing facts. *Journal of Educational Psychology, 80*, 268–278.

Programme for International Student Assessment (PISA). (1999). *Measuring student knowledge and skills: A new framework for assessment.* Paris: Organisation for Economic Co-operation and Development. Retrieved January 25, 2002, at http://www.pisa.oecd.org/pisa

Programme for International Student Assessment (PISA). (2007). *Science competencies for tomorrow's world: Executive summary.* Paris: Organisation for Economic Co-operation and Development. Available at http://www.oecd .org/dataoecd/15/13/39725224.pdf

Redfeld, D. L., & Rousseau, E. W. (1981). A meta-analysis of experimental research on teacher questioning behavior. *Review of Educational Research, 50*(1), 237–245.

Rhoder, C. (2002). Mindful reading: Strategy training that facilitates transfer. *Journal of Adolescent & Adult Literacy, 45,* 498–512.

Richek, M. A. (2005). Words are wonderful: Interactive, time-efficient strategies to teach meaning vocabulary. *The Reading Teacher, 58*(5), 414–423.

Robinson, F. P. (1970). *Effective study* (4th ed.). New York: Harper & Row.

Ross, B. H. (1987). This is like that: The use of earlier problems and the separation of similarity effects. *Journal of Experimental Psychology, 13*(4), 405–437.

Routman, R. (1996). *Literacy at the crossroads: Crucial talk about reading, writing, and other teaching dilemmas.* Portsmouth, NH: Heinemann.

Ryan, R., & Deci, E. (2000). Self-determination theory and the facilitation of intrinsic motivation, social development, and well-being. *American Psychologist, 55,* 68–78.

Schoenfeld, A. H. (Ed.). (1994). *Mathematical thinking and problem solving.* Hillsdale, NJ: Erlbaum Associates.

Schuster, L., & Canavan Anderson, N. (2005). *Good questions for math teaching: Why ask them and what to ask, Grades 5–8.* Sausalito, CA: Math Solutions Publications.

Secretary's Commission on Achieving Necessary Skills (SCANS), U.S. Department of Labor. (1991). *What work requires of schools.* Washington, DC: U.S. Government Printing Office.

Sibley, R., & Kagan, M. (2005). *Higher level thinking questions: Secondary mathematics.* San Clemente, CA: Kagan Publishing.

Silberman, M. (1996). *Active learning: 101 strategies to teach any subject.* Boston: Allyn & Bacon.

Silver, E. A., Kilpatrick, J., & Schlesinger, B. (1990). *Thinking through mathematics: Fostering inquiry and communication in mathematics classrooms.* New York: College Board.

Solomon, I. (1995). Analogical transfer and "functional fixedness" in the science classroom. *Journal of Educational Research, 87*(6), 371–377.

Sousa, D. (2001). *How the brain learns* (2nd ed.). Thousand Oaks, CA: Corwin.

Stahl, S. A. (1999). *Vocabulary development.* Cambridge, MA: Brookline Books.

Stahl, S. A., & Fairbanks, M. M. (1986). The effects of vocabulary instruction: A model-based meta-analysis. *Review of Educational Research, 56*(7), 72–110.

Stahl, S. A., & Nagy, W. E. (2006). *Teaching word meanings.* Mahwah, NJ: Erlbaum Associates.

Stanovich, K. E. (1986). Matthew effects in reading: Some consequences of individual differences in the acquisition of literacy. *Reading Research Quarterly, 21,* 360–407.

Steen, L. A. (1988, April 29). The science of patterns. *Science, 240,* 611–616.

Steen, L. A. (Ed.). (1990). *On the shoulders of giants: New approaches to numeracy.* Washington DC: National Academy Press.

Steen, L. A. (Ed.). (2001). *Mathematics and democracy: A case for quantitative literacy.* Prepared by the National Council for Education and the Disciplines. Princeton, NJ: The Woodrow Wilson National Fellowship Foundation.

Stone, C. L. (1983). A meta-analysis of advanced organizer studies. *Journal of Experimental Education, 51*(7), 194–199.

Sullivan, P., & Lilburn, P. (2002). *Good questions for math teaching: Why ask them and what to ask, K–6.* Sausalito, CA: Math Solutions Publications.

Tishman, S., Jay, E., & Perkins, D. (1993, Summer). Teaching thinking disposition: from transmission to enculturation. *Theory Into Practice, 32.*

Tomlinson, C. A. (1999). *The differentiated classroom.* Alexandria, VA: Association for Supervision and Curriculum Development.

Tovani, C. (2004). *Do I really have to teach reading? Content comprehension, Grades 6–12.* Portland, ME: Stenhouse Publishers.

Umstatter, J. (2004). *Words, words, words: Ready-to-use games and activities for vocabulary building, Grades 7–12.* San Francisco: Jossey-Bass.

Vaca, J., Vaca, R., & Gove, M. (1987). *Reading and learning to read.* Boston: Little Brown.

Van de Walle, J. A., & Lovin, L. H. (2006). *Teaching student-centered mathematics, Grades 5–8.* Saddle River, NJ: Pearson Education.

White, B., & Frederikson, J. (1998). Inquiry, modeling, and metacognition: Making science accessible to all students. *Cognition and Instruction.*

White, T. G., Graves, M. F., & Slater, W. H. (1990). Growth of reading vocabulary in diverse elementary schools: Decoding and word meaning. *Journal of Educational Psychology, 82,* 281–290.

Whitin, D. J., & Whitin, P. (2004). *New visions for linking literature and mathematics.* Urbana, IL: National Council of Teachers of English; Reston, VA: National Council of Teachers of Mathematics.

Whitin, P. (2002). Leading into literature circles through the sketch-to-stretch strategy. *The Reading Teacher, 55,* 444–450.

Willis, J. (2009). *Inspiring middle school minds: Gifted, creative, and challenging.* Arizona: Great Potential Press, Inc.

Willoughby, T., Desmarais S., Wood, E., Sims, S., & Kalra, M. (1997). Mechanisms that facilitate the effectiveness of elaboration strategies. *Journal of Education Psychology, 89*(4), 682–685.

Wormeli, R. (2009). *Metaphors & analogies: Power tools for teaching any subject.* Portland, ME: Stenhouse Publishers.

Worsley, D., & Mayer, B. (1989). *The art of science writing.* New York: Teachers and Writers Collaborative.

Zimmerman, S., & Hutchins, C. (2003). *7 keys to comprehension: How to help your kids read it and get it!* New York: Three River Press.

Zinsser, W. (1988). *Writing to learn.* New York: Harper & Row.

Zwiers, J. (2004). *Building reading comprehension habits in Grades 6–12.* Newark, DE: International Reading Association.

CLASSROOM LITERATURE

Aker, S., & Karlin, B. (1990). *What comes in 2's, 3's, and 4's?* New York: Children's Publishing Division.

Anno, M., & Anno, M. (1983). *Anno's mysterious multiplying jar.* New York: Penguin Putnam Books.

Burns, M. (2008). *The greedy triangle*. New York: Scholastic.

Calvert, P. (2006). *Multiplying menace: The revenge of Rumpelstiltskin (a math adventure)*. Watertown, MA: Charlesbridge Publishing.

Chambers, V. (2002). *Double Dutch: A celebration of jump rope, rhyme, and sisterhood*. New York: Hyperion Books for Children.

Clemens, A., & Reed, M. (2006). *A million dots*. New York: Atheneum Publishing.

Clement, R. (1995). *Counting on Frank*. Boston: Houghton Mifflin.

Demi. (1997). *One grain of rice*. New York: Scholastic.

Ellis, J. (2004). *What's your angle, Pythagoras? A math adventure*. Watertown, MA: Charlesbridge Publishing.

Gardner, H. (1993). *Multiple intelligences: The theory in practice*. New York: Basic Books.

Giganti, P. (1999). *Each orange had 8 slices*. New York: Mulberry Books.

Hoban, T. (2000). *Cubes, cones, cylinders, & spheres*. New York: Mulberry Books.

Hopkins, L. B. (2001). *Marvelous math: A book of poems*. Tucson, AZ: Good Year Books.

Jenkins, S. (2004). *Actual size*. Boston: Houghton Mifflin.

McCallum, A. (2006). *Beanstalk: The measure of a giant (a math adventure)*. Watertown, MA: Charlesbridge Publishing.

McGrath, B. B. (1994). *The M & M's counting book*. Watertown, MA: Charlesbridge Publishing.

Neuschwander, C. (1997). *Sir Cumference and the First Round Table (a math adventure)*. Watertown, MA: Charlesbridge Publishing.

Neuschwander, C. (2001). *Sir Cumference and the Great Knight of Angleland (a math adventure)*. Watertown, MA: Charlesbridge Publishing.

Neuschwander, C. (2003). *Sir Cumference and the Sword in the Cone: A math adventure*. Watertown, MA: Charlesbridge Publishing.

Neuschwander, C. (2004). *Sir Cumference and the Dragon of Pi (a math adventure)*. Watertown, MA: Charlesbridge Publishing.

Nolan, H. (2001). *How much, how many, how far, how heavy, how long, how tall is 1,000*. Morton Grove, IL: Albert Whitman and Co.

Palotta, J., & Bolster, R. (1999). *The Hershey's milk chocolate fractions book*. New York: Scholastic.

Palotta, J., & Bolster, R. (2002). *Hershey's milk chocolate weights and measures*. New York: Scholastic.

Palotta, J., & Bolster, R. (2003). *Apple fractions*. New York: Scholastic.

Pappas, T. (1993). *Fractals, googols, and other mathematical tales*. San Carlos, CA: Worldwide Publishing/Tetra.

Pinczes, E. J. (1993). *One hundred hungry ants*. New York: Houghton Mifflin.

Pinczes, E. J. (1995). *A remainder of one*. New York: Houghton Mifflin.

Pinczes, E. J. (2001). *Inchworm and a half*. New York: Houghton Mifflin.

Schwartz, D. M. (1999). *If you hopped like a frog*. New York: Harper Collins.

Schwartz, D. M. (2003). *Millions to measure*. New York: Harper Collins.

Schwartz, D. M. (2004a). *G is for Googol*. New York: Harper Collins.

Schwartz, D. M. (2004b). *How much is a million*. New York: Harper Collins.

Scieszka, J., & Smith, L. (1995). *Math curse*. New York: Penguin Books.

Shannon, G. (1995). *Stories to solve*. New York: Harper Collins.

Silverthorne, S., & Warner, J. (2007). *One-minute mysteries and brain teasers: Good clean puzzles for kids of all ages*. Eugene, OR: Harvest House Publishers.

Sobol, D. J. (1991). *Two-minute mysteries*. New York: Scholastic.

Tang, G. (2001). *Grapes of math*. New York: Scholastic.

Tang, G. (2002). *The best of times: Math strategies that multiply*. New York: Scholastic.

Tang, G. (2003a). *Math appeal*. New York: Scholastic.

Tang, G. (2003b). *Math-terpieces: The art of problem-solving*. New York: Scholastic.

Tang, G. (2004). *Math fables*. New York: Scholastic.

Tang, G. (2005). *Math potatoes: Mind-stretching brain food*. New York: Scholastic.

Treat, L. (2004). *You're the detective! Twenty-four solve-them-yourself picture mysteries*. Jaffrey, NH: David R. Godine, Publisher.

Weber, K. (1996). *Even more five-minute mysteries: 40 new cases of murder and mayhem for you to solve*. Philadelphia: Running Press Kids.

Weber, K. (2005). *Cleverly crafty five-minute mysteries*. Philadelphia: Running Press Kids.

Wells, R. E. (1993). *Is a blue whale the biggest thing there is?* Morton Grove, IL: Albert Whitman and Co.

Wells, R. E. (2000). *Can you count to a googol?* Morton Grove, IL: Albert Whitman and Co.

Index

Note: The names of specific activities are in italics.

Accommodation, 18, 19
Acting activities, 40, 98
Active learning, 132, 140–141
Algebra, 51, 57, 175
Algorithms, 38
Allen, Janet, 113, 114–115, 159
Allington, Richard, 10, 118
Analogies, 31
Analytical thinking, 30
Anchor lessons, 64–65
Anderson, Nancy Canavan, 76–77
Angles activity, 13–14
Answers to homework, 14–15
Anticipation Guide, 26–27, 172, 203
Anxiety, 118
Art activities, 27, 32, 39, 135
Assessment
    Bridge to the Learning, 139
    formative assessments, 96, 157–159, 167
    Gradual Release in Mathematics,
        159–161, 165–167
    questions for, 70, 128
    student self-assessment, 161–162, 167
    See also Exit tickets; Independent
        application
Assessment Standards for School Mathematics
    (NCTM), 165, 166
Asssimilation, 18–19

Background knowledge
    about, 18–19
    activating and building, 19–22, 138
    activities, 22–28, 93–94, 147–148
Barnes, Douglas, 119
Baseball video clips, 17
BDA Predicting and Inferring, 63
Beck, I. L., 103, 104

Beers, Kylene, 54, 60, 67, 154
Bell, B., 158
Black, P., 158
Bridge to the Learning
    activities, 141–148
    defined, 137–138
    key ideas, 139–141
    purpose, 138–139
    questions, 71, 128
    sample lesson plans, 180, 183–184, 188,
        191, 196, 198–200
Bringing Words to Life (Beck, McKeown,
    and Kucan), 104
Building Academic Vocabulary (Marzano
    and Pickering), 111
Bynner, J., 4

Calculation errors, 167
Calculator activities, 32
Cartoons, 108, 109
Category classification
    about, 30
    Circle the Category, 25, 110
    Classifying Numbers Matrix, 45
    Name That Category, 111
    Organize and Classify Concepts, 135
Census activity, 27, 134, 203
Circumference activity, 47–48
Citizenship, 3–4
Classification. *See* Category
    classification
Classroom Instruction That Works (Marzano,
    Pickering, and Pollock), 84–85
Clock Partners, 164–165
Cloze activities
    about, 20–21
    Interactive Cloze, 86, 89, 141–142

216

Collaboration
    importance of, 117–120, 160
    key ideas, 120–122
    research findings, 120
    standards, 122–123
    See also Guided practice
Common Core States Standards Initiative, 6
Comparisons
    about, 29–32
    activities, 32–35, 59, 113
    examples of, 108
Compass Rose groupings, 162–163
Comprehension, 10, 139
Concept Circle, 112, 144–145
Concept Ladder, 114–115
Concept Maps, 90
Conceptual errors, 167
Conjecture example, 135
Connections, 28, 172
Consensus, 99–100
Cook, Marcy, 136
Cornell note taking, 86, 87–89
Counting activities, 24, 32
Cowie, B., 158
Craft of teaching, 177–178
Cross-curricular activities, 41
Cues, 138

Data analysis, 57, 175
Debrief
    activities, 26, 95, 98, 116, 169–176
    Bridge to the Learning incorporated
        into, 142–145
    importance of, 168–169
    questions, 72–73, 128
    sample lesson plans, 181, 189, 197
    See also Exit tickets; Summarization
Decimals, 50–51, 175
Declines in recall, 85
Definitions, 28
Diagrams, 39
Differences. *See* Comparisons
Differentiation, 95
Division, 23, 180–187
Does Numeracy Matter? (Bynner &
    Parsons), 4
Double-Dutch Chants, 99, 111
Drawing Pictures/Diagrams, 39
Dual-coding model of information
    storage, 36

Early elementary activities
    background knowledge, 22–25
    kinesthetic activities, 40

    manipulatives, 44–46
    measurement, 12–13
    nonlinguistic representations, 42–43
    note taking, 88
    patterns, 58–60
    read alouds, 49–52
    similarities and differences, 32
Early Elementary Purpose and Focus
        statements, 129
Einstein, Albert, 68
Elapsed time sample lesson, 188–194
Employment oppportunities, 4
English language learners, 49
Errors, 166–167
Escher, M. C., 27, 44
Estimation
    about, 10–12
    Estimate With Little Ones, 23
    Estimation Moment, 14
    Good Number Sense and Estimation, 133
Evaluation of the Learning, 170–171
Examples and Nonexamples, 28, 144
Exit Tickets
    about, 96–97, 169–170
    activities, 27, 98
    sample lesson plans, 181, 189, 197
Expectations, 106–107
Experiments and hypotheses
    about, 55–57
    Experimental Inquiry, 65
    Experiment With Generating a Formula,
        27–28
    Experiment With Rates and Scales, 46–47
    Generating and Testing Hypotheses, 62–63
Exploratory talk, 119–120

Fake reading, 155
Feedback for students, 165–167. *See also*
    Assessment
"Fix-up" tools, 11–12
Flash cards, 41
Focus lessons. *See* Modeled instruction
Forecasting. *See* Prediction
Formative assessment, 96, 157–159, 167
Four Corners, 41
Fraction activities
    Fractions With 2-Color Counters, 43
    Journaling Prompts, 175
    read alouds, 50–51
Frayer Model, 114
Frontloading, 20, 27, 147–148

Gallagher, M. C., 7–8, 150
Gear, Adrienne, 55, 67, 153

Generating Interactions Between Schema and Text (GIST), 100–101, 172

Geoboards, 32

Geometry, 51, 57

Gerlic, I., 37

GIST (Generating Interactions Between Schema and Text), 100–101, 172

Good Questions for Math Teaching: Why Ask Them and What to Ask, K–6 (Sullivan & Lilburn), 76

Good Questions for Math Teaching: Why Ask Them and What to Ask, 5–8 (Schuster & Anderson), 76

Goudvis, A., 67

Gradual Release in Mathematics
  importance of, 149–150
  model of, 150–151
  research findings, 152–153
  sample lesson plans, 180–181, 185–187, 188–189, 192–194, 196–197, 201–202

Graphic organizers
  Cite Your Evidence T-Charts, 66–67
  questions for evaluating, 42
  summarizing activity, 31
  types, 44
  Venn Diagrams, 33
  vocabulary activity, 105

Graphic representations. *See* Nonlinguistic representations

Graphs
  Generate Questions, 136
  Graphing With Your Feet, 40
  journaling and, 94–95, 175
  Skittles and Graphing, 74

Greet and Go, 41–42, 112, 143

Group instruction. *See* Guided practice; Small-group instruction

Guesstimates, 11–12. *See also* Estimation

Guided practice, 138, 151, 152, 153, 159–165. *See also* Small-group instruction

Habits to ignite, 7

Half Snacks, 24

Handbook of Research on Mathematics Teaching and Learning (NCTM), 159–160

Handfuls #1 and #2, 59

Harvey, S., 67, 79–80

Harwayne, Shelley, 141, 169, 178

Heavier or Lighter? 32

Hierarchies, 34, 82

Homework answers, 14–15

Hot Seat, 77–78

How Many Pockets Is the Class Wearing Today? 59

How Many Popcorn Kernels Can Fill a Cube? 59

How Many Stars Can You Draw in a Minute? 59

How Many Ways? 46

Human Continuum, 171–172

Human Number Line, 40–41

Human Scatterplot, 41

Hyde, A., 10, 12, 19, 38, 169

Hypotheses. *See* Experiments and hypotheses

Icebreakers, 164–165

I Do, You Watch. See Modeled instruction

Ignition
  activities, 133–136
  exit tickets as, 27
  focus questions, 128
  importance of, 130–131
  key aspects, 131–132
  sample lesson plans, 180, 182, 188, 190, 195–196

I Learned/I Wonder Two-Column Notes, 77

I Model—Think-Aloud
  about, 150
  sample lesson plans, 154–157, 180, 185, 188–189, 192, 196–197, 201

Importance determination
  about, 79–82
  activities, 98–101
  note taking and, 84–85

Independent application, 151, 152, 153, 167

Inference
  about, 54–55
  BDA Predicting and Inferring, 63
  Ignition activities, 136
  Inference Versus Math Fact, 61–62
  Inferring Thinking Stems, 65–66
  Object Lessons in Inferring, 64–65

Informational text, 65

Inner conversations, 9–10

Inside/Outside Circle, 41

International comparisons, 2

Invention, 57

I Spy, 32

Jausovec, N., 37

Jellybean Jar, 24

Jingles, 99

Johnson, David, 120

Johnson, Robert, 120

Journals
  benefits, 92
  implementing, 93–97
  Journaling Prompts, 174–176
  Math Journals, 173
  3-2-1 Journal Entry, 98, 173
Joyce, Jaime, 134

Keene, Ellin, 97
Kinesthetic activities, 40–42
Know/Want/Learn (KWL), 24–25
Kucan, L., 103, 104
KWL (Know/Want/Learn), 24–25

Language. *See* Vocabulary; Word activities
Leftovers Again! 174
Lesh, R., 38
Lesson components, 125–126. *See also*
    Bridge to the Learning; Debrief;
    Gradual Release in Mathematics;
    Ignition; Purpose and Focus
Lesson plans
  critical reading, 154–157
  division, 180–187
  elapsed time, 188–194
  prism area, 195–202
Let's All Go to the Movies, 193–194
Lilburn, Pat, 76
Line-ups, 165
Lists, 25, 39–40, 110
Literacy and numeracy, 4–5

Manipulatives
  activities, 28, 43–49, 144
  benefits, 38
  importance of, 21
  questions, 42
Marzano, R. J., 30, 36, 56–57, 84–85, 107,
    108, 110, 111, 120, 158, 166
Mathematics and Democracy
    (Steen), 5
Math facts and inferences, 61–62
Math sense moments, 14
Matrixes, 33, 45, 112
"Matthew Effect," 104
McGregor, T., 65, 66–67
McKeown, M. G., 103, 104
Meaningful feedback, 165–167
Measurement
  activities, 12–14, 33, 47–49, 59
  patterns and, 57
  read alouds, 51
Mental images. *See* Visualization
Mental math, 16–17, 134

*Metacognitive Self-Talk to Maintain Mental
    Stamina*, 62
Metaphors, 30, 35, 107
Middle school activities. *See* Upper
    elementary/middle school activities
Miller, D., 83
Miscommunication, 166–167
Missing information activities, 135
Mix and Match, 41
Mixed ability teams, 162–163
Mnemonics, 108, 109
Modeled instruction
  about, 76, 150
  group behavior, 162
  I Do, You Watch, 153–157
  research findings, 152
  sample lessons, 154–157, 180, 185,
      188–189, 192, 196–197, 201
Multiple-meaning words, 148
Multiplication, 46, 50
Music, 135
Mysteries, 13, 61

Name That Category, 111
National Council of Education and the
    Disciplines (NCED), 3
National Council of Teachers of
    Mathematics (NCTM)
  *Assessment Standards for School
      Mathematics*, 165, 166
  *Handbook of Research on Mathematics
      Teaching and Learning*,
      159–160
  *Principles and Standards for School
      Mathematics*, 149
  *Professional Standards for Teaching
      Mathematics*, 122–123, 165
  recommendations of, 37
National Research Council, 149
NCED (National Council of Education
    and the Disciplines), 3
NCTM. *See* National Council of Teachers
    of Mathematics
Nonlinguistic representations
  about, 36–38
  activities, 42–49
  key ideas, 38–42
  read alouds, 49–52
  vocabulary instruction, 108–109
Note taking
  about, 84–85
  concept maps, 90
  Cornell method, 86, 87–89
  online resources, 91

SQ3R method, 89–90
three-column, 90–91
two-column, 77, 90–91
See also Cloze activities
Numbering Off, 165
Number relationships/number sense
Build Number Sense and Division, 23
encouraging, 133
Journaling Prompts, 175
patterns and, 57
read alouds, 49–50
rounding, 16
Numbers, Numbers, Where Are They, 22
Number Surgery, 23
Numeracy, 1–6

1–2–3, Green Light, Yellow Light, Red Light, 162
$100,000 Pyramid game show, 111
Online resources for note taking, 91
Overviewing, 99

"Parking Lot of Questions" Poster, 78
Parsons, S., 4
Pass the Plate, 114
Patterns
about, 57–58
Does Anyone See a Pattern? 43
early elementary activities, 58–60
Identify Sets of Objects, 43
key ideas, 31–32
Making Necklaces, 58
Pattern Block Art, 32
Pattern Dance, 40
Recognizing and Continuing Patterns, 34–35
upper elementary/middle school activities, 60–67
0–99 Patterns, 43
Pauk, Walter, 86
Pearson, P. D., 7–8, 150
Penguins and Polar Bears, 60
Percents, 50–51, 175
Perfect Partners, 163
Pi activity, 47–48
Piaget, Jean, 18
Pickering, D. J., 30, 84–85, 108, 110, 111, 120, 166
Pictographs, 39–40
PISA (Program for International Student Assessment), 2
Pointillism, 44
Pollock, J. E., 30, 84–85, 108, 120, 166

Polygons, 44
Popham, W. James, 157
Postassessment, 25
Postconcept Check, 26, 115–116, 143–144, 172
Posters, 24–25, 65–66, 78
Post-its, 78
Preassessment, 25
Preconcept Check, 26, 115–116, 143–144, 172
Prediction
about, 53, 54
Bridge to the Learning, 139
Cookie activity, 48
Greet and Go, 41–42, 112, 143
inference compared to, 55
journaling and, 94
See also Inference; Patterns
Preplans, 69
Preteaching, 20–21, 147
Previewing, 138
Principles and Standards for School Mathematics (NCTM), 149
Prism sample lesson, 195–202
Problem solving
about, 56
Analyze and Evaluate, 136
Compose Problems, 99
Highlight Similar Problems Students Have Solved, 34
journaling prompts, 175
Problem-Based Learning, 100
Provide for Flexible Thinking, 34
questions, 75
Professional Standards for Teaching Mathematics (NCTM), 122–123, 165
Program for International Student Assessment (PISA), 2
Prompts, 93–95, 97, 175
Proportional reasoning, 50
Protractors, 13–14
Purpose and Focus, 127–129

Questions
about, 68–69
Bring Any Important Questions You Have to the Table, 74–75
Central Question, 77, 142–143
Essential Question Revisited, 170
Focus Question, 142
Hook Students by Providing a Thought-Provoking Question, 133–134
key ideas, 71–73
Questions Never End, and That's a Good Thing, 78

Questions on Sticky Notes, 78
"Questions That Keep Going Around in My Head" Poster, 78
Questions to Monitor and Repair Understanding, 75
research findings, 69–71
student-generated, 74
teacher-generated, 69
unanswered, 70
What's the Question? 100

Race for a Flat, 44, 46
Random teams, 163–165
Raps, 99
Read alouds, 49–52
"Reading the World," 60–61
Real-world application, 16, 21, 28, 134
Recall, declines in, 85
Reflection, 97
Representation of the Lesson, 174
Review of prior skills, 133
Rhymes, 108, 109
Riddles, 58–59
Rockwell, Norman, 36–37

Say Something, 98
Scaffolds, 139
Scanning, 64
Scatterplots, 41
Scavenger hunts, 13, 80–81
Schoenfeld, Alan H., 2–3
Schuster, Lainie, 76–77
Science of patterns, 57
Scriven, Michael, 158
Scrolling, 64, 65, 141
Secret rules, 34
Self-assessment, 161–162, 167
Sentence frames, 20–21, 147
Sentence starters, 96
Shape activities, 32, 63
Shared practice, 151, 152
Show Multiplication, 46
Signac, Paul, 44
Silent Conversation, 100
Similarities. See Comparisons
Simplify, 34
"Size 'em Up": Measuring Angles, 13–14
Skimming, 64, 99, 141
Skits, 40, 98
Skittles and Graphing, 74
Small-group instruction, 181, 189, 197. See also Guided practice
Snap It, 46
Solving a Good Mystery, 61

Sort Shapes on a Geoboard, 32
SQ3R note taking, 89–90
Standards, 6. See also National Council of Teachers of Mathematics
Statistics, 175
Steen, Lynn Arthur, 5, 57–58
Students
  declines in recall, 85
  evaluating learning, 170–171
  generating questions, 74
  self-assessment, 161–162, 167
  supporting each other, 22
Stump the Teacher, 78, 174
Subtraction, 24–25
Sullivan, Peter, 76
Summarization
  about, 82–83
  Four to Six Word Summary, 100
  GIST, 100–101
  note taking and, 84–85, 86
  Say Something, 98
  Sum It Up, 99
  Summaries in Headline Fashion, 98
  Writing Summaries, 173
Synthesis of information, 83–85

Tables, 39–40
Talk a Mile a Minute, 111
T-charts, 24–25, 44, 66–67, 77
Teach-alouds, 154
Teacher-generated questions, 69
Teacher modeling. See Modeled instruction
Teaching an Adult at Home, 173–174
Tessellation, 44
Textbook Scavenger Hunt, 80–81
T.H.I.E.V.E.S., 145–146
Think-alouds
  about, 16–17, 76, 150
  sample lessons, 154–157, 180, 185, 188–189, 192, 196–197, 201
Thinking maps, 105–106
"Thinking That Keeps Going," 61
Think-Pair-Share, 119
Third International Mathematics and Science Study (TIMSS), 149
Three-column note taking, 90–91
Three Facts and a Fib, 27, 143, 172–173
3-2-1 Journal Entry, 98, 173
Thumbs Up, Thumbs to the Side, Thumbs Down, 162
Time measurement, 13
TIMSS (Third International Mathematics and Science Study), 149

Tovani, Cris, 139, 153, 158
Transformative Assessment (Popham), 157
True Statement? 33
Try-a-Tile/Logic With Numbers (Cook), 136
Turn and Talk, 119
Two-column note taking, 90–91

Unanswered questions, 70
Understanding of mathematics, 9–17, 61
Unfamiliar language, 20
Upper elementary/middle school
    activities
    background knowledge, 25–28
    Cornell note taking, 87
    kinesthetic activities, 40–42
    manipulatives, 46–49
    measurement, 13–14
    nonlinguistic representations, 44
    patterns, 60–67
    read alouds, 49–52
    similarities and differences, 33–35
Upper Elementary/Middle School
    Purpose and Focus statements, 129

Venn Diagrams, 33
Visualization
    Concept Maps, 90
    as frame of reference, 22
    Ignition examples, 134
    nonlinguistic representations,
        38–39, 44, 49
    Representation of the Lesson, 174
Vocabulary
    activities, 41–42, 110–116, 143
    habits, 103–104
    importance of, 102–103
    key ideas, 104–108
    meaning in math settings, 22
    See also Unfamiliar language; Word
        activities

Vocabulary Objects, 112
Volume, 23
Voting With Your Feet, 25–26, 42

We Do, I Support. *See* Shared practice
We Do It Together, 181, 186–187,
        189, 197, 202
What If? 42–43
What I Knew/What Is New T-Chart, 24–25
What Really Matters for Struggling Readers
        (Allington), 10
What's As Big As Me? 12–13
What's the Question? 100
What's the Title? 100
"What We Wonder" Poster, 78
*"When Are We Ever Going to
        Use This?"* 28
Whip Around, 172
William, D., 158
Willis, Judy, 40
Wonderings, 78
Word activities
    Create a Working Word Wall, 35
    Cross-Out Strategy, 98
    Multiple-Meaning Words, 148
    Word Hunt, 106
    Word Sort, 25, 34, 110
    Word Surgery, 63–64, 105
    Word Toss, 142
    Word Wizard, 110
Working Answer Keys, 14–15
Wormeli, Rick, 56, 121, 140–141
Writing to Learn (Zinsser), 92

*You Try It, I Support—Small-Group
        Instruction*, 181, 189, 197

0–99 Patterns, 43
Zinsser, William, 92
Zoom-In to Nonfiction Text Features, 65